W9-BVY-791

DI BRUNO BROS.

HOUSE
OF
CHEESE

A GUIDE TO

WEDGES, RECIPES, AND PAIRINGS

Tenaya Darlington

PHOTOGRAPHY BY

Jason Varney

RUNNING PRESS
PHILADELPHIA · LONDON

© 2013 by Tenaya Darlington
Photographs © 2013 by Jason Varney
Published by Running Press,
A Member of the Perseus Books Group

All rights reserved under the Pan-American and International Copyright Conventions
Printed in China

This book may not be reproduced in whole or in part, in any form or by any means,
electronic or mechanical, including photocopying, recording, or by any information
storage and retrieval system now known or hereafter invented, without written
permission from the publisher.

Books published by Running Press are available at special discounts for bulk
purchases in the United States by corporations, institutions, and other organizations.
For more information, please contact the Special Markets Department at the Perseus
Books Group, 2300 Chestnut Street, Suite 200, Philadelphia, PA 19103, or call (800)
810-4145, ext. 5000, or e-mail special.markets@perseusbooks.com.

ISBN 978-0-7624-4604-9
Library of Congress Control Number: 2012942524

E-book ISBN 978-0-7624-4833-3

9   8   7   6   5   4   3   2   1
Digit on the right indicates the number of this printing

Cover and interior design by Joshua McDonnell
Edited by Kristen Green Wiewora
Typography: Accanthis, Avenir, Bembo, and Govenor

Running Press Book Publishers
2300 Chestnut Street
Philadelphia, PA 19103-4371

Visit us on the web!
www.runningpresscooks.com

In Memory of Daphne Zepos, who ignited our passion for so many "little gems" produced by American artisans and by cheesemakers throughout the world.

7   Acknowledgments

10   **Foreword:** The Di Bruno Bros. Story

15   **Preface:** The Birth of a Cheese Courtesan

17   **Introduction:** How to Pick a Hunk

25   I.   Baby Faces

39   II.   Quiet Types

65   III.   Free Spirits

87   IV.   Vixens

117   V.   Mountain Men

141   VI.   Stinkers

163   VII.   Rockstars

179   VIII. Wise Guys

209   IX.   Sugar Mamas

225   X.   Pierced Punks

244   **Appendix:**
      Useful Books, Websites, and Organizations

246   **Cheese Glossary**

ACKNOWLEDGMENTS

This book never would have been written without the trust, encouragement, and absolutely stunning support from everyone at Di Bruno Bros. I can't imagine a kinder or more passionate group of people. Huge thanks to Kristen Green Wiewora at Running Press for lighting on this idea with such a vengeance and to the world's most valiant agent, Amy Williams, for shepherding this project into the fold.

William and Emilio Mignucci at Di Bruno Bros. believed in this book from its inception, and cheesemonger Hunter Fike welcomed me behind the counter for a year of tasting and talking. His friendship and written contributions were so essential. Ezekial Ferguson, who handed me my first cheese sample six years ago, read every draft, cheered us on, and broke out the camp stove in the back of the Italian Market store to help recipe-test grilled cheese.

Special thanks to Chef Rob Sidor and everyone in the kitchen at Di Bruno Bros. on Chestnut Street for developing many of the recipes for this book. And to everyone on staff who contributed pairing ideas, suggestions, and enthusiasm, thank you: Adam Balkovic, Dan Black, Mark Bomalaski, Evan Bortzfield, Rebecca Brumberg-Frimmer, Melanie Fortino, Jamie Hoffman, Richard-Luis Morillo, Ian Peacock, Jamie Png, Rocco Rainone, Matt Shankle.

Finally, to the cheesemakers who produce the beautiful wheels described within these pages, you have my undying gratitude. For all the evenings you spend in the milk barn and all the mornings you rise to cut curd, know that you bring so much pleasure to countless delighted eaters.

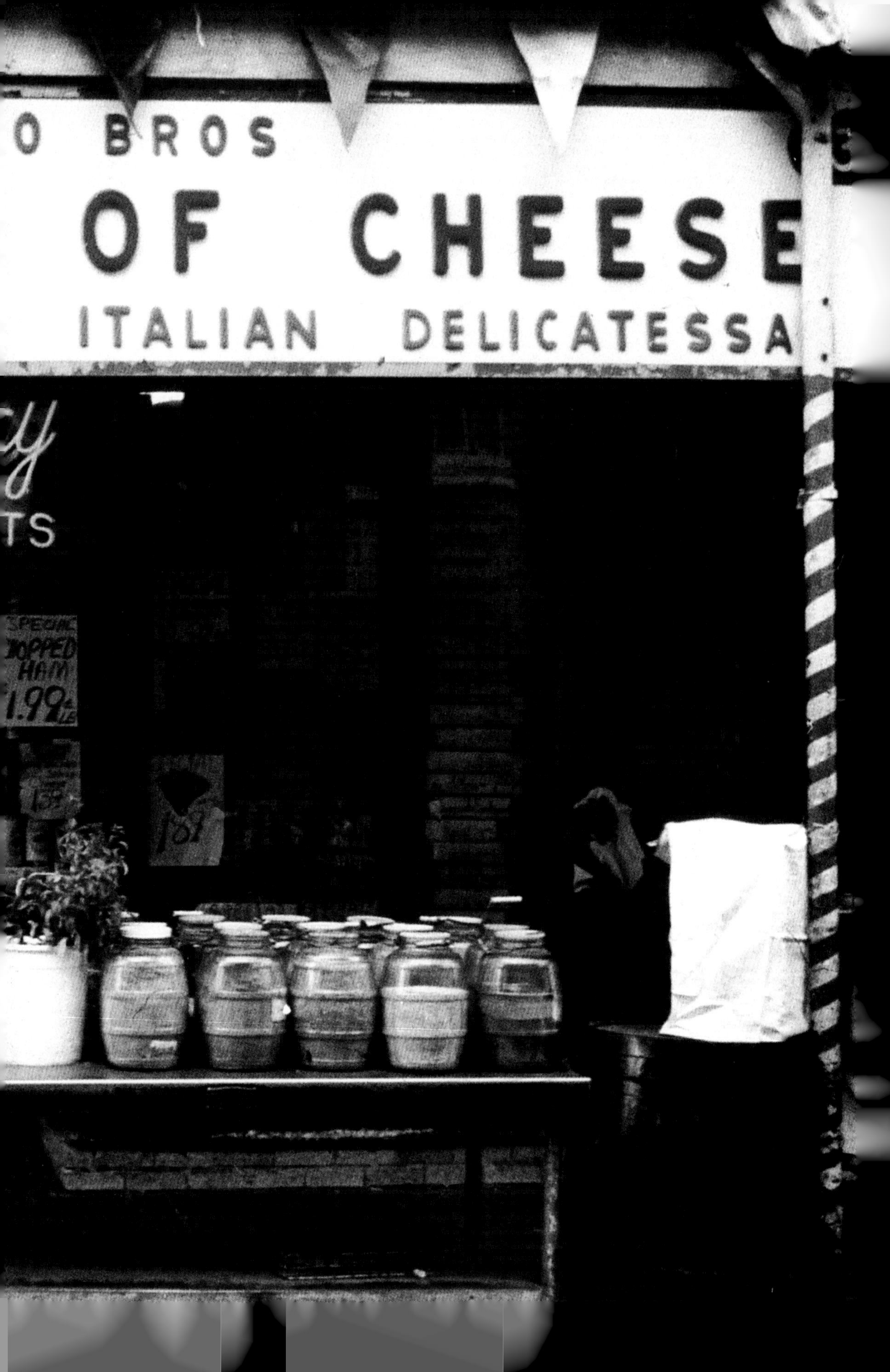
O BROS
OF CHEESE
ITALIAN DELICATESSA
TS
SPECIAL
HAM
1.99

FOREWORD:

THE DI BRUNO BROS. STORY

Just as so many stories of American family business begin, ours opens with Ellis Island as the picturesque background. Two immigrant brothers with third-grade educations from the southern Italian region of Abruzzo crossed into America with their siblings and very few belongings. Danny and Joe Di Bruno came to America searching for streets paved with gold. What they found were the cobbled streets of Philadelphia (roughly the same thing). What Danny and Joe may have lacked in formal education and wealth, they made up for with work ethic. The two brothers were innovative entrepreneurs who found great opportunity in the food business.

Ninth Street and the Italian Market became a home and an incubator for Danny and Joe as they set out to open a small grocery in the heart of the Italian population of Philadelphia. It was 1939, the same year that *Gone with the Wind* won Best Picture. Relying on their gut instincts, the brothers immediately began to celebrate "great people" by treating every customer like family. Customers still come into our stores today with stories of how their mother or grandmother went to Danny and Joe's shop with her last five dollars and left with two heaping bags of groceries. Danny and Joe planted roots in the neighborhood, and they flourished.

As time carried on and the world became a smaller place, supermarkets began to encroach on Danny and Joe's humble neighborhood. Recognizing this new business dilemma, Danny and Joe once again relied on their entrepreneurial spirit and gut instinct to find a solution. The answer arrived as Danny broke into a 200-lb wheel of cave-aged Emmentaler while vacationing in Switzerland. The irresistibly complex structure of this cheese produced by Swiss artisans gave Danny the idea to complement the Di Bruno Bros. practice of celebrating great people by celebrating great food.

Fueled by their new culinary pioneering spirit, the Di Bruno Bros. committed all their energies into explaining to their customers the merits and history of new cheeses like Parmigiano Reggiano and why it surpassed the infamous green can of ambiguously labeled (and frightfully shelf-stable) "Parmesan." Customers took notice, and Di Bruno Bros. quickly became recognized locally and beyond as Philadelphia's destination for culinary enthusiasts.

Danny and Joe grew old and proud of both of their countries and their business. Soon, two young nephews—Emilio and I—began to toy with the idea of taking over the family business. We were young and enthusiastic. Just like Danny and Joe, we decided to go with our gut instinct and expand. The time was right. The Food Network was entering homes everywhere, and Philadelphia was in need of gourmet food establishments to serve visitors of the new Pennsylvania

Convention Center. When we were ready, we took a jump and opened our doors to Center City at a brand-new Rittenhouse location.

With a fully functioning market, and the original 900-square-foot shop now up and running, things moved quickly. We were celebrating great people, great food, and now great business. Our company of 23 employees grew at an exponential rate to almost 275. With this growth came a new form of leadership that fit our culture: servant leadership. Servant leaders prioritize the needs of their colleagues and those they serve. Very humbly, they lead by serving.

Born into the Di Bruno family, we were raised to serve our customers and our community. Influential business minds such as Danny, Joe, Aunt Rita, and others imparted their intuition and knowledge on us any chance they had. We soaked everything up like sponges, and when the time came, we used that information to best serve our employees. Now, as we have expanded to four retail locations, an import and e-commerce warehouse, and a commissary kitchen, we still practice servant leadership to keep the ideals of Danny and Joe alive.

The community of Philadelphia and the specialty food community have equally influenced us in our journey. Companies such as Zingerman's and Neal's Yard Dairy inspire us daily to continue our ongoing mission of culinary pioneering. With a true reverence for our friends and colleagues across the country and world producing amazing quality products, we stock our shelves with their food. From decadent truffle honey slathered on a piece of Brie de Normandie, to Salami di Abruzze sliced so thin you can see through the fat pockets, we love what we do. Our employees are constantly looking for the next best pairing of a new cheese coming in from the Caves of Jasper Hill and accompaniments from around the world.

When we do find a perfect pairing, there is a celebration, and we share our culinary pioneering with our customers. This is the reason we come to work every day and are so proud of holding up the legacy of Di Bruno Bros. This is why we celebrate great people, great service, and most importantly. . . great food. We hope this book brings you a little closer to the people you love as you plan your next graduation party, holiday meal, or family gathering. Thank you for letting us celebrate with you.

—William Mignucci, Jr.
President, Di Bruno Bros.

PREFACE:

THE BIRTH OF A CHEESE COURTESAN

A few years ago, I was like you, standing at the cheese counter, intimidated by all those Italian hunks and weepy little French guys. I am speaking, of course, about cheese. As a newly transplanted Wisconsinite living in Philadelphia, I thought I knew a few things about curds and whey—I'd sampled a lot of cheese at farmers' markets and was the sort of person who could spend half an hour at the natural foods store browsing the dairy case—but I was unprepared for the vast selection before me at Di Bruno Bros. I felt like I'd just walked into a party where I didn't recognize a single face.

Behind the counter stood a few burly, bearded types. Cheese bouncers? I was sure they could smell my fear. Just as I was turning in my boots to slink away, one of them spoke. "Would you like a taste?" My mouth went dry. Surely he would size me up as a Cheddar Head and make me feel like a girl from the sticks. Or, maybe he'd come on like a sommelier and pressure me into buying something I couldn't pronounce, much less afford. So I simply said, "I like strong cheese."

The cheese bouncer turned and reached his inky biceps up toward a cooler, and for a moment I thought he was resuming his daily duties, too annoyed to respond. But no, he withdrew a moldy oldy from a line-up of blues and began scraping at the surface with a tiny plastic spoon. "We just got this in," he said, offering a taste. "It's a new wheel of Carles Roquefort, and we can't stop eating it back here. It's epic."

And so I was baptized. That spoonful of Roquefort hit my tongue, turned my mouth silky, and popped my eyes open with its wild, sweet fire. That was the day I learned about Jacques Carles, a Frenchman in his nineties who still uses freshly baked bread to harvest the blue mold for his wheels—just like the original makers of Roquefort. I also discovered that the bouncers behind the counter were called "cheesemongers" and that they loved what I loved: to eat and tell stories.

A week later, I returned to Di Bruno Bros., this time with a notebook. As a former journalist, I felt compelled to chronicle my visits and record every taste. The timing couldn't have been better. A nationwide renaissance in cheesemaking was just beginning to make the news, and the cheesemongers—sensing my obsessive nature—plied me with books, articles, and even videos on the subject. Best of all, when a hard-to-find dream wheel arrived, they alerted me by text message: *Winnimere is in—hurry over!* I felt like the Diane Fossey of cheese.

Friends who enjoyed the fruits of my fascination urged me to start a blog, and so I did, Madame Fromage (madamefromageblog.com). At first, I tried to keep it under wraps because it seemed patently ridiculous, but as posts drew comments from cheesemongers, and sometimes even from cheesemakers, I realized that I had stumbled into a new community—not just in Philadelphia, but online. After a year, I became the resident freelance cheese blogger for Di Bruno Bros.

Over time, it became clear: I had found my niche, not just as a cheese understudy, but as a cheese courtesan. Wherever I went, people wanted to talk cheese—and not just at the cheese counter. By the photocopier. In the community garden. Next to the jukebox. At the dog park. And they didn't just want to talk cheese: they wanted to understand how to taste it. My stoop became an extended cheese counter for neighbors in need of party advice; at work, colleagues filled my office to ask for cheese recommendations—and to eye my bulging lunch bag. I finally installed a mini "cave" under my desk and offered noontime tastings under the auspices of the Saint Joseph's University English Department. Even students joined in for these studious samplings.

This book is my attempt to bring the secrets of the cheese counter into your kitchen, and to put tasting notes and pairing advice into your hands. If I have learned one thing in my six years of nibbling and scribbling, it's that you don't need to be an expert in order to enjoy cheese. You just need an enthusiastic guide. Whoever you are—novice, dabbler, thrill-seeker, geek—consider this your invitation to the world's most luscious cheese party.

Within these pages, you'll find:

- **170 of the most loved and requested cheeses from the counter at Di Bruno Bros.**
- **Ideas for pairing cheese with wine, beer, and cocktails**
- **Menus for special occasion cheese boards**
- **Tips on how to buy, serve, and store cheese**

Now, come with me. I have a few hunks for you to meet.

—Tenaya Darlington,
a.k.a. Madame Fromage
Madamefromageblog.com

INTRODUCTION:

HOW TO PICK A HUNK

You never forget your first love; mine was a blue cheese. For you, it may be a sweet, nutty type or a muscle-y Italian with a dense rind. Because the purpose of this book is to help *you* find the cheese of your dreams, it's not organized like other cheese guides, which often group selections by milk types or rind styles. Instead, the cheeses are grouped by personality. What you hold in your hands is essentially a matchmaker's directory to the most luscious dairy in the world. If a cheese made it into these pages, it's because we—the cheesemongers of Di Bruno Bros. and I—felt that it was exceptional, a cheese with character. Once you have a look around, you'll see what we mean.

If you're the kind of person who loves rich friends, try hanging out with Vixens (page 87). If loud talkers make you nervous, let us set you up with a Quiet Type (page 39). And if you're the sort who welcomes a risk, a dare, a bedeviling suitor, well, just head straight for Pierced Punks (page 225). Along the way, you'll find tips, recipes, and pairing ideas to sweeten the experience.

Our hope is that you will flip through these pages in much the same way that you might wander through a party after a cocktail or two: with a flirtatious spirit. It doesn't matter if you're still in a relationship with Velveeta, as long as you have an open mind. Just be forewarned: you probably won't find your supermarket steadies in these pages, and that's because our goal is to surprise and amaze you. Part of enjoying cheese, after all, is its seductive nature. Intriguing beauties await. Curious?

Here's your key to the party:
  Baby Faces: fresh, unaged
  Quiet Types: approachable, subtle
  Free Spirits: sunshiny, herby (mostly goat's milk)
  Vixens: rich, decadent
  Mountain Men: bold, Alpine
  Stinkers: whiffy, boozy
  Rockstars: rare, revered
  Wise Guys: old school, mostly Italian
  Sugar Mamas: sweet, desserty
  Pierced Punks: blues

Now let's start with a quick tour:

NAVIGATING THE COUNTER

Keep in mind that every cheese shop is essentially a dairy spa: some cheeses crave air, while others need help coping with age. It's the job of a trained cheesemonger to attend to everyone's needs, to decide which cheeses need a little time to ripen among the rafters and which cheeses are ready for you to devour.

Fresh cheeses are usually stored in a cooler near the counter—here you'll find your Baby Faces (page 25), your Vixens (page 87), and your Stinkers (page 141), too. They need to be eaten soon. Anything dangling from the ceiling or sitting on a shelf unrefrigerated is probably "mature"—a Wise Guy (page 179) or a Mountain Man (page 117). They're good for camping trips, long walks on the beach, or extended stays in your crisper. Read How to Talk to a Cheesemonger (page 23) and embrace the cheese shop for what it is: a place to soften and relax.

THE CHEESEMONGER'S TRADE

Discovering a rare cheese that no one knows about yet is half the fun of perusing a well-stocked counter. That's why cheesemongers will go to the ends of the earth to stock little-known wheels from independent producers, many of whom dedicate themselves to raising their own animals and making cheese by hand. Often these folks are highly skilled, like musicians, and fans fill their inboxes with beseeching requests.

In his Cheesemonger Notes for this book, Hunter Fike—a longstanding Di Bruno Bros. monger—will give you a glimpse of how he has sweet-talked some of the legends in the business, along with other behind-the-scenes tips and insights. If you want to taste some of Hunter's favorites, check out Rockstars (page 163).

AMERICAN VS. IMPORTED

It used to be that the best cheeses came from Europe, and many people still have a bias against any cheese labeled "American." Understandable. As a country, we have gone Dr. Seuss on cheese—stuffing it with fillers and dyes, putting it into pumps, and stirring every imaginable whacky ingredient into it, from bacon bits to blueberries.

Just know that American cheese, like beer in this country, is coming out of its ugly adolescence and fueling a very interesting scene. Look beyond the Kraft Single and you'll find a world of "craft" cheese that has experienced a major growth spurt in the last decade. There are now over 800 licensed artisan cheesemakers in the United States, according to Jeff Roberts, author of *The Atlas of American Artisan Cheese.* Compare that to roughly 150 back in 2000.

BUILDING A CHEESE BOARD

Use the cheese boards at the end of each chapter to pull together picnics, holiday spreads, and themed tastings. If you get into the dairy spirit, you might even decide to set aside one night a month to try some cheeses with friends. Send them on a mission to find hunks from different countries or from different milk types, and then settle in for a night of exploring. Call it "Palate Development" and everyone will think you're taking a design class.

Over time, you'll be amazed by how much you can learn just from setting aside time to taste. It's kind of like training your eyes to read lips or your ears to recognize pitches. Once you train your taste buds, you will never look at food—not even a bowl of popcorn—in quite the same way. Check out the section on How to Taste Cheese (page 139), and use the lexicon if you need to spice up your vocabulary.

RAW VS. PASTEURIZED

You may have heard about raw (unpasteurized) milk in the news, so let me explain a few things. First, the FDA requires all raw-milk cheese to be aged at least sixty days, so all of the cheeses listed in this book are perfectly legal. After sixty days, it's believed that any potentially harmful bacteria will have expired.

Secondly, cheesemakers tend to have a very different view of raw milk from the general population. Pasteurization kills *everything* in milk, not just bacteria and enzymes, but also flavor. It also changes the chemical make-up of milk. As a cheesemaker once explained: making a cheese with pasteurized milk is like trying to bake a cake with hardboiled eggs.

Next time you're at the cheese counter,

ask for a sample of raw-milk cheese. You'll probably notice that it's quite complex, whereas many pasteurized cheeses can taste "flat" or "one note." On the whole, cheesemongers tend to be raw-milk cheese junkies, so don't be afraid to quiz them about their personal attachments.

CONFRONTING ALLERGIES, LOVE HANDLES, AND CHOLESTEROL

Understanding how certain foods, like cheese, affect the body can be confusing. If you're lactose sensitive, here's my advice: meet some Wise Guys (page 179) and Sugar Mamas (page 209). Most of these are hard cheeses, and hard cheeses are free of lactose except for an occasional trace. Cabot, an award-winning cheese company based in Vermont, actually markets its aged Cheddar as "lactose free." If you can eat their Clothbound Cheddar (page 165), you can probably eat any well-aged cheese.

If fat and cholesterol are your mortal enemies, let me point out one observation and a fact: few people who make and sell cheese are obese, even though they sample cheese all day. That's because people tend to savor bites of high quality cheese rather than gorging. If you bear this in mind, you'll understand why nibbling reverently from a lovely cheese board at dinner is much better for you than sitting before the television with a large pizza. As for cholesterol, a 3.5-ounce piece of cheese has a quarter of the cholesterol in an egg—and twice as much protein. So put that in your backpack and take a hike.

A WORD ON PAIRINGS

All of the cheeses in this book come with suggestions for beer, wine, and sometimes spirits, because who wants a nosh without a little sparkle? You'll also find more general pairing lessons (labeled Cheese 101) at the end of each chapter so that you can begin to play around with some ideas of your own.

Keep in mind that cheeses can vary in taste depending on the season and their state of ripeness; I've tried to account for that in my recommendations, but don't be afraid to deviate. And if you discover a new combination that makes your mind reel and your knees sway, feel free to drop a comment on the Di Bruno blog (www.dibruno.com/blog) or stop by the counter to share your discovery. Who doesn't love to nerd out on a good cheese pairing?

How to Host a Cheese Party

A good cheese board, like a good party, needs a mix of friends. If you invite a Vixen, you might also want to invite a Rockstar. Free Spirits and Sugar Mamas—they usually get along, too. Here are a few things to remember:

• Always serve cheese at room temperature so you can taste the full range of flavors. Think about it: would you serve stone-cold chocolate?

• For a balanced cheese plate, pick three to five contrasting cheeses. You can go for a variety of milk types (goat, cow, sheep), or work off a theme, like French, Italian, or Spanish cheeses. It's also fun to play up the seasons and serve cheeses that match local fruit or jam from the farmers' market. Check out the guide to pairing cheese and fruit (page 222).

• Don't worry too much about how you arrange your cheeses. If you eat them in order of soft to hard, you can be pretty sure you won't burn out your palate on a sharpie right away. For that reason, it's best to eat blues last.

• Both wine and beer pair well with cheeses. When in doubt, pick a white; reds can be a little pushy, especially with mild creamies. Beer is incredibly forgiving and usually cheaper than wine, so if you need to wing it, grab a variety pack and play around with flavors Mr. Potato Head–style.

• Here's a handy hostess tip: Think "light and fresh" before dinner (try mozzarella or soft goat, or stack the decks with Brie and Champagne). Think "dark and stormy" after dinner (grab blues and butterscotchy Goudas to pair with thick elixirs, like port and dark beer).

• Hold the herbed crackers, my friend. Plain baguette is a girl's best friend. Otherwise, go for water crackers, petit toasts, or oaty biscuits—none of which will detract.

• Condiments, oh condiments. A few olives, dried apricots, or nuts can turn a droopy wedge into a dream. Don't be afraid to play around with pairings. You can never go wrong with honey and fresh pears or apples.

• Fancy utensils? Not necessary. It is nice to serve each cheese with its own knife, though, so that flavors don't cross-pollinate.

• A final word: Take a risk on at least one cheese when you have people over. It always makes for interesting conversation. Personally, I recommend a Pierced Punk (page 225).

DIY Cheese Boards

If you don't have any nice cutting boards, there are plenty of creative stand-ins, and you probably have some of them hiding in a dark closet. A piece of slate and some chalk makes it easy to label your cheeses so that guests will remember the fabulous wedges they tasted at your house.

    Clay or ceramic tiles
    Retro dinner plates
    Old china saucers from your grandmother
    Cake stands
    Remaindered marble
    Terracotta plant saucers
    Holiday platters
    Book covers wrapped in butcher paper

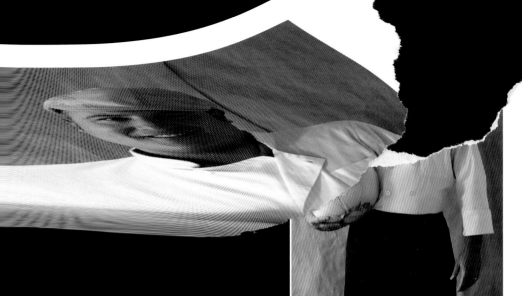

HOW TO TALK TO A CHEESEMONGER

Contrary to popular belief, cheesemongers are not ogres. They're not interested in judging your cheese knowledge: they just want to make you happy. So, for your first lesson in cheese, let's go over a few terms and suggestions.

• Walk up to the counter and look lost. Cheesemongers, like forest rangers, want to help you. Admit that you don't know anything, and they'll take you by the hand.

• Be adventurous. If you're scared of blues, say so. But don't cling to Jarlsberg.

• Once you discover a cheese you like, tell the cheesemonger you want to try something similar. There are roughly eight styles of cheese—fresh, bloomy, washed rind, soft, semisoft, firm, hard, blue—once you discover one you like, explore the field.

• If you don't know whether to eat the rind, ask. Many rinds, like those fuzzy sweaters around Brie, look a bit funky but are perfectly edible, and you'll notice that the rind often contains the most flavor. But if it doesn't appeal to you, don't eat it. No hard feelings.

• If you want to see a cheesemonger get excited, ask, "So, what do you like?" You'll get to try the most interesting cheeses that way.

• Ask for pairing tips. Cheesemongers graze all day, and they're often wonderful cooks who attend tastings and secret, service-industry parties full of unthinkable delights. Most of them can rattle off cheese and wine pairings like it's no big thang.

• Eat the samples. As you taste them, make a mental a note of the flavors. If you have trouble placing a flavor, ask the cheese-monger, "What am I tasting?" so that you get a little instruction. This is a great way to develop your palate.

• If you're on a budget, let the cheesemonger know. Splurge on one or two delicacies, then pick something affordable. In cheese land, you really do get what you pay for. Exquisite cheeses are expensive because they are usually made by hand on a farm by someone who has lots of furry little mouths to feed.

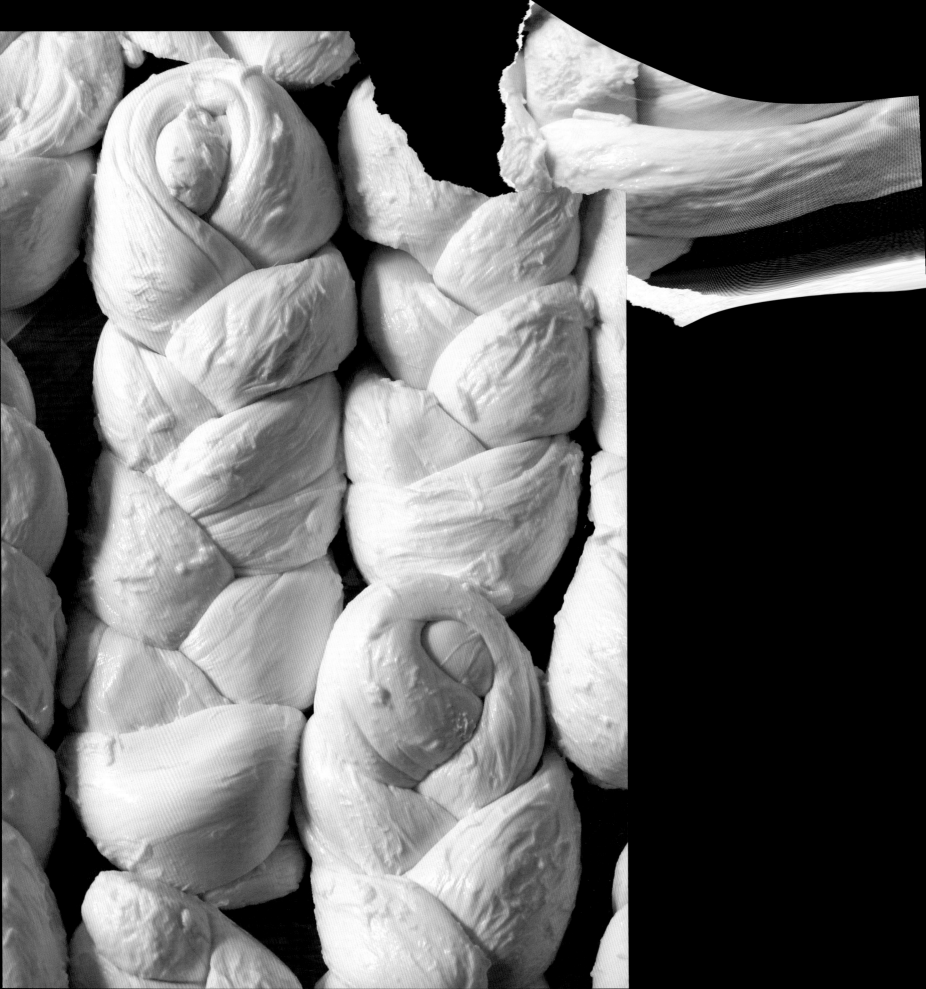

CHAPTER I

BABY FACES

(fresh, unaged)

These young, fresh cheeses are mellow and easygoing. They're a great place to start if you're shy, and they're perfect for a summer evening when garden-ripe tomatoes and peaches need bedfellows. Pop the cork on Prosecco or rosé, and you're good for eating and drinking the night away.

Burrata | Burrata with Heirloom | Tomatoes | **Capricho de Cabra** | Goat Cheese Terrine with Fig Jam and Pesto | **Mascarpone** | **Mozzarella** | **Ricotta** | Cheese Board: Tapas on the Patio | Cheese 101: How to Pair Cheese and Wine

BURRATA

ITALY, COW'S MILK

PERSONALITY: Mozzarella with soul—a rare treat with a dreamy center.

Burrata is to the cheese world what the dumpling is to Asian cuisine: the ultimate comfort food. Within each pouch of noodle-soft mozzarella is a center filled with cream and, sometimes, truffle shavings or fresh herbs. Airy and cloud-light, this fresh cheese is meant to be drizzled with olive oil, sprinkled with sea salt and black pepper, then sopped up with bread. Over the last few years, burrata (pronounced Boo-RAH-ta) has become something of a dairy darling, especially in restaurants. Along the East Coast, you're likely to find it on summer menus served with heirloom tomatoes; on the West Coast, with sea urchin.

Di Bruno Bros. has made burrata in house for decades. It's tied off with leek leaves and kitchen twine, just as custom dictates in Puglia, where this cheese originates. The twine holds the pouch together, and the leeks are used to help gauge freshness. Buy burrata when the leaves are emerald bright; when the leaves turn spotty or brown, toss the burrata out. Great burrata is plush, luxuriant, and cooling—a gentle balm after a sun-drenched day at the beach.

Good matches: To serve, set your burrata on a lipped plate, remove the leaves, and cut the cheese in half, vertically. Drag hunks of baguette through the cream and serve them to your beloved, preferably in a hammock.

Wine/beer: Pick up something sparkly, unless you're serving antipasti, in which case you can ramp up to a spicy red or something fruity and supple. Young Chianti or Barbera work well with fresh cheeses. So does an icy cold Pilsner.

THE HUMBLE BEGINNINGS OF BURRATA

History is riddled with proud, noble cheeses that have had their names slandered by mass-produced knock-offs. We've all seen them, pre-shredded, canned, or cryovac-ed, populating the dairy aisle of your local grocery store; Cheddars, Parmesan, and Swiss that bear little resemblance to their handmade originals.

But the timeline of burrata is the inverse of this familiar tale. It was originally created in the 1920s by a manufacturer in Puglia, who would take the scraps from production, whip them, and stuff them into the center of mozzarella. It was a clever way to use what would otherwise become waste, and their heavier mozzarella could be sold for more money.

Burrata existed in relative obscurity, remaining unknown to anyone outside of southern Italy. However, in recent years several artisan producers have begun to realize burrata's full potential, and exquisite burrata is now produced throughout Italy and the United States.

-CHEESEMONGER HUNTER FIKE

BURRATA with HEIRLOOM TOMATOES

This variation on a Caprese salad is a Di Bruno Bros. classic. Serve it with grilled bread, olives, and Prosecco for a light appetizer or a summery lunch. It's easily doubled or halved.

SERVES 4

1 pound heirloom tomatoes cut into bite-size pieces (or about 2 cups halved cherry tomatoes)

8 basil leaves, sliced into ribbons

¾ cup balsamic vinegar

3 tablespoons extra-virgin olive oil

2 garlic cloves, minced

Sea salt and freshly ground pepper

2 burrata, about 12 ounces each

1 loaf rustic Italian bread, cut in thick slices and grilled or toasted

Toss the tomatoes with the basil and balsamic. While they sit, make a quick garlic oil—just heat the olive oil in a frying pan over medium-high heat for about a minute, then add the minced garlic. You don't want it to brown, so as soon as the garlic begins to sizzle, remove the pan from the burner.

Pour the hot garlic oil over the tomatoes and season with salt and pepper. Arrange the tomato mixture on four plates, and slice the burrata vertically in half. There's cream inside, so make sure you do this on a cutting board or plate. Arrange the halved burrata on top of the tomatoes. Serve with thick slices of grilled or toasted bread.

CAPRICHO DE CABRA

SPAIN, GOAT'S MILK

PERSONALITY: A contortionist—versatile, young, and game for anything.

Everyone needs a go-to soft goat cheese. It's light on the palate and easy on the stomach, which makes it suitable for breakfast or late-night snacking. Capricho de Cabra, from Murcia, is widely recognized as one of the best chèvres on the market. Unlike some commercial brands that taste "bucky" (like the smell of goats) or feel grainy, this spreadable dream is mild and clean tasting with a smooth, clayey texture. It's also one of the more affordable softies.

Murciano goats give Capricho de Cabra its silky appeal: this breed, native to southeastern Spain, is famous for its rich milk. If you want something a little tangier, try Caña de Cabra (page 67), an aged goat cheese with a bloomy rind. It comes from the same maker.

Good matches: Use Capricho de Cabra for crumbling on salads or pastas, or for baking. This is a great cheese to spread on toasted bread or sandwiches, too. For a quick appetizer, stir in some fresh herbs and schmear the mixture on baguette rounds. Try adding some tapenade, roasted red peppers, or a sprinkle of pink or gray salt for color.

Wine/beer: Pick a light white, like Sauvignon Blanc, or a citrusy wheat beer.

GOAT CHEESE TERRINE
with FIG JAM and PESTO

This layered appetizer works well with Capricho de Cabra (page 30), or seek out a local chèvre. In summer or winter, this is a great party dish—it's quick to assemble and easy to make ahead. Serve it with baguette rounds or Semolina Crackers with Sea Salt (page 100). If you want to make your own pesto, see the recipe on page 185.

SERVES 6 TO 8

4 ounces (1 stick) unsalted butter, at room temperature

1 pound fresh goat cheese (approximately 2 cups), at room temperature

Sea salt and freshly ground pepper

$^{1}/_{2}$ cup basil pesto

$^{3}/_{4}$ cup fig jam

$^{1}/_{2}$ cup walnuts or pecans, toasted and coarsely chopped

Line the inside of a very deep 4-cup bowl with plastic wrap, allowing the edges to drape over the sides. Cream the butter and fresh goat cheese in a mixing bowl for 3 minutes, until fluffy. Add a dash of salt and pepper, to taste.

Spoon one-third of the goat cheese into the plastic-lined bowl, and spread it evenly with a spatula to form your first layer. Top this with a layer of pesto, but don't spread it all the way to the edge (it will seep out on its own), followed by a second layer of goat cheese (there will be three total). Add the fig jam, followed by a final tier of goat cheese.

Cover the dish with a layer of plastic wrap. Chill for 2 to 4 hours, or until set.

Before serving, remove the top layer of plastic wrap and invert the bowl onto a plate, then remove the bowl and the plastic liner. Garnish with the toasted nuts.

MASCARPONE

ITALY, COW'S MILK
PERSONALITY: A lingerie model, rich and almost unbearably smooth.

In the United States, mascarpone rarely appears except in desserts, like tiramisù, but in Italy mascarpone (rhymes with "NASCAR-pony") is a staple. Its creamy consistency is the texture of whipped butter, and it can be spread on toast in much the same way. If you're a fan of cream cheese, you'll clutch your bosom when you taste this close cousin, which is many times more luscious. In fact, it's really not a cheese—it's satin.

Mascarpone is made from cream without the addition of rennet, a coagulant used in cheese-making. Technically, this means mascarpone isn't really a cheese at all; it's more akin to yogurt. In Italy, this sweet stuff is tucked into ravioli, spooned onto grilled fruit, or swirled into soups as a final garnish. For a snack in certain parts of Italy, mascarpone is served in ice cream bowls, topped with sugar, grated dark chocolate, and finely ground coffee beans. Meow.

Good matches: Use mascarpone as you would cream cheese or whipped cream. Spread it on scones or toasted challah, or serve it with fresh berries and a touch of honey. Check out the Tapas on the Patio cheese board (page 35).

Wine/beer: Prosecco or a bubbly Belgian beer is the magic choice here since effervescence is the key to unlocking rich, fatty cheeses.

Mascarpone Frosting

One Di Bruno Bros. customer swears by mascarpone for topping cakes. She combines equal parts mascarpone and Nutella, then spreads it across sheet cake or brownies. You can also stir some cinnamon into plain mascarpone and press it between amaretti. A thin layer of apricot preserves makes for a most exquisite sandwich cookie.

MOZZARELLA

ITALY, COW OR BUFFALO MILK
PERSONALITY: **A true baby face, round and soft with a sweet character.**

Great mozzarella should always taste pillowy and ephemeral. This light texture is achieved by stretching warm curds into long ribbons—a process that is similar to pulling and spinning wool to make yarn. The method was developed around Naples in the second century when water buffalo milk was plentiful. Old timers still ask for "mozzarella di bufala" at the cheese counter, and when it's available, this rare treat is worth trying. It's complex in flavor, and the texture is sensuous.

When you buy fresh mozzarella, eat it straight away. The longer it sits around, the more it congeals into a tough little cue ball. If you ever get the chance to try warm mozzarella right out of the vat, go for it. You'll melt into your shoes.

Good Matches: You don't need much more than a loaf of crusty bread, some good olive oil, and a fresh tomato. For a summer cheese plate, add an assortment of olives, fresh basil, prosciutto, and melon or peaches. For an irreverent cheesemonger favorite: slice a glazed yeast doughnut lengthwise and stuff it with mozzarella di bufala.

Wine/beer: Pick up a bottle of Prosecco, or opt for a Pilsner or lager. A cold Peroni always works well.

RICOTTA

ITALY, COW, GOAT, OR SHEEP'S MILK
PERSONALITY: **The kid sister of the family—sweet, likable, and amenable to almost everything.**

Fresh ricotta should be airy and light, like the featherbed of an angel. The key is buying it fresh from the cheese counter or making it yourself, an easy-peasy achievement as long as you use quality, fresh milk. This is an un-aged cheese, best eaten soon after it's made. Commercially prepared ricotta can be grainy and tasteless, but the real deal is fluffy—like perfectly cooked grits—with a mild, milky taste and smell.

Ricotta is rich in protein and low in fat, which makes it a useful alterative to cream cheese or butter, especially for spreading on toast or sandwiches. It's made from whey, a byproduct of cheesemaking, and the name literally means "recooked." In Italy, ricotta is used in pastries, like cannoli, or in savory dishes, like *pasta al forno* (baked pasta). Aged and salted, it's sold as ricotta salata, which can be grated or cubed. Both fresh ricotta and ricotta salata are great summer cheeses that accentuate ripe tomatoes.

Good matches: On the patio, set out a dish of fresh ricotta with a bottle of good olive oil, some sea salt, and grilled Italian bread. For dessert, serve a scoop of fresh ricotta over peaches or berries, followed by a drizzle of honey and some toasted almonds. Use ricotta salata—which is firm and salty—much as you would feta, crumbled over heirloom tomatoes, watermelon, or salad greens.

Wine/beer: Try a glass of dry rosé. A light beer is a good choice for ricotta appetizers.

CHEESE BOARD: Tapas on the Patio

Fresh cheeses always taste good in spring and summer, alongside fresh herbs and farmers' market produce. They're light, mild, and great for outdoor entertaining. Set out some Burrata with Heirloom Tomatoes (page 28), or for a festive evening, serve an array of these combinations. They pair well with Christmas lights and a bottle of Prosecco or rosé. A pitcher of sangria or mojitos would also be smashing.

Ricotta with Fresh Herbs, Lemon Zest, and Olive Oil

Mix some lemon zest and a selection of chopped herbs (basil, thyme, and chives are nice) into some fresh ricotta (page 34). Scoop it into a shallow bowl, and drizzle with olive oil, salt, and cracked pepper. Serve with baguette rounds or grilled bread for dipping.

Mascarpone with Peaches, Basil, and Speck

Toast some baguette rounds, then schmear each one with mascarpone. On each round, add a piece of thinly shaved speck (or prosciutto), a slice of ripe peach, and a basil leaf. Drizzle with olive oil and a crank of white pepper.

Grilled Bread with Fresh Tomatoes, Garlic, and Ricotta Salata

Light up the grill. Cut a baguette lengthwise, drizzle it with olive oil, and grill it cut-side down until it has nice marks. Then top it with a roughly chopped mixture of fresh tomatoes, minced garlic, and crumbled ricotta salata. Add fresh basil or oregano as a garnish.

Mascarpone and Anchovy Toasts

Top petit toasts with a layer of mascarpone, half an anchovy, a dab of Dijon mustard, and a pinch of finely chopped red pepper or purple onion—in that order. Add a sprig of dill for color.

CHEESE 101: How to Pair Cheese and Wine

Learning how to pair wine with cheese takes practice, which is why it's always good to pick the brain of a cheesemonger—especially one who looks a little flush. Don't forget that beers work well with cheese, too, and so do cocktails and, oh hell, even certain teas, especially green teas and smoky oolongs. Don't stop exploring the realm of pairings. It's always fun to make a gorgeous discovery.

- When in doubt, go for a white. White wine is forgiving and easier to pair with cheese than reds. Among lacto nerds, the most cheese-friendly wine is said to be an Alsatian Gewürztraminer. It's sweetly aromatic and a little spicy, so it makes friends easily.

- Choose a wine that matches the strength of your cheese. A Sauvignon Blanc with a young goat cheese is sublime—both are a bit fragile. A Cabernet needs a busty hard cheese to keep it in check.

- Consider terroir. Cheese, like wine, exhibits the flavors of its origins. If you pick out a Basque cheese, try to find a wine from the same part of the country—say, a Rioja from northern Spain.

- Red wines work well with hard, crystalline cheeses. Take that Parmigiano Reggiano or Pecorino and sic a dark, blood-red master on it.

- Use the descriptors on the back of the wine bottle. If you pick out a wine with cherry notes, say, imagine what kind of cheese might pair well with actual cherries. Hopefully, you'll think of cheesecake, which will lead you to a triple crème. A "brambly" wine might make you think of camping; you'd be right to pick out a rustic cheese, like a little wheel of leaf-wrapped Banon (page 88).

- Dense, fatty cheeses, like triple crèmes, benefit from effervescence. Think of Brie and Champagne. The bubbles cleanse your palate between bites. For this same reason, Italians often nurse Prosecco while snacking on hunks of aged Parm.

HERE ARE SOME FAVORITE PAIRINGS:

White Wine Matches

Champagne/Prosecco: Bries and triple crèmes, like Brie de Meaux (page 89)
  or Délice de Bourgogne (page 95)

Sauvignon Blanc: young to medium-aged goat cheese, like Valençay (page 82)

Chardonnay: medium to sharp Cheddar, like Cabot Clothbound Cheddar
  (page 165)

Pinot Grigio: Alpine cheeses, like Comté (page 121) or Beaufort (page 119)

Gewürztraminer: funky cheeses, like Munster (page 152)

Riesling: aged goat cheeses, like Ticklemore (page 110)

Sauternes: salty blues, like Roquefort (page 92)

Red Wine Matches

Rosé: ricotta (page 34) or mozzarella (page 34)

Pinot Noir and Burgundy: nutty cow's milk cheeses, like Gruyère (page 125)

Bourdeaux: earthy clothbound Cheddars, like Avonlea (page 164)

Côtes du Rhône: French stinkers, like Epoisses (page 143)

Barbera d'Asti: Fontina (page 125) or Taleggio (page 158)

Merlot: aged sheep's milk cheeses and Wise Guys, like Ragusano (page 196)

Amarone: Parmigiano-Reggiano (page 189), Piave (page 190)

Port: earthy blue cheese, like Stilton (page 234)

For notes on pairing cheese with beer, see page 176. For notes on pairing cheese with digestifs, see page 242.

CHAPTER II

QUIET TYPES

(approachable, subtle)

The hunks in this chapter are mild and friendly, but it doesn't mean that they're wallflowers. In fact, some of the most revered cheeses are quite delicate, like Idiazábal (page 49) and Ossau-Iraty (page 56), two Spanish lovers prized for their understated flavors. These are great party cheeses, special enough to impress chowhounds but gentle enough to appease finicky friends.

Abbaye de Belloc | Appleby's Cheshire | Berkswell | Caramelized Endive Marmalade | Camembert du Bocage | Cantal | Garrotxa | Haystack Queso de Mano | Idiazábal | Mahón | Manchego | Manchego and Marcona Almond Pesto | Mimolette | Mrs. Kirkham's Tasty Lancashire | Nevat | Nuvola di Pecora | Ossau-Iraty | Pantaleo | Petit Basque | Seven Sisters | Wensleydale | Cheese Board: Desk Bento for One | Cheese 101: Alone with Olives: A Novice's Guide

ABBAYE DE BELLOC

FRANCE, RAW SHEEP'S MILK

PERSONALITY: Graceful and complex, like a monk enrobed in rustic silence.

As you eat this cheese made by the Benedictines of the Abbaye de Notre-Dame de Belloc, think of blanched almonds and brown butter. This much-loved quiet type from the western Pyrénées is gentle and sweetly nutty without the mutton-chop antagonism that sometimes pops up in cheeses made from sheep's milk. Thank the red-nosed Manech ewes that graze around the abbey; quality milk and skillful monks contribute to the superb balance of flavors here.

Note the rind, which looks like the sheath of a Brazil nut (its vaguely reddish color comes from a good rubdown with paprika). The ivory paste should be firm and smooth, like fresh sheets on a farmhouse bed. If you're a fan of Ossau-Iraty (page 56), a popular Spanish cheese, be sure to try this version. It's loosely based on the same recipe, but Abbaye de Belloc bears the distinction of being a monastic French sheep's milk cheese—a rarity.

Good matches: Offer this with a touch of golden honey and some rustic bread. On a cheese plate, beware of overshadowing this gem with too many strong flavors. Keep it simple with almonds, fruit, and a handful of other mellow sweeties. Try serving thin slices atop a lightly dressed salad of butter lettuce and pears.

Wine/beer: This is a versatile cheese when it comes to wine. Rosé works perfectly, so do most summery whites, or if your wedge of Abbaye de Belloc is punchy from age, pop the cork on that bottle of Chateau Margaux you've been saving. Midas Touch, a saffron-kissed ale from Dogfish Head, is a stunning side.

APPLEBY'S CHESHIRE

ENGLAND, RAW COW'S MILK

PERSONALITY: Cheddar's granddad, a ruddy sea captain with a mellow disposition.

Before there was Cheddar, there was Cheshire. In fact, records show that this is England's oldest cheese. First mention appears in the Domesday Book of 1086 A.D., and later, ship captains' logs reveal that Cheshire was a favorite on long ocean voyages—probably because it traveled well. Like other clothbound cheeses, it's a dense form of sustenance. It's also protein-packed and surprisingly mild.

Today the loveliest Cheshire comes from Lucy Appleby's farm in Shropshire, where it's formed into large drums and wrapped in calico. If you have a hankering for something earthy and easygoing, give it a try. Like traditional British Cheddar, it has a hint of rustic tang, but on the whole, Cheshire is milder and moister. If Cheddar is a tiger, then Cheshire is the family cat. Don't be alarmed by the bright orange coloring; the pigment comes from a natural dye extracted from the annatto plant.

Good matches: Cut off hunks of Cheshire with your pen knife and layer them over warm apple pie. Or, enjoy a wedge alongside fall fruit. This is an excellent cheese for melting on thick toast, especially with a schmear of caramelized onions.

Wine/beer: Pair this with a young Zinfandel, a mild brown ale, or a spot of single-malt scotch.

THE HISTORY OF ANNATTO SEED EXTRACT

In nineteenth century England, well before the two wars decimated farmhouse cheese production, nearly every single dairy farm was making some form of cheese. While Cheddar, Caerphilly (page 170), and Wensleydale (page 60) were all popular, nothing was made in such great quantity as Cheshire. Imagine going to the market in town every morning, and having ten different Cheshires from which to choose. How do you decide? Aside from visiting a different producer every day, or trying them all at once, it had to have been difficult to pick one over the other.

With that in mind, one producer had the genius idea of adding annatto seed extract to his curds. The coloring agent made his Cheshire shine with a reddish-orange hue, but did not alter the flavor. When his Cheshire started attracting customers, his competitors started adding annatto as well. So what began as a marketing ploy became common practice, and these days you would be hard pressed to find a Cheshire without the extract added.

–CHEESEMONGER HUNTER FIKE

BERKSWELL

ENGLAND, RAW SHEEP'S MILK
PERSONALITY: A stoic figure with a biscuity crust and firm interior.

Berkswell is a sweet and subtle cheese with a reptilian appearance. The wheels are shaped like flying saucers with distinct markings: imprints from the colanders in which the curds are drained. The Fletchers, a sixth-generation dairy family, began making this unique cheese at their home, Ram Hall, in the West Midlands back in the '90s. Now it's a much-loved English specialty, appreciated for its seasonality and subtle flavor.

In spring, you'll find Berkswell to be lactic and fruity; in fall, the profile changes dramatically, turning musky. As the pasture diet of the ewes changes, so does the taste of the milk. If you're a fan of Manchego (page 51), you'll find Berkswell to be a nuanced next step for your palate. The texture is similarly firm, but the taste pulls in both sweet and savory notes, like a beautifully caramelized roast.

Good matches: Berkswell is just the right cheese to serve alongside a rustic stew. It also pairs well with potatoes. In summer, take it on a picnic with rosemary bread and fresh fruit.

Wine/beer: Pair with a Côtes du Rhône or a wheat beer.

CHEESEMONGER NOTE: THE BEAUTY OF BERKSWELL AND SCOTCH

In 2010, we hosted a Scotch and cheese pairing conducted by Rory Stone, maker of Strathdon Blue (page 240). Because the art of pairing Scotch with cheese was still in its nascent stages, the format of the event was more open forum than instruction. We presented six Scotches and six cheeses, with enough cheese for guests to taste each cheese with each Scotch. The results were very surprising.

While we thought that the bigger cheeses—Ardrahan (page 142), Keen's (page 171) and Montgomery's Cheddars (page 172) and Stichelton (page 174)—would stand up to the big, burly Scotches, the near unanimous favorite was Berkswell. Perhaps the sheepy flavors so evocative of eponymous Scottish wool had something to do with it, but what was sure was that the subtleness of Berkswell seemed to cut the alcohol bite while elevating the peaty, smoky flavors. This has been my go-to Scotch pairing ever since.

- CHEESEMONGER HUNTER FIKE

CARAMELIZED ENDIVE MARMALADE

Endive, a bitter green that looks like a tiny elongated cabbage, forms the bulk of this curious spread, which gains its sweetness from honey and finishes with roasty notes of caramelized onion. Serve with Berkswell (page 44) and other firm sheep's milk cheeses for an unusual sweet-savory pairing.

MAKES 2 CUPS

¼ cup vegetable oil
6 Belgian endive, roughly chopped
3 shallots, peeled and thinly sliced
2 garlic cloves, minced
2 tablespoons unsalted butter
¼ cup honey
Zest and juice of 1 orange
Sea salt and white pepper

Heat a large skillet over medium-high heat, and add the vegetable oil. When the oil begins to smoke, place the endive in the pan. Cook for 6 to 8 minutes, stirring every 30 seconds or so to develop caramelization.

Reduce the heat to low, then add the shallots, garlic, butter, honey, orange zest, and orange juice. Let the mixture cook down for 1 hour, until it's golden brown. Check it from time to time, and add a little water if it gets too dry. Don't be tempted to crank up the heat. Slow cooking is key here to "melt" the ingredients. Add salt and pepper to taste.

Cool the marmalade completely before serving. Covered and refrigerated, this will last for one week.

CAMEMBERT DU NORMANDIE

FRANCE, COW'S MILK

PERSONALITY: A heartthrob of buttery mushrooms with roll-in-the-hay freshness.

Too often Camembert gets lost on party platters amid a lot of fancy fixings, and by the end of the night its carcass-like rind serves as a reminder that surface mold is still misunderstood. Word to all: a good Camembert needs very little fuss, and yes, the rind is perfectly edible. In fact, it's the most flavorful part of the cheese, full of mushroomy goodness and hints of cracked pepper.

Camembert hails from Normandy, where it's made, by law, with raw milk. In the States, the FDA requires all young cheeses to be pasteurized, and since Camembert is an adolescent wünderkind, the wheels available to us here are a little different from the opulent rounds you may have sampled in France. That said, you must try Camembert du Normandie, one of the tastiest pasteurized versions on the market. Let it come to room temperature, then inhale its buttery, fungal scent as you dig in. When ripe, Camembert—even in America—can be glorious.

Good Matches: The French eat Camembert with baguette and walnuts. Make like the French.

Wine/beer: Pick a beverage based on the ripeness of your Camembert. For a young wheel: Champagne. For a medium-ripe wheel, a hard cider from Normandy will bring tears to your eyes. A well-aged wheel can tame a Côtes du Rhône. Favor beer? Grab a Belgian Dubbel.

How to Know When Camembert is Ripe

Camembert ripens from the outside in, so look to the color of its surface for clues. A perfectly white Camembert is young and will be mild in flavor, dense in texture. As the cheese ripens, stippling appears on the rind and the surface will look less like velvet and more like beige corduroy. Most people favor a Corduroy Camembert—the flavors deepen, and the center turns wicked fudgy, almost runny. If you smell ammonia on your Camembert, it's beginning to turn. Eat it *maintenant*!

CANTAL

FRANCE, COW'S MILK
PERSONALITY: The Gérard Depardieu of cheese—a burly quiet type.

When people ask for a mild or medium Cheddar, Cantal comes to mind. It's *not* a Cheddar, but it is vaguely reminiscent of the rugged farmhouse-style cheeses that come out of Somerset where real British Cheddar is made. In fact, rumor has it that French missionaries actually brought Cantal to Somerset, inspiring the first Cheddar. (Just don't bring this up in a pub on a hot night, or fur might fly.) Cantal comes in keg-like wheels with a rustic rind, and its taste is buttery with just a hint of tang. As a table cheese, this gentle giant can enliven an otherwise humdrum lunch. It also melts like a dream.

Cantal takes its name from a mountain range within the Massif Central, where it originates. Early references to this cheese go back more than 2,000 years—long before Roquefort—when Pliny the Elder wrote about it in his 37-volume *Naturae Historiae,* the first encyclopedia. Today, Cantal is a name-controlled cheese, prized by the French. Look for a young wheel that's been aged two to six months (*doré*) for medium sharpness. For a spunkier version, ask for a sample that's been aged more than six months (*vieux*). It will have a reddish rind.

Good matches: Plane this onto sandwiches or set out a hunk with some dry-cured salami, preferably one that's not too peppery. Apples or apple jelly pair well, and so do walnuts. Cantal is fantastic on a grilled cheese sandwich destined for dipping into tomato soup.

Wine/beer: Pair this with a fruity Beaujolais or white Bordeaux. Otherwise, nab a wheat beer and head for the hills.

GARROTXA

SPAIN, GOAT'S MILK
PERSONALITY: A puckish dandy in a velvetine jacket—eccentric and beguiling.

Spain is famous for its hard sheep's milk cheeses, which makes this goaty buddy something of an anomaly. Its flavor profile is also unusual: imagine Brazil nuts, the scent of lemongrass. These notes can be bold or subtle, depending on the ripeness, so always ask for a taste of Garrotxa (pronounced Gah-ROH-cha). If you're a dogged lover of caprine delights, this is a must try. It's especially good for a Sunday lunch when you want to wake up a sleepy palate and invigorate a plate of cold cuts and olives.

Here's how to recognize this fairy nubbin: Garrotxa's rind is brown and fuzzy, like a layer of fine velvet. This is an edible coat, but some find it off-putting. No matter. Focus your attention on the ivory paste, which is smooth and clean tasting. Garrotxa is a fairly new cheese, first made in the 1980s, and while it's very popular in Northern Spain, it's just beginning to put its paws on American cheese plates. Serve it at a party, and you'll be ahead of your fashionable friends.

Good matches: Serve this as a table cheese alongside Catalan olives, a dish of walnuts, golden honey, and Spanish ham. For a special evening, pair it with a few Spanish cheese sidekicks, like Monte Enebro (page 78), Idiazábal (page 49), and Valdéon (page 240).

Wine/beer: Garrotxa yearns for summery Vinho Verde, Cava, or a lemony wheat beer

HAYSTACK QUESO DE MANO

UNITED STATES, RAW GOAT'S MILK
PERSONALITY: **Summery, almost flowery, like a jam-band lover in overalls.**

It's hard to stop with the superlatives when it comes to this raw goat cheese from Longmont, Colorado. It's full of flavor—nutty and herbaceous—and yet delicate, making it a dream cheese to serve alongside spring and summer produce. If you want a smooth, firm Manchego-like cheese that captures the terroir of the Rockies, this is your next breath of heaven.

Queso de Mano is handmade by Jim Schott, an educator who left his job in the late '80s to launch a goat farm with his wife. Just as he was getting started, his wife died of cancer and his college-age daughter, Gretchen, stepped in to help. Their beautiful cheeses quickly won awards, and in 2005, *Saveur* listed this as one of fifty best artisanal cheeses in America. An interesting fact: Haystack Mountain Creamery supports a prison work program by purchasing goat's milk from the state pen in Canon City. Now that's collaboration.

Good matches: Figs, apricots, honey, and homemade preserves are lovely additions to this subtle cheese. For a mountain cheese plate, add smoked trout, blackberries, and tender greens.

Wine/beer: Pair this with a Sauvignon Blanc or Gamay Beaujolais. A wheat beer or fruit beer also works well. Good Juju, a ginger-kissed beer from Colorado's Left Hand Brewing Co., is an especially fine pairing.

IDIAZÁBAL

SPAIN, RAW SHEEP'S MILK
PERSONALITY: **An enthralling romantic who prefers the smoking table in the back.**

Pronounced *iddy-ah-THAW-ball*, this Basque cheese is nutty and buttery with a trace of wood smoke. Imagine a mountain campsite with still burning coals in the fire pit—can you smell grass? Wooly ruminants? Yup, then you've got Idiazábal in mind. Although this cheese shares similarities with Manchego (page 51), its smoky quality is unique, and so is the richness of the milk from indigenous Lata sheep. Originally, shepherds hung wheels of Idiazábal in their chimneys to cure, and although wheels are hung in more conventional smoke rooms today, this is still a rustic beauty.

In Spain, Idiazábal is highly prized. Its name-controlled status means that supply is limited but that the quality is excellent. The rind can be nut-brown or saffron-yellow, but the interior should be beige or white. Forget the tricky pronunciation and dive right in. Faint caramel notes make this an unforgettable cheese at the end of a big meal.

Good matches: Make this the centerpiece of a Spanish cheese plate, along with olives, quince paste, and Serrano ham. Or, try shaving it over asparagus, pasta, or leafy salads. After dinner, serve it with nougaty hunks of Spanish Turrón.

Wine/beer: Pair this with a medium-bodied Spanish red, like a Rioja or Navarra. A Pilsner or pale ale also works well. After dinner, try it with a dark lager.

MAHÓN

SPAIN, COW'S MILK
PERSONALITY: A friendly Spanish "Cheddar" that plays well with others.

When it's young, this cheese from the sea-swept island of Menorca is fruity and fudgy, a good match for olives and cured meats. Aged, or *curado,* Mahón morphs into something quite interesting: a firm, flaky cheese with luxuriant apricot notes and plenty of nutty warmth. Mahón Curado is especially appealing to Cheddar lovers who enjoy the toasty aroma of a well-aged Cabot (page 165); after six to eight months, the sea air turns this otherwise ordinary morsel into sweet-salty epiphany. Break out the sherry and the love poems. (We suggest Frederico Garcia Lorca's "Romance Sonambulo" as an ideal pairing.)

You can always tell a Mahón from its rind, which is amber from the application of olive oil and paprika. These ingredients are rubbed into the surface of the cheese as it ages, a tradition that extends back at least a century. Although this is a name-controlled cheese, you'll find that the taste and quality vary widely, depending on the maker. Avoid the bland supermarket variety dipped in orange wax, and look for a wheel of golden Mahón glistening with crystals.

Good matches: A really good hunk of Mahón is worthy of a party. Light some skull candles, and set out Serrano ham, Spanish olives, Marcona almonds, and dried figs or fig cake. Then cue the guitars.

Wine/beer: Fruity Spanish reds love to nuzzle up next to this one. Try a Tempranillo, a spicy Rioja, or, best of all, a Clos Lojen made from the indigenous Spanish grape variety, Bobal. On a hot night, an IPA is stellar.

CHEESEMONGER NOTE: THE MAGIC OF MAHÓN AND IPA

In the course of our hundreds of beer and cheese pairings, we have identified a few absolutes. One of them is that any good farmhouse Cheddar paired with any craft IPA will, at worst, be really good. At best, this pairing is transcendent, elevating both beer and cheese to heights unattainable in their own rights. But pairing IPA and Cheddar on a weekly basis can get redundant, so eventually we forced ourselves to eat and drink outside the box.

We like to think of Mahón as the Cheddar of Spain, if for no other reason than that it is an aged, sharp cow's milk cheese. Mahón's sharpness comes through as grapefruit citrus, and paired with an apricot-y IPA like Dogfish Head 60 Minute, the combination is sublime. This is easily one of my all-time top 10 pairings.

—CHEESEMONGER HUNTER FIKE

MANCHEGO

SPAIN, SHEEP'S MILK

PERSONALITY: A bathing beauty, oil-slathered and striking but rather shy.

Manchego is always touted as Spain's most famous cheese, probably because Cervantes alluded to it in *Don Quixote*. For all its literary cachet, Manchego is rather timid, preferring to hide behind olives or quince paste rather than take center stage. If you are grilling or chilling, this is a fine accent on a snack plate, but it definitely needs companionship. Play off its olive and almond notes, its salted-butter undertones, especially with red wines and cured meat.

The dark, plaited rind of Manchego is its most striking attribute. Originally, this hard cheese was formed in woven grass molds, and although plastic forms are used today, the wheels still come with those tweed-like impressions and a glistening coat of olive oil. A well-aged wheel should pop with the taste of acorns and wild grass, which are part of the diet for the durable Manchega sheep that roam La Mancha's high plateau. Their fatty milk gives this cheese its heft, and at fifty percent fat, you'll notice Manchego bead with "sweat" once it warms to room temp. Don't let it bask on a cheese board for too long.

Good matches: Manchego pairs well with dates, honey, almonds, olives, cured Spanish ham, and roasted red peppers. In Spain, it's traditionally served with thin slices of *membrillo*, or quince paste. Try it in pesto (see recipe, page 53).

Wine/beer: Go for a glass of Cava or Rioja. A malty beer with a tinge of sweetness works well, and so does a glass of sherry. With a savory pairing, try a gin cocktail. Really.

Grilled Figs with Manchego

Next time you're BBQing outdoors, try grilling fresh fig halves and serving each one draped with a slice of Manchego. The cheese will soften over the warm figs, and the flavors will mingle beautifully. It's a good idea to toss the figs in a little olive oil before you put them on the grill rack so they don't dry out. Once you plate these and add the cheese, try a few cranks of black pepper and a drizzle of honey, but only if you really want to wow the neighbors.

MANCHEGO and MARCONA ALMOND PESTO

Rich sheep's milk cheese pairs well with roasted almonds. In this Spanish twist, the two come together with peppery arugula and lemon zest to make a bright-tasting pesto that is perfect for linguine with shrimp, baked fish, or roasted cherry tomatoes and olives tossed with penne. For breakfast, I love to spread this pesto on toast and top it with a soft-boiled egg.

MAKES 1¼ CUPS

3 ounces arugula (about 2 cups, packed)
1 tablespoon lemon zest
2 tablespoons lemon juice
½ cup roasted Marcona almonds
¼ pound Manchego, grated (1½ cups)
2 small garlic cloves
Sea salt, to taste
½ cup extra-virgin olive oil

Place everything but the olive oil in a food processor or blender and combine until roughly chopped. Then, with the blade running, slowly add the olive oil until the mixture is well combined. For a rough pesto, use a mortar and pestle.

Note: Marcona almonds are available at many grocery and specialty food stores. If you can't find them, substitute toasted almonds, preferably skinless.

MIMOLETTE

FRANCE, COW'S MILK
PERSONALITY: **Gnarly looking but imminently gentle, like a young punkster.**

Mimolette looks like an asteroid. It's a squat sphere with a cratered surface that's generously pocked by tiny robots, also called cheese mites. That's right, I just said cheese mites. These nearly microscopic organisms naturally exist in cheese caves, and Mimolette just happens to be one of their favorite snacks. Don't worry, you won't eat the rind anyway. It's the bright orange paste that tastes so good—sweet, delicate, and slightly smoky. Look for a well-aged wheel with plenty of crystallization. Literally, it should sparkle.

Since the seventeenth century, Mimolette has been a specialty of northern France. The region borders the Netherlands, home to super subtle cheeses like Edam and Gouda, and Mimolette is, in fact, something of a knock-off. Word has it that Louis XIV banned the importation of Gouda, so the people of Flanders revolted by making their own version, Mimolette. To confuse matters, Mimolette tastes vaguely Cheddar-ish but without the rampant acidity, and it's often sold as a waify Cheddar to nervous types. Embrace its wild rind and blaze orange color, but don't expect to be electrified by flavor. Despite its rogue appearance, this is a deeply mild cheese, very appropriate for children.

Good matches: Toss shaved Mimolette onto salads for color, or grate it over risotto. On a cheese plate, pair it with candied hazelnuts, roasted pumpkin seeds, or dried cranberries. For an appetizer, melt slices on sourdough toasts with thinly sliced tomato.

Wine/beer: Savor this with a Châteauneuf du Pape or a spicy wheat beer with hints of coriander and citrus. A saison or toasty French Bière de Garde would be very appropriate.

MRS. KIRKHAM'S TASTY LANCASHIRE

ENGLAND, RAW COW'S MILK
PERSONALITY: **A fetching teetotaler, affectionately known as "the floofy monster."**

When you take a bite of Lancashire, think of crumb cake. The curds are made from three days of milking, then milled like grain so that they hang loosely together. At the cheese counter, the texture is often likened to "butter crumble," but the Brits favor the word "floofy." Hence, the nickname "floofy monster" for this rather delicate, citrus-bright cheese that is brushed with butter and bound in cloth.

Lancashire is a territorial style of cheese, meaning that it's named after the region where it originated. During World War II, it was banned, like many territorial styles, so that cheesemakers could focus on producing "government Cheddar." Traditional Lancashire all but disappeared until the 1980s when Mrs. Ruth Kirkham resurrected her grandmother's recipe and began making it the old way: with raw milk and animal rennet. Today, this historic cheese is produced by Ruth's son, Graham. It's a must-try for Cheddar aficionados and persnickety Anglophiles.

Good matches: A cheese this delicate is perfect for brunch or tea, alongside biscuits and jam or chutney. It can also anchor a ploughman's lunch; serve it with whole grain bread, mustard, cured meat (try landjäger), and crisp apples.

Wine/beer: This cheese needs a light, fruity wine or a proper British ale. Be gentle with it, as it's easily overpowered.

NEVAT

SPAIN, SHEEP OR GOAT'S MILK
PERSONALITY: A heavenly bombshell of
sweet sheep's milk, interesting and elegant.

Nevat is the kind of cheese that makes you stop
before a cold case and draw in a breath. It looks
like a snowdrift, like achingly white cake. No
wonder its name is drawn from the Catalan
word for "snowy." Made by the esteemed Spanish cheesemaker Josep Cuixart, this sheep's milk
cheese combines the earthiness of Brie with the
citrine softness of a young goat cheese. The flavor palate is wild: think of wet leaves under
fresh snowfall.

　　Since this cheese ripens from the outside
in, you'll notice a beautiful creamline just below
the downy surface. The more of this runny layer
you see, the more pungent this cheese will be.
The paste within is almost like ricotta, clean
tasting and clayey. This kind of variation in texture and flavor makes for a complex cheese. Try
tasting the peppery rind, then the creamline,
then scoop out the soft center. You'll notice that
each layer is distinct. Eaten together, they create
a spectacular forest pillow.

Good matches: Nevat's earthy character is
best offset by simple sides, like honey and walnuts or fresh fruit. Try it on walnut bread,
alongside fresh or dried figs.

Wine/beer: Pair this with a wheat beer or
Duvel, or lean on a Spanish sparkler.

NUVOLA DI PECORA

ITALY, SHEEP'S MILK
PERSONALITY: Pudding-soft and fairytale-
like, a sheep cheese for princes.

From northern Italy's Emilio-Romagna region,
this bloomy sheep's milk cheese is notable for
its custardy texture and a downy rind that's
imprinted with a quilted pattern. If you were
going to die with a cheese at your bedside, it
should be this one. The name literally means
"sheep clouds," so think *fluffy, glorious, gentle,
sweet*. The taste calls to mind steamed cauliflower, lemons, and lush grassy meadows with
just a whiff of hay.

　　Nuvola di Pecora is unique because it's one
of the few bloomy cheeses (think Brie-style)
made entirely from sheep's milk. In 2010, it won
a gold medal at the World Cheese Championships, a huge boon. If you're a fan of Taleggio
(page 158), an Italian cheese also made in this
square format, you'll find Nuvola similar, but it
provides a much milder, more luxurious experience without the pungent, room-filling aura.

Good matches: For a revelation, try warm
ciabatta bread and blackberry jam. Otherwise,
keep it simple. This one needs little adornment,
other than a few fresh berries. Di Bruno
cheesemongers think its best eaten as is, with a
spoon.

Wine/beer: Seek out a white from the Veneto
region, or an effervescent Saison Dupont.
Sheep's milk cheeses really coat the mouth, so
anything with bubbles—i.e. cava, Champagne—
will cleanse the palate and create balance.

OSSAU-IRATY

FRANCE, RAW SHEEP'S MILK
PERSONALITY: **The grandfather of Basque cheeses, nutty but distinguished.**

Although the name can be hard to remember, Ossau-Iraty (OH-so EAR-ahty) is one of those remarkable cheeses that looms large in your mind once you sample it. If you're unfamiliar with Basque cheeses, start here. Ossau-Iraty holds sacred status in the Pyrénées, where scientists have uncovered cheese-cooking pots that date back to 5000 B.C.—they were likely used to make this recipe. Today, this is a name-protected cheese produced only by small village cooperatives that still depend on shepherds to move their ewes through high mountain pastures for grazing.

Like other sheep's milk cheeses from this region, Ossau-Iraty has distinct notes of toasted almonds and green olives. The texture is firm. The color is white, nearly translucent, like a set of antique pearls. Because the smell is redolent of freshly ground wheat, this is an especially good cheese to pair with beer.

Good Matches: Eat this in the park with a handful of Marcona almonds and some succulent Spanish olives, preferably with fall leaves rustling in the background. Cherry preserves are a classic pairing for this cheese in Spain.

Wine/beer: Try a Trappist beer or red ale, like Philadelphia Brewing Company's Rowhouse Red. A traditional Basque wine, like Irouléguy, is ideal. Otherwise, pick a Pinot Noir.

PANTALEO

ITALY, GOAT'S MILK
PERSONALITY: **A Sardinian flirt, the darling of the cheese counter.**

At Di Bruno Bros., Pantaleo is known as "the converter" because it has won over so many despotic goat cheese haters. The reason is probably because it tastes like sunshine and pistachios, without any goaty flavor. The paste is firm and smooth. The smell is citrusy. Think of preserved lemons. It's almost as if you can smell the island of Sardinia on the rind: the salty sea air, the rocky terrain.

This is a great cheese for noshing. Pack a hunk in your lunch or hack off a slice to munch on while you're cooking. Goat's milk cheeses are lighter than cow's milk or sheep's milk cheeses, so you won't spoil your supper. For that same reason, Pantaleo makes a good "grating cheese" if you're watching your cholesterol and need an alternative to Parmigiano or Locatelli. In Sardinia, this cheese is something of an anomaly since the island is known for its rich Pecorinos, and yet Pantaleo has its worshippers. One cheesemonger I know claims this is the one cheese she always keeps in the house—it's her midnight snack.

Good matches: Try using Pantaleo in pesto, or grate it over summery pastas, salads, or steamed asparagus. For a stunning cheese plate, add apricots, pistachios, a light-colored honey, mild green olives, charcuterie, and rosemary bread.

Wine/beer: Lean on a summery white, like an unoaked Chardonnay. Otherwise, Rioja. Beer fans should try a fruity American Pale Ale.

CHEESE JUDGING

In November 2011, Ossau-Iraty was named Best Cheese in the World at the World Cheese Championships. What do judges look for when identifying the best cheese in the world? It starts with feel. Judges will break off a small nugget and roll it between their fingertips, excreting some of the fat and releasing the aroma. Excessive oil or dryness are demerits. Like Goldilocks's porridge, it has to be just right.

Next, they take a deep whiff, hoping to smell the land and the animal's diet. These are marks of a true farmhouse cheese. It should be manipulated as little as possible so as to highlight the abundant flavors of the milk.

The third component is taste. Like the aroma, the flavors should convey a "sense of place," or *terroir*, proudly exclaiming their origin. Perhaps the judge's criteria are best, albeit briefly, expressed by English poet W. H. Auden:

> A poet's hope: to be,
> like some valley cheese,
> local, but prized elsewhere.

For more on this subject, see "How to Taste Cheese" on page 139.

—CHEESEMONGER HUNTER FIKE

PAIRING CHEESE AND SEAFOOD

One of the most irritating kitchen "rules" is the one that states you should never mix seafood and cheese. Seriously? I have heard this commandment recited ad nauseum by nearly ever celebrity chef, but I will never be convinced of its validity. Have these people never heard of a tuna melt, or lobster mac and cheese, or shrimp and feta?

If you have been brainwashed by the automaton-like repetition of this dictum and are dubious about breaking out of your (crustacean) shell, try Pantaleo on just about anything. First of all, you should trust that it works because it is made on an island in the Mediterranean. Where else would a cheese be made to work with seafood? Second, the flavors are just right: lemon, salt, pepper, a hint of pistachio. They represent the quintessential profile of what you might work into any seafood dish. Try it once and you will be hooked for life.

—CHEESEMONGER HUNTER FIKE

PETIT BASQUE

FRANCE, SHEEP'S MILK

PERSONALITY: Your mother's sheep's milk cheese, delectable and accessible.

This oversized muffin of a cheese is just what you want on a picnic or at an outdoor concert. It's all almonds and caramel. Some have even likened it to crème brulée since it has notes of sea salt, vanilla, and brown butter. Like the dessert, it has a dark golden rind and a paste that is bone-white and milky.

Petit Basque is a relative newcomer to the cheese party. It appeared in 1997 as a gateway sheep's milk cheese for the American market, and while it bears a strong resemblance to Ossau-Iraty (page 56) it's sweeter and nuttier—not to mention softer—giving it wide appeal. Because of its small format, it also ripens faster than other Spanish cheeses in its class, making it, oh, a touch cheaper. Never a bad thing.

Good matches: Prepare a picnic of cured meat, green olives, toasted almonds, and apricots or plums, or serve Petit Basque for dessert, along with nectarines and amaretti cookies.

Wine/beer: Try a glass of Tempranillo. If beer calls to you, reach for an American Pale Ale, a lager, or a frothy goblet of Bière de Garde.

Petit Basque Salad with Cherries and Almonds

In the Basque country, nutty sheep's milk cheeses like this one are often served with tart cherry preserves. For a take-off on this pairing, try adding dried cherries and toasted almonds to a salad topped with Petit Basque. You can cube the cheese into "croutons" or use a vegetable peeler to create shavings. A light dressing prepared with a fruity vinegar rounds out all the flavors.

SEVEN SISTERS

UNITED STATES, RAW COW'S MILK
PERSONALITY: Cream and summer grass—
it's Laura Ingalls Wilder with a rind.

Seven Sisters is produced on one of the most pristine dairies in Chester County, Pennsylvania. The farm, called Doe Run, includes 700 acres of rolling prairie, and nothing disturbs the peace except for birdcall and the occasional bell clanking against the neck of a meandering ruminant. If you don't taste covered wagons and knitted shawls in this firm, buttery cheese made by Kristian Holbrook, you're not tasting carefully enough.

Fans of Gouda and firm Alpine cheeses will appreciate this curious hybrid. It's got sugary high notes and savory, oniony undertones. Young, it's moist and waxen. After a year, crystallization appears and the paste turns dense and Cheddary. At either stage, it's lovely, a perfect picnic cheese or summer-afternoon splurge.

Good matches: Set out a basket of apples and some homemade bread. A touch of apricot jam pairs nicely. So do candied pecans. Di Bruno cheesemongers love this on a turkey club.

Wine/beer: The cheesemaker recommends dry cider. For a young batch of Seven Sisters, try a Chardonnay or a lager from Victory, a brewery close to Doe Run Farm. Older, sweeter wheels need a Pinot Noir or a pint of Lancaster Milk Stout.

WENSLEYDALE

ENGLAND, COW'S MILK
PERSONALITY: A buttercup of a cheese,
popular with the *Wallace & Gromit* crowd.

This British classic has been the subject of so much televised hilarity (even Monty Python gets in on the action), and yet it's a rather serious cheese with origins that date back to a group of twelfth century Cistercian monks from Roquefort, France, who emigrated to England after the Norman Conquest. They built a monastery in Wensleydale and began producing a cheese of the same name, a blue much like their beloved Roquefort. Over time their recipe was cleverly British-ized into a purring, Cheddar-like creature, probably when the monastery dissolved in 1540 and local farmers took over production. It was a well-known style until World War II, when the British government required all milk to be regulated for rationing.

Today, a creamery in Hawes has revived traditional Wensleydale. Like the old days, it's made with animal rennet and tucked into clothbound drums. Don't fall for fakes made outside of Yorkshire. At Di Bruno Bros., Wensleydale comes from Neal's Yard in London, where the affineurs take care to ripen it perfectly. The smell of real Wensleydale calls to mind lemon yogurt, and the crumb is as tender as freshly baked coffee cake. Mild and delicate, this is a cheese that children take to and grannies murmur over. Cue up some animated shorts, and feast away.

Good matches: British cheese authority Patricia Michelson suggests serving young Wensleydale with honey and plums. The British often eat it at tea time, with biscuits, scones, or fruitcake.

Wine/beer: Pick a crisp, fruity white or a wheat beer. You might also nab a hard British cider if you want to stick with tradition.

CHEESE BOARD: Desk Bento for One

If you keep a small cutting board in your desk drawer at work, it's easy to make a cheese plate come true. Just tote the ingredients to the office in a tiffin or bento box. If you have a mini fridge, you can even keep an assortment of olives, jams, and nuts on hand. Who knows, you might even start a secret cheese-tasting society at work. Here are some enlivening combinations to suit your style:

The Creative Director
Pantaleo (page 56), pistachios, hard-boiled egg, radishes, baguette rounds

The Day Laborer
Cabot Clothbound Cheddar (page 165), smoked landjäger salami, apple, grainy mustard, whole wheat bread

The Sensualist
Délice de Bourgogne (page 95), sour cherry preserves, bacon, dark chocolate, French roll

The Purist
Fresh ricotta (page 34), fresh thyme sprigs, sea salt, honey, walnuts, flatbread

The Workaholic
Stichelton (page 174), dried figs, biscotti, candied pecans, flask of Scotch

The Shopaholic
Seven Sisters (page 60), raw almonds, celery, fiber crackers, dried apricots, preferably stashed in a pretty handbag

The Monocle
Mascarpone (page 32), tin of herring, Dijon mustard, jar of capers, petit toasts

CHEESE 101: Alone with Olives: A Novice's Guide

Use olives like punctuation. Toss them onto a cheese plate to create a cleansing pause between slivers. If you need a rule of thumb, remember that smallish olives tend to pack a lot of punch, while bigsters tend to be meaty but mellow. Pair accordingly.

Alfonso: The Wine Drinker's Choice

Plump purple Alfonsos from Chile are cured in wine. They're easygoing and juicy, not too strong. Try them with a wine-washed cheese, like Tuma Persa (page 204).

Calabrese: The Hot Mix

Set out these spicy green olives with a buttery sheep's milk cheese, like Manchego (page 51), and some hot sausage, then cue the Latin beats. Lemony, fresh tasting.

Castelvetrano: Best for Breaking in Newbies

Mild and meaty, these go well with any mellow beastie. You'll know them by their marble-like shape and bright green, almost turquoise hue. Try them with Ossau-Iraty (page 56).

Catalan: The Salami of Olives

Big and spicy, these look like small green limes. Pair them with cured meats and gutsy cheeses, like really ripe Garrotxa (page 48) or hard cheeses.

Cerignola: The "Rocky" of Olives

Hunky Cerignolas from southern Italy pair well with Parm (page 189) and provolone. They're mild, huge, and wildly luminescent—the color of a golf green.

Greek Mammoth: Most Likely to Impress

Need we say more? They're dark, thick-skinned, and pungent. Fling them on a pizza or salad, or pair them with a bright, citrusy cheese like Pantaleo (page 56).

Kalamata: Little Plums

These sweet maroon-black gems are briny and fruity. Suck them down with Greek feta (page 73), toss them on salads, or bake them with chicken.

Niçoise: Charlemagne's Choice

Small and assertive, these bead-shaped olives are dark and smoky. Break out the anchovies, marinated artichokes, and a hard, zesty friend like Cantal (page 48).

Picholine: The French Accent

From Provence, these delicate commas are mild, herby, and vaguely citrusy. They're great when you want just a little something—try them with Carre du Berry (page 69).

Sicilian: The Martini Maker

Stuff these with Gorgonzola Piccante (page 237) or toss them in a drink. They're briny like an oyster and muscle-y like a dark-eyed Sicilian.

CHAPTER III

FREE SPIRITS
(sunshiny, herby)

These are great picnic mates and beach buddies, especially if you bring along a six-pack. They're friendly and summery—well, okay, some of them can be a little tarty (goat's milk can be that way), but mostly they're mild and light on the stomach.

Acapella | Bijou | Bûcheron | Caña de Cabra | Baked Caña de Cabra with Pine Nuts and Honey | Carre du Berry | Crottin de Chavignol | Feta (Bulgarian) | Pickled Feta with Cerignola Olives and Strawberries | Humboldt Fog | Lazy Lady La Petite Tomme | Leonora | Rhubarb Refrigerator Jam | Monte Enebro | Old Kentucky Tomme | Sea Smoke | Selles-sur-Cher | Shellbark Sharp II | Fig and Goat Cheese Crostini | Valençay | Wabash Cannonball | Cheese Board: An All-Goat Blow-Out | Cheese 101: How to Pair Cheese and Honey

ACAPELLA

UNITED STATES, GOAT'S MILK
PERSONALITY: **A boys' choir conducted by a goat cheese provocateur.**

Eating this heavenly puck of soft-ripened goat cheese is on par with listening to the most ethereal vespers. It is a cheese that hums. You have to close your eyes to imagine this: a snowy cake of goat cheese, rolled in ash—just a dusting, to help form a thin, soft crust. It adds yeasty warmth to an otherwise icy cool experience. Touch Acapella with a single finger, and it dimples, then springs back—just like dough.

Korean-born scientist and pianist Soyoung Scanlan makes Acapella at her farm in Petaluma, California. As a cheesemaker, she's gained a worshipful following from folks like Thomas Keller of The French Laundry and Liz Thorpe of Murray's Cheese. Thorpe, who writes about visiting Scanlan's dairy in *The Cheese Chronicles* intones, "How this woman learned to make cheese is impressive. She knew the structure of fat but nothing of cheesemaking, so she went to Europe and tasted five to seven cheeses every day, very intently, and from their flavor and texture started writing recipes for how she thought they were made." Need I say more?

Good matches: Serve this hard-to-find cheese to your most special friends, preferably without fanfare, unless you want to play some Tallus Scholars.

Wine/beer: Pick a Sonoma County sparkling wine or a sweet, bready wheat beer.

BIJOU

UNITED STATES, GOAT'S MILK
PERSONALITY: **A tender button, softly poetic, like Gertrude Stein.**

As its names suggests, Bijou (French for *jewel*) glows like a pearl. This dainty round of spreadable week-old goat cheese is light and luscious with a thin, edible veil of "netting" around it (*membrane* would be more accurate, but that sounds unpleasant). Even if you don't love goat cheese, you may be swayed by this American take on France's esteemed Crottin de Chavignol (page 70). It's made by one of the most decorated U.S. cheesemakers, Allison Hooper of Vermont Butter and Cheese Creamery, who started her business in 1984 with a patch of dirt and a church loan.

Hooper is known for her tender touch—a skill that yields velvety soft textures and impossibly thin rinds. Although she has expanded her business over the years to meet demand, her cheeses have retained a mild, sweet-smelling quality and a delicate, floral taste that is on par with the best small-batch goat cheeses anywhere. Together with her partner Bob Reese, she supports seventeen small family farms in Vermont and Canada.

Good matches: You can bake Bijou and use it as a topper for lightly dressed greens or serve a little round on a cheese board with honey and jam. To bake Bijou, Hooper recommends placing a round on top of a baguette slice and popping it under the broiler for two to three minutes.

Wine/beer: Serve with a glass of Sauvignon Blanc or Gewürztraminer. Belgian Tripels and wheat beers also work nicely.

BÛCHERON

FRANCE, GOAT'S MILK
PERSONALITY: A classic French chanteuse with just a hint of heartache in her voice.

Goat cheeses range from marvelously mild to hot 'n' wild. This one's a dialed back doozy. It bears the distinction of being one of the first French goat cheese imports in America, back before anyone could say *chèvre*. Call it the original goat log. It's milder than its femme fatale alter ego, Caña de Cabra, but it's got more boom-boom than the very twee Capricho de Cabra (page 30). On a nice day, when you're having an "Umbrellas of Cherbourg" moment, grab a chipped plate and eat this cheese on your fire escape while humming something appropriately melancholy.

Bûcheron gains its flavor from a downy coat of Brie-like white mold, which works its fingers through the cheese from the outside in. As time passes, the exterior darkens and a creamline forms a beige halo below the rind. The center remains dense and flaky, the color and consistency of freshly-packed snow. Flavors of citrus and flint shine through with just a touch of tang.

Good matches: On a cheese plate, serve Bûcheron with fresh fruit and honey, or go for radishes and pickled beets. In spring, core out fresh radishes, fill them with Bûcheron, and top them with chives for a French-inspired appetizer.

Wine/beer: Pour a sparkling wine, or go for a flinty Sauvignon Blanc or rosé. A citrusy wheat beer fits this cheese like a glove.

CAÑA DE CABRA

SPAIN, GOAT'S MILK
PERSONALITY: A Spanish dancer, light on her feet but full of *duende*.

On a hot summer night, few things are lovelier than discovering a round of Caña de Cabra on a tapas platter. This tangy goat cheese from Murcia is clayey and bright, like a good spa mudpack, and its taste is refreshingly lemony and light. In Spain, it's often a vehicle for local honey, which balances the acidity, but it's also good with in-season trappings, like fresh fruit and crisp white wines.

Caña de Cabra is a young thing that ripens with age. You can tell a lot from its coat, which starts off kitten-white and tips toward butterscotchy after six or seven weeks. You'll want to taste it in order to tell where it's at. If you prefer the taste of lemon yogurt, make sure you pick a young round. If mushrooms and earth turn you on, reach for a sliver with some straw-colored stippling. For a milder goat log, try the more delicate Bûcheron.

Good matches: To experience the pleasures of a cheese pairing that replaces the salted nut roll of childhood memory, serve Baked Caña de Cabra with Pine Nuts and Honey (see recipe, page 68).

Wine/beer: A glass of Sauvignon Blanc or white sangria will mix perfectly. Wheat beers love this cheese.

BAKED CAÑA DE CABRA
with PINE NUTS and HONEY

This appetizer is so easy, you can make it in your toaster oven. Serve it on the patio for tapas, along with Spanish wine, Serrano ham, melon, and plump green olives. Toast up plenty of baguette rounds for dipping.

SERVES 2 TO 4

1 (2-inch) round of Caña de Cabra
2 to 3 tablespoons honey, for drizzling
2 to 3 tablespoons pine nuts, toasted
Baguette rounds, toasted

Preheat the oven to 200°F.

Set the goat cheese in an oven-safe crock and bake it for about 15 minutes, or until the cheese softens. Keep an eye on it so it doesn't liquefy. The edges may brown a little, but the cheese shouldn't get too oozy.

Remove the crock from the oven, and top the cheese with honey and toasted pine nuts. Serve warm with toasted baguette rounds.

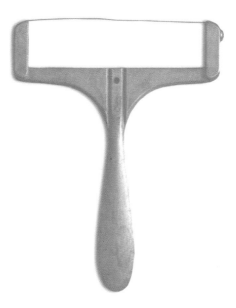

CARRE DU BERRY

FRANCE, GOAT'S MILK

PERSONALITY: Like spring incarnate, a goat cheese worthy of Persephone.

Picture a Klondike Bar for grown-ups: a square of impeccable goat cheese rolled in herbes de Provence and pink peppercorns. Carre du Berry is the kind of cheese you want to eat on a park bench in spring or share with a new infatuation. The herby aroma calls to mind pretty things: rain, new shoots, nests. And the taste is, well, purely refreshing, like citrus zest mixed with snowfall. If the French have cornered the market on goat cheese, it's because of cheeses like this. It might as well have been assembled by elflings.

Carre du Berry hails from the Loire Valley, a region that is famous for its lush pastures. Few areas of the world produce goat cheese this pristine: no goaty tang, no "bucky" whiffs here. The same region is also known for Selles-sur-Cher (page 80) and Valençay (page 82), both of which are rolled in ash—very dramatic. Carre du Berry doesn't come cloaked in darkness. Its coat of herbs enhances the grassy notes in the milk and infuses each bite with splendid flavor. At Easter time, this is an especially picturesque cheese to serve at brunch.

Good matches: Serve Carre du Berry with warm rolls for breakfast or with crackers before dinner. To pair it with other spring cheese highlights, add a small leaf-wrapped Banon (page 88) and a rustic wedge of Tomme de Savoie (page 135). With some fresh strawberries and a dish of walnuts, you will have a beautiful little French cheese board.

Wine/beer: Beaujolais or rosé will work beautifully with this cheese, and so would a wheat beer.

Cheese for Breakfast or Brunch

Here are a few cheese pairings that are lovely before noon; try them all together for a sumptuous spread, or carry a couple of them to your room for a decadent breakfast in bed: Moses Sleeper (page 106) with blackberry jam, Carre du Berry with toast and smoked trout, Selles-sur-Cher (page 80) with fresh raspberries, mascarpone (page 32) with preserves and scones, ricotta (page 34) with honey and blueberries.

CROTTIN DE CHAVIGNOL

FRANCE, GOAT'S MILK
PERSONALITY: Elfin and elegant, like a
character from the pages of Tolkien.

If you've never come across this dainty toad-
stool-like cheese before, you might be a little
taken aback by its wrinkly surface. Fear not: it's
a gentle marshmallow, at least when it's young.
Aged crottins turn peppery and a little angsty.
Ask your cheesemonger to help you gauge the
strength of this cheese before you set about
selecting pairings. You can also take ageing into
your own hands and let this cheese sit out on
your counter (under a glass dome, please) for a
few days.

In France, these compact cheeses were
often served as quick snacks during the grape
harvest; they originated in the hamlet of Chavignol, a well-known winemaking region. Today,
they're popular picnic fare, often enjoyed on
rounds of baguette with a schmear of butter.

Good matches: Try popping a couple crottins
under the broiler and serving them warm atop
lightly dressed greens. Otherwise, give a drizzle
of honey and cue up some Jacques Brel.

Wine/beer: Flinty Sancerre from the Loire
Valley is a classic pairing, but wheat beers work
well, too. Noted British cheese writer Patricia
Michelson suggests Scotch (an Islay) as a pairing for mature crottins—the smoky character
common in Islay soothes the feisty acidity. Sit
back and let peat mingle with barnyard.

FETA (BULGARIAN)

BULGARIA, SHEEP'S MILK
PERSONALITY: An unassuming star, not too
salty, with a huge fan club.

No doubt there will be quibblers here since so
many countries produce feta, including France
and Israel, not to mention Greece. Sorry,
Greece! At the risk of peeving whole nations, I
will say this: Bulgarian feta is the creamiest.
Hopefully, we can agree there. If you are one of
those people who have been buying foam
hunks of grocery-store feta your whole life,
only to crumble it on the occasional watery
salad, wake up and smell the Bulgarian ewe's
milk. Once you discover it, you will never go
back to dry, salty ceiling tiles of commercial-
grade stuff.

Let it be known that there are also a grow-
ing number of great American feta makers. Look
for them at farmers' markets, particularly among
the goat people. Feta can be made from any
kind of milk, but goat's milk lends itself especially well to bright, acidic feta that's especially
good for marinating (see recipe, page 73).
Because it's a brined cheese, feta keeps almost
indefinitely in your fridge. If you buy a tub of it
in summer and keep it around, you'll probably
invent ten new uses for it, from baking it into
casseroles to eating it fresh on everything from
greens to watermelon.

Good matches: Feta is a brilliant mate. It
pairs well with lamb, mint, olives, figs, and
roasted red peppers Try crumbling it onto salads
or baking it with whole dates at 350°F for 20
minutes, then drizzling it with honey.

Wine/beer: The straightforwardness of this
cheese calls for a straightforward slosh: go for a
mellow white or red, or pick a pilsner.

FETA (BULGARIAN)

PICKLED FETA with CERIGNOLA OLIVES and STRAWBERRIES

Briny feta is pickled, then tossed with plump olives and strawberries for a bright, juicy salad. Since the feta needs five days to cure in the fridge, this is a great make-ahead dish. Use Greek feta if you want neat cubes; Bulgarian feta is divine, but it needs to be handled carefully as it's very soft and crumbly. Whip up this recipe for a picnic, or serve it after a day on the beach when salt and sun are still on everyone's mind. Glasses of Processo or Saison are a perfect accompaniment.

SERVES 6 TO 8

FOR THE PICKLE:

3 cups Champagne vinegar or white balsamic vinegar

1/2 cup granulated sugar

2 tablespoons coriander seeds

2 tablespoons mustard seeds

1 medium shallot, sliced

4 whole garlic cloves

4 sprigs cilantro

2 pounds feta, diced or crumbled (roughly 6 1/2 cups)

FOR THE SALAD:

1 pound Cerignola olives (red, green, or black), pitted and cut in half

1 pound fresh strawberries, hulled and cut in quarters

1/4 cup extra-virgin olive oil

1/4 cup cilantro, chopped

12 ounces baby spinach

Salt and white pepper

To prepare the pickle, combine the vinegar, 3 cups of water, sugar, coriander seeds, mustard seeds, shallot, garlic, and cilantro in a small saucepan. Bring the pickling liquid to a boil over medium-high heat, reduce to a simmer, and allow the contents to cook for 5 minutes. Remove the pot from the heat and let it cool completely.

Place the feta in a large mixing bowl or divide it between two 1-quart jars, and pour the cool pickling solution over the cheese. Make sure all of the feta is completely submerged. (If you use quart jars, you will have a little bit of extra brine left over, which you can use for a salad dressing.) Cover the feta and refrigerate it for at least five days.

To prepare the salad, remove the pickled feta from the liquid and drain it on paper towels. In a salad bowl, toss together the olives, strawberries, olive oil, chopped cilantro, and spinach. Stir in the feta, then season with salt and pepper, if desired.

Note: This dish should be served fresh as the strawberries will begin to break down and lose color over time. Use any leftover pickling solution to drizzle over salad greens.

HUMBOLDT FOG

UNITED STATES, GOAT'S MILK
PERSONALITY: A trippy beauty with a texture like Joan Baez's voice.

Not many cheesemakers in America have been at it as long as Mary Keehn. In the 1960s, she started out with a cabin in southern Humboldt County, California and a pair of goats named Hazel and Esmeralda. After her daughters were born, she built a robust herd—thanks to a run of 4-H projects—and launched her own company, Cypress Grove. Today, her most iconic cheese, Humboldt Fog, has become a mainstay on many artisan cheese plates.

Anyone who's tasted, or seen, this stunning cheese knows that there's nothing quite like it. A horizontal layer of ash bisects each clay-like cake, a hat tip to the view from Keehn's creamery. Think of fog rolling across white surf. As each wheel begins to age, a creamline forms just below the rind—a lovely characteristic. Try tasting that all by itself: it's pleasantly peppery. The rest of the paste is light, lemony, mushroomy, and perfectly balanced. In 2010, Keehn sold her business to the Swiss company Emmi, but she remains at the helm and is revered as one of our country's first small-batch goat cheesemakers.

Good Matches: Humboldt Fog's lush profile is a marvelous foil for berries, pears, or honey. Its striking appearance makes it a good choice for entertaining. Some people have been known to serve it in place of wedding cake since it's icing-white, layered, and rather festive.

Wine/beer: Grab a wheat beer, like Philadelphia Brewing Company's Walt Wit. A rosé or California Chenin Blanc works well, too.

THE RISE OF AMERICAN CHEESE

When we first started selling Humboldt Fog in the mid-nineties, we caught some flak for trying to sell an American cheese that cost more than most imports. We expected it, to be honest. At the time, the American artisan cheese landscape was barren, and customers expected to pay no more than ten dollars a pound for anything made in The States.

But Humboldt Fog *warranted* the price tag. Not only was it of exceptional quality, but it was widely available, campaigning nationwide as the flag bearer of small American cheese producers. Nowadays, with domestic cheese garnering as much acclaim as its European counterparts I still look to Humboldt Fog as the cheese that broke down walls and led the charge.

-CHEESEMONGER HUNTER FIKE

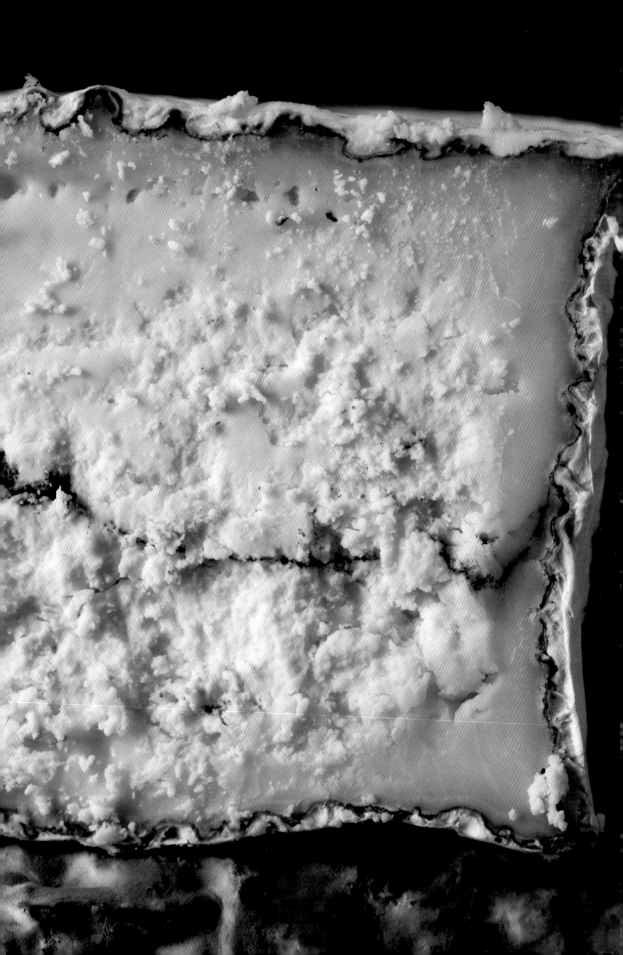

LAZY LADY LA PETITE TOMME

UNITED STATES, GOAT'S MILK
PERSONALITY: Off-the-grid Brie made by an intrepid dairy goddess.

La Petite Tomme is just what it sounds like: a little cupcake of goat cheese that's lush and oozy in the center, at least when it's ripe. It has a mild aroma and a very delicate taste that evolves with each bite. Hay, sweet grass, and mushrooms poke through, creating a complex and sumptuous treat from Vermont.

This cheese is just one of many unusual creations from Laini Fondilier, a back-to-the-lander who runs an organic creamery supported by solar and wind power. Her cheesemaking operation started with one Nubian goat back in 1987, after Fondilier spent two years apprenticing cheesemakers in France. Since then, she has upped her herd to about forty, built two underground cheese caves, and released at least a dozen wildly beloved selections that often reflect her politically driven sense of humor: Barick Obama, Condisend, Bi Partisan, Biden his Time, and Fil-A-Buster, to name a few. If you want a glimpse of life at Lazy Lady Farm, pull up the website (lazyladyfarm.com), where you can see a complete list of critters and view every aspect of the dairy, from the barn to the cheese room. There's a lot of TLC going into every wheel, a good reflection of the small-batch cheesemaking spirit that's taken hold in the United States.

Good matches: Find some impeccable bread, preferably made with wild yeast, and then eat La Petite with abandon. Berries pair well, so does raspberry jam. For a study in contrast, sample it with Humboldt Fog (page 74).

Wine/beer: Pour a summery white or something bubbly. Wheat beers and lambics love this tomme's wild side, and so does hard cider.

LEONORA

SPAIN, GOAT'S MILK
PERSONALITY: A head-turning blonde on a lemon cake bender

Traditionalists will point to France as the seat of goat cheese glory, but the caprine beauties coming out of Spain deserve special attention, Leonora in particular. Put this gooey delight on a cheese plate and your friends may think you are serving up a heavily frosted dessert. Leonora looks like baked Alaska. It comes in a rectangular cake with a meringue-like rind made of *Geotrichum*, a mold that's used in making Camembert. Here, it lends a hint of white pepper to an otherwise cloud-like lemon bomb.

Leonora is probably the one gooey goat cheese your Aunt Doris will like because it's mild and creamy. It comes from a farmstead producer in León, the northernmost province of Spain. In early spring, the lady goats devour the first tender greens that come into view, drawing the loveliest of flavors into their milk. Look for hints of citrus zest and wildflowers in this cheese. Then curl up on a deck chair and dream of rolling hills and long siestas.

Good matches: Serve this decadent wedge with berries, cherries, kiwi slices, honey, or jam. If you need an after-dinner cheese for the Easter table, Leonora can take down any lamb cake.

Wine/beer: Because this cheese is fairly acidic with a twinge of pepper in the rind, you'll want a crisp Sauvignon Blanc or a Grüner Veltliner. If you prefer beer, reach for a saison.

RHUBARB REFRIGERATOR JAM

Rhubarb is one of the first spring fruits to emerge on the shelves of produce stands and markets in late March and early April, right around the same time that goat cheeses are coming into their prime. This recipe makes a beautiful pink jam that offsets the tang in lemon-bright goat cheeses, like Leonora (page 76). If you prefer a saucy jam, leave out the gelatin.

MAKES 1½ CUPS

3 cups rhubarb cut in 1-inch segments (5 to 6 thin stalks or about 3 thick ones)
1 cup granulated sugar
3 tablespoons grenadine
1 teaspoon powdered gelatin (optional)

Combine the rhubarb, sugar, and grenadine in a medium saucepan and cook over low heat for 20 minutes, stirring to prevent browning. The rhubarb will become soft and very juicy, and the color will turn a deep scarlet. You'll want to reduce the mixture to about half the original amount.

Remove the pan from the heat and whisk in the gelatin (if using) until it dissolves. Place the hot jam in a blender or food processor and process it for 1 to 2 minutes, or until it turns smooth.

Pour it into a lidded jar or decorative bowl, and store it in the refrigerator until you're ready to use it. Well-sealed, this will keep in the fridge for 1 to 2 months.

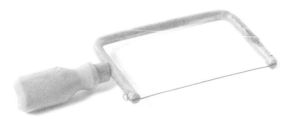

MONTE ENEBRO

SPAIN, GOAT'S MILK
PERSONALITY: The "Snow White" of goat cheese—porcelain skin meets black coiffeur.

This unique goat cheese from Avila looks like an inverted Humboldt Fog (page 74). The paste is bright white, like densely packed snow, while the surface is stippled with a thin layer of edible black ash and *Penicillium roqueforti*, the same mold that's used in blue cheese. The smell of Monte Enebro calls to mind river stones; the taste is bright and flinty with a finish of white pepper. It's gorgeous, both in appearance and in flavor. It's a fairytale, a real princess.

Monte Enebro only has one source, the Spanish cheesemaker Rafael Baez and his daughter Paloma. Baez developed this cheese in 1983, and he makes it by hand, forms it into logs, and ships it to the States after several weeks of ageing. As it ripens, a creamline forms under its surface, and the flavors intensify. This is a gorgeous cheese for entertaining. No one will forget it.

Good matches: Enjoy this with honey and baguette, alongside almonds or fresh berries. This looks stellar on a cheese plate, especially among other Spanish wedges.

Wine/beer: Try a Sauvignon Blanc, Chenin Blanc, or a light Spanish sherry. Or, reach for a Belgian-style saison.

OLD KENTUCKY TOMME

UNITED STATES, RAW GOAT'S MILK
PERSONALITY: A good selection for the Kentucky Derby, sunshiny and not quite tame.

Tomme-style cheeses are always rustic, and this special round from southern Indiana is no different. Judy Schad raises her own goats and makes cheese from their unpasteurized milk, which means that the flavor profile in a tomme like this yields complex undertones. Here, you'll find sweet cream mixed with wet leaves and mushrooms, followed by a gentle bite on the finish. The flavors build gradually rather than assaulting the tongue—this is a walk in the forest rather than an airdrop. Very pleasant, very sumptuous. The texture is smooth, Brie-like with a rind that is dappled beige or gray.

Schad began making cheese back in the eighties, before raising goats was fashionable. Today, she's viewed as a pioneer of the artisanal cheese movement in the United States. Her farm is home to a happy herd of about 500 goats, including Alpine, Nubian, and Saanen breeds. If you like this cheese, check out her Wabash Cannonball (page 83).

Good matches: Schad recommends serving this cheese with grilled apples and onions; they bring out the sweetness and the bite. On a cheese plate, Old Kentucky Tomme is especially nice with tomato jam or chutney and toasted walnuts.

Wine/beer: This is a versatile cheese, especially with whites; try a Chenin Blanc, a Chardonnay, or Sauternes. Wheat beers work well. The cheesemaker recommends Goose Island Oktoberfest.

SEA SMOKE

UNITED STATES, GOAT'S MILK

PERSONALITY: *Alice in Wonderland* meets a goat's milk tuffet.

If Humboldt Fog (page 74) were a cupcake, it would look like Sea Smoke, a cheese developed by Debbie Mikulak to honor her favorite seaside haunt, the Maine Coast. Today, Debbie is retired from cheesemaking, and Sea Smoke is under the care of an enterprising couple, Will and Lynne Reid, who left the Philadelphia suburbs to take over Debbie's farm in Chester County. They still make this muffin-sized goat cheese as Debbie did, with a streak of ash and a delicate sweet taste that smacks of spring rain and slightly peppery watercress.

One detail worth mentioning: the rind enrobing this cheese is veil thin, a highly revered achievement among the cheese intellegentsia. If you've ever eaten a mochi ball at a Japanese restaurant, you will be able to imagine the texture of this sheer girdle. It's tasteless but gummy, in a good way. When people first see Sea Smoke, they often take a step back: it looks more like something you'd find in an old forest than in a cheese case. The Reids also make a beautiful, subtle goat log, called Baby Bloomer, which is worth seeking out.

Good matches: Halve Sea Smoke and set it atop a spring salad of tender greens, fiddleheads, and strawberries. Petals would not be out of place. On a cheese plate, keep it simple with fresh berries and baguette rounds.

Wine/beer: A wheat beer, like Philadelphia Brewing Company's Walt Wit, pairs well, and so does a flute of Prosecco.

ON FRENCH VERSUS AMERICAN GOAT CHEESE

When my wife and I were trying to decide where to go on our honeymoon, I had only one stipulation: we had to go near cheese. Ultimately, we settled on the Loire Valley, and their celebrated chèvres were the staple ingredient of my every meal.

Our pictures of magnificent chateaux and medieval cathedrals are an excellent way to reminisce, but never have I so vividly remembered my time in France as the first time I tasted Sea Smoke. Its lemony tang was balanced perfectly by a barnyardy, damp hay earthiness that perfectly reflected the Loire terroir. The texture was cloud-like.

There are plenty of fantastic American goat cheeses, so my implication that this is the "most French" is not intended to imply that it is the best. But it's knack for teleportation will keep Sea Smoke in the heart of this Francophile forever.

—CHEESEMONGER HUNTER FIKE

SELLES-SUR-CHER

FRANCE, GOAT'S MILK
PERSONALITY: The Catherine Deneuve of goat cheese, fresh and flawless.

If goat cheese makes you nervous, let Selles-sur-Cher (sell-sur-SHARE) be your gateway drug. This quintessential cheese from the Loire Valley—picture lush meadows and happy goats nibbling wildflowers—is the gold standard for glorious chèvre. It's rolled in ash, which neutralizes the acidity in the milk to create a beautifully balanced cheese. You won't taste any "goaty tang," just a delicate, clean taste. Think spring dew.

Selles-sur-Cher can be eaten at any stage. Young, this small wheel has a snow-packed look when cut. Aged, it gains a butter-colored veil around the rind and becomes molten within. Both stages are desirable. The latter is more flavorful.

Good matches: Nothing is better for breakfast than fresh raspberries and Selles-sur-Cher. The combination looks stunning, too—black, white, and red. If you don't have raspberries, substitute raspberry jam. For an appetizer, serve this cheese with blanched spring vegetables, like baby carrots and peapods. It can also be crumbled over mixed greens studded with strawberries.

Wine/beer: Fresh goat cheese is incredibly flexible. For something refreshing, serve it with a wheat beer on the patio. Otherwise, Sauvignon Blanc or Sancerre are perfect.

SHELLBARK SHARP II

UNITED STATES, GOAT'S MILK
PERSONALITY: Sparky, edgy, a longhaired type with attitude.

In Philadelphia, Pete Demchur is a legend. He's the area's first goat cheesemaker and a real DIY guy. He builds all his own equipment, welding it by hand, to produce some of the area's most interesting goat cheese. Shellbark Sharp II, an aged chèvre that benefits from an extra-long spell in the ageing cave, is his hallmark. It's crumbly, like a feta, but not as salty. And it's far zestier than most soft goat cheeses, though you couldn't exactly call it spicy. Let's just say it has depth. Think herbs-and-citrus *maximus*.

Pete Demchur lives in Chester County, where he maintains a herd of about seventy Nubians and produces a variety of goat's milk products, from kefir to a wildly peppery crottin that's a menu staple at Philadelphia's own Southwark Restaurant. Demchur and his sister, Donna, are also fixtures at local farmers' markets. If you like this cheese, look for their custardy Maysiola, a loose interpretation of Robiola (page 107), named after their favorite nanny goat.

Good matches: The Demchurs often sample Shellbark Sharp II with buckwheat honey and slices of Asian pear—outstanding compliments. For an appetizer, try Fig and Goat Cheese Crostini (page 81).

Wine/beer: Pour a glass of Vouvray or a heady lager. This is one goat cheese that can even stand up to a smoked beer, if you want to explore contrasts.

FIG AND GOAT CHEESE CROSTINI

Serve these little toasts at a BBQ or cocktail party with Prosecco, wheat beer, or Mojitos. If you can't find Shellbark Sharp II (page 80), substitute Leonora (page 76) or Caña de Cabra (page 67).

SERVES 6 TO 8

1 baguette, sliced into half-inch rounds
4 tablespoons extra-virgin olive oil
1/2 pound Shellbark Sharp II
Buckwheat honey, for drizzling
1 pound dried mission figs, sliced
1/2 cup chopped walnuts, toasted
Fresh thyme, for garnish
Freshly ground black pepper

Preheat the broiler on high.

Place the baguette rounds on a cookie sheet, then brush or drizzle them with olive oil. Pop them under the broiler for 3 to 5 minutes, or until the edges are browned. Remove the tray from the oven, flip the baguette rounds over (tongs are good for this), then return the tray to the oven to brown the other side.

Top each toasted round with a schmear of goat cheese, followed by a drizzle of honey. Add a slice or two of dried fig and a few toasted walnuts. Sprinkle with fresh thyme leaves and black pepper.

VALENÇAY

FRANCE, GOAT'S MILK
PERSONALITY: A wizardy cheese, shaped like a pyramid—very Harry Potter.

At peak ripeness, Valençay is the consistency of dense snow, moist but powdery. In its younger stages, Valençay is wet, like rum-soaked cake. Both are delicious. Both suggest patio parties, spring flings, and magical thinking. Were Harry Potter to wave his wand and develop a cheese, it would no doubt be black and shaped like a stunted sorcerer's cap, the very shape of Valençay.

The black exterior comes from a light coating of ash—it's tasteless but striking, and some say it neutralizes the acidity of the goat's milk. Others will tell you it's just part of Valençay's iconic appeal, alongside its shape; supposedly, Napoleon used his sword to lop off the tip. Valençay epitomizes Loire Valley goat cheese: it's ethereal, balanced, and redolent of tender grass blades. You shouldn't taste any tang, which makes it very kid-friendly.

Good matches: Valençay is wildly versatile. Serve it with berries, crumble it over salad greens, or slather it on baguette rounds topped with sautéed ramps or light-colored honey. Because spring milk makes the best fresh goat cheese, Valençay always goes well with the first farmers' market produce. It's also lovely for breakfast served with peach or apricot preserves.

Wine/beer: A flinty Sauvignon or rosé will never let you down. A wheat beer is delightful, especially one with bright, herbaceous notes.

A Note for the Goat Cheese-Averse

If you know someone who professes to dislike goat cheese, know that they have probably been scarred by a poor-quality chèvre. Explain to them that good goat cheese should taste balanced, never sickeningly sour or "bucky" (like the smell of a male goat), then soothe your beloved with one of the tender morsels in this chapter. If he or she still recoils, pour them a glass of flinty Sauvignon Blanc or pass them a jar of honey. Both create pairing magic. You might even say that fresh goat cheese without honey is like a bed without sheets.

WABASH CANNONBALL

UNITED STATES, GOAT'S MILK
PERSONALITY: **A sprite with downy wings.**

Few cheeses can be called adorable, but Judy Schad's 3-ounce puffball of goat cheese dredged in ash and stippled with pretty white mold is just that. Is it a cheese, or is it a dark chocolate truffle rolled in powdered sugar? Try to resist putting the whole thing in your mouth. The experience would probably make you float for a moment, but everyone around you would be irate. These little bombs can be hard to come by, but they are worth seeking out as you would a precious new night cream. Texturally, the two substances are similar—fluffy, almost aerated—but of course the Cannonball is much more replenishing.

Look for a hint of citrus, followed by baby soft pepperiness. This is hand-made goat cheese at its finest and most inventive. Schad won Best of Show at the American Cheese Society for this delicacy back in 1995, which is not an easy feat. Her technique is impeccable, but of course, that's what you get from a cheese pioneer. In addition to running one of the oldest farmstead goat dairies in the country, Schad earned a Ph.D. in Renaissance Literature, which might explain why she chooses the most delightful names for her creations. In addition to Wabash Cannonball, she makes Crocodile Tear and Old Kentucky Tomme (page 78).

Good matches: Save this for a momentous cheese board. In winter, its snowball-ish appearance is a lovely accent on holiday cheese boards. Try garnishing it with holly or rosemary sprigs. Serve it with figs or Rhubarb Refrigerator Jam (recipe, page 77) any time of year.

Wine/beer: The flavor profile of this cheese changes between weeks three and five, so ask your cheesemonger about its age. When it's young, pair it with Sauvignon Blanc; the cheese will be mellow and moist. Otherwise, try a Sauternes or Moscato to offset the slight pepperiness.

CHEESE BOARD: An All-Goat Blow-Out

Goat cheeses are easy to digest and wonderful to serve in spring and summer. This board gives you the chance to try goat's milk in all its forms, from fresh chèvre to a lush blue. Serve wheat beers or lambics, or pick out a minerally white, like a Sauvignon Blanc or Sancerre. As you sample these, it may help you to refer to the section on tasting cheese (page 139), which includes a lexicon.

Carre du Berry (page 69)   Crottin de Chavignol (page 70)

Monte Enebro (page 78)   Midnight Moon (page 216)

Cremificato Verde Capra (page 234)

Suggested Accompaniments: Fresh berries, a tossed salad with radishes and herbs, blanched asparagus drizzled with olive oil and lemon juice, pickled ramps or fiddleheads, grilled or fresh figs, honey, Rhubarb Refrigerator Jam (page 77), rosemary bread, water crackers.

CHEESE 101: How to Pair Cheese and Honey

Most cheeses pair well with honey, but goat cheeses—like the ones in this chapter—are ideal honey companions. If you think about it, bees draw pollen from many of the same plants that animals graze on in pastures, so it's no wonder that "milk and honey" fit together like a pair of hands. Many cultures that make cheese have developed regional honey pairings, like Tuscany's affinity for Pecorino Toscano (page 195) and Acacia honey.

With so many kinds of honey available, it's fun to experiment with flavors. Keep your eye out at farmers' markets where you may find cranberry honey, sage honey, and even blueberry honey, depending on where you live. Here are a few combinations to play around with if you enjoy a touch of sweetness with your cheese:

Floral Honey and Goat Cheese

Light colored honeys from clover blossoms, orange blossoms, or wildflowers are generally sweeter and more delicate than amber or darkly hued honeys. They are perfect to drizzle over mild Capricho de Cabra (page 30) or a lemony wedge of Leonora (page 76). For a cheese plate, pick a variety of Quiet Types and Free Spirits, and offer a jar or two of light-colored honey that guests can sample with different cheeses. Serve almonds and pears or apricots on the side. Flat bread, scones, or baguette rounds would work well. You could even serve tea, as goat cheese pairs well with green or rose-black tea.

Buckwheat Honey and Cheddar

The malty notes in amber honeys, like buckwheat, are for pairing with complex, nutty cheeses like clothbound Cheddar, or tart goat cheeses like Shellbark Sharp II (page 80). If you're serving the sort of cheese you might pair with dark beer, consider going with a molasses-dark honey. Its toasty notes play well off ploughman's lunch fare, like apples, brown bread, and rustic hunks of Keen's Cheddar (page 171), Vermont Shepherd (page 175), or Wensleydale (page 60).

Truffle Honey and Pecorino

Firm, salty Pecorinos always pair well with honey. Any kind will do, but truffle honey is especially fine. Its mushroomy accent plays well off Pecorino's light note of lanolin, a natural oil found in wool and a flavor associated with sheep's milk cheese. In Italy, honey from native Acacia trees makes a classic pairing for local Pecorinos. The flavor is light but lingering.

Fruity Honey and Parmigiano Reggiano

Parmigiano is often described as a "fruity" cheese because it's sweet and even a little sour at times, like a pineapple. If you ever get a chance to pair it with cranberry honey, the combination is just perfect. At a dinner party where you don't want guests to fill up on appetizers, try setting out a simple hunk of Parmigiano Reggiano (page 189) along with a jar of interesting honey, preferably cranberry or truffle (a small jar of truffle honey won't set you back more than a few bucks). Encourage your guests to break off hunks of Parm and dip them into the honey. The complexity in that single bite will be the talk of the night.

Honeycomb and Blue Cheese

The veining in blue cheese creates an interesting textural surface, which is visually enhanced by pairing it with a hunk of honeycomb—pure honey, still encased in waxy cells. The wax is edible, and when eaten with a hunk of Roquefort (page 92) or Point Reyes Original Blue (page 239), the combination of salty-sweet and creamy-toothsome is striking. For a stunning dessert course, serve a hunk of blue cheese and whole honeycomb cut into cubes. You might also serve baguette rounds, sliced pears, and toasted walnuts to create a cheese board that encourages guests to keep nibbling.

Cheese and Honey Recipes

For dishes that feature honey, try **Grilled Figs with Manchego** (page 51), **Baked Caña de Cabra with Pine Nuts and Honey** (page 68), **Fig and Goat Cheese Crostini** (page 81), and **Dessert Grilled Cheese** (page 230).

CHAPTER IV

VIXENS

(rich, decadent)

You know these ladeez—ultra-rich and luxurious? Leave them alone in your house and they'll gorge themselves on strawberries and drink all of your Champagne. If you appreciate naughty types, you'll fit right in with these triple crèmes.

Anton's Red Love | Banon | Brie de Meaux | Baked Brie with Pears and Apricots | Carles Roquefort | Casatica di Bufala | Constant Bliss | Délice de Bourgogne | Harbison | Peach Balsamic Compote | Hummingbird | Semolina Crackers with Sea Salt | Kunik | La Serena | La Tur | Largo | Moses Sleeper | Noble Road | Robiola Bosina | Saint Marcellin | Seal Bay | Sottocenere | Ticklemore | Truffle Tremor | Weybridge | Winnimere | Cheese Board: An Evening in Paris | Cheese 101: How Cheese is Made

ANTON'S RED LOVE

GERMANY, COW'S MILK
PERSONALITY: The bodice-ripper of
washed rinds—naughty but nice.

You haven't seen cheesy packaging until you've
seen the label on Anton's Red Love, a Taleggio-
like square from Bavaria. The photograph on
the balsa wood box looks like the cover on a
Harlequin Romance: a buxom maiden with
braided hair feeds a runny wedge to a bearded
chap with a big grin. Turns out, the bearded
chap really is named Anton. He may go down
in history as the first European cheesemaker to
embrace sexy ad campaigns, and it works.
Anton's Red Love is one sexy beast.

In texture, ARL is like a cream-filled Bis-
marck. The exterior is bready and chewy, while
the interior remains pudding-soft, like Bavarian
cream. The taste is pleasantly mellow for a
washed-rind cheese: milky, lightly stinky, with a
floral hook. Think of a picnic in a pasture.
You've got your fresh bread, your soft blanket,
your cows chewing cud in the distance. If you
want to introduce your special someone to a
second-base stinker, this is the cheese to please.
If it helps, tell her Anton named this cheese
after his wife, a flaming redhead—true story. He
also makes a cheese called Bavarian Blonde.

Good matches: Pair this with crusty bread
and berry preserves. Because this cheese is big
and buttery, we think it's ideal for breakfast in
bed. On a cheese board, try serving it with
another Bavarian cream cake, Chiriboga Blue
(page 233).

Wine/beer: Pour a glass of Riesling or a Belgian Strong Ale.

BANON

FRANCE, GOAT OR COW'S MILK
PERSONALITY: A bunting of leaf-wrapped
joy, perfect for camping trips.

Cheese wrapped in leaves always promises to be
gorgeous. As the leaves break down, the dairy
within turns woodsy and supple. Peel open this
little package of earthy pleasure and you can't
help squealing like a Girl Scout. Banon is to the
cheese world what foil-pack dinners are to
young campers dressed in green smocks.

Don't be surprised if you taste a touch of
booze. After Banon gets swaddled in chestnut
leaves, the whole puck is dunked in eau-de-vie, a
delicious spirit. It's rumored that Roman
Emperor Antonius Pius was so hooked on Banon
he ate himself to death. To make sure your Banon
is ripe, give it a squeeze; it should give beneath
your fingers. If not, it may be astringent and
chalky inside, a sign of unripeness. The color of
the leaves is also a good indicator: a well-aged
Banon will have brownish leaves. For a stateside
specialty, look for Capriole Farm's O'Banon,
Indiana's version of Banon with leaves that have
been macerated in Woodford Reserve Bourbon.
Yee-haw!

Good matches: Serve this before or after a
Provençal-inspired supper richly accented with
herbs and seafood. All you need is a baguette to
scoop out Banon's soft insides. If you pack this
cheese on a camping trip, take along walnuts
and apricots or blackberries.

Wine/beer: Rosé is lovely, and so is a French
white or sparkling wine. If your Banon is very
ripe, draw out the savory notes with a Rhône
red. A malty beer or a spot of Cognac works
well, too.

BRIE DE MEAUX

FRANCE, COW'S MILK

PERSONALITY: A delicate 'tween in a shearling jacket—moody and impulsive.

First, the sad truth about Brie in America: most of it tastes like a rubber Frisbee. Your average supermarket Brie is nothing like the glorious moons Charlemagne swooned over in 774 B.C., nor is it anything like the luxe, grassy wheel you might have melted for in Paris during a recent junket. In the United States, it's illegal to import young raw-milk cheese, and true Brie is just that: an unpasteurized adolescent. The Brie that comes in from France is pasteurized to meet FDA requirements, and it's made in factories, rather than on small farms—a factor that definitely affects taste.

All this to say: Brie de Meaux from the family-run Fromagerie Rouzaire just outside of Paris produces some of the best Brie for export. Ask a trustworthy cheesemonger to help you select a pudgy diskette, since textures and flavors vary wildly depending on the season and the age of the wheel. Perfect Brie is fleeting, which means that the Brie de Meaux you buy today is not the same one you will buy tomorrow. Still, this tends to be a silky, mushroomy creature—lovely for eating by the spoonful. Some cheesemongers prefer it to ice cream. If you can't find Brie de Meaux, look for its likeminded cousin, Brie de Nangis.

Good matches: Sauté some mushrooms and ready a baguette, or set out jams and berries. Just remember, Brie is no good cold. Let it relax on the counter for a half hour at least, or put it in a pie pan and heat it gently in the oven, then serve it with sliced pears and toasted, slivered almonds. Around the holidays, try Baked Brie with Pears and Apricots (page 90).

Wine/beer: Brie always likes bubbly, but a Côte de Rhône or unoaked Chardonnay can work magic as well. Otherwise, seek out a yeasty and effervescent ale.

When to Eat the Rind

There is a simple rule of thumb about rinds: if a rind appeals to you, eat it; if it doesn't appeal to you, don't fret. As long as the rind isn't dipped in wax, it's fair game. Keep in mind that the rind often contains the most flavor. That's the case with Brie: its slightly spongy surface tastes peppery, a nice contrast to the mushroomy cream filling underneath. If a party guest leaves you with a pile of Brie rinds, simply broil them on baguette rounds, then drizzle them with honey or fig jam for a midnight snack. Add some cracked pepper and toasted nuts or green apple slivers, and you will wish for many more rind-fearing friends.

BAKED BRIE with PEARS and APRICOTS

Forget the baked Brie of yore. This one is like an overstuffed purse full of glistening nuts and preserves. Make it ahead of time for a holiday party, or serve thick slices for dessert with coffee or glasses of Riesling.

SERVES 8 TO 10

1 medium Bosc pear, diced
½ cup dried apricots, chopped
½ cup dried figs, chopped
½ cup dried cranberries
½ cup chopped walnuts
1 cup apricot jam
2 sheets puff pastry
1 wheel Brie (2.2 pounds or 1 kg)
1 egg yolk

Note: For a smaller Brie (8 ounces), use one sheet of pastry dough and halve the fruit mixture. Baked Brie can be served warm or at room temperature.

Preheat the oven to 400°F and line a lipped cookie sheet or baking dish with parchment paper. You can also use a 12-inch pie pan or a large springform pan. (A wheel of Brie of this size is 9 inches across, so this will give you plenty of room.)

In a bowl, combine the pear, apricots, figs, cranberries, walnuts, and apricot jam until well mixed.

Unfold the puff pastry on a lightly floured surface, and roll out both sheets of dough so that they are about an inch wider on all sides than they were originally. You'll want to be able to encase the Brie between the two sheets and crimp the edges well.

Place the wheel of Brie in the center of one of the pastry sheets, then spoon the fruit mixture onto the cheese, using a spatula to spread it out in an even layer.

Drape the second sheet of puff pastry over the fruit-topped cheese, and crimp the edges shut. (You may want to trim off the corners with kitchen scissors.) Make sure you seal the puff pastry well so that the Brie doesn't ooze out in the oven. Do not make any holes in the dough.

Combine the egg yolk and 1 tablespoon of water in a small dish, then brush the mixture over the surface of the pastry with a pastry brush.

Bake the Brie for 15 to 20 minutes, or until golden brown. Let it rest for 10 minutes before serving.

CARLES ROQUEFORT

FRANCE, SHEEP'S MILK
PERSONALITY: The dominatrix of blue cheese—wildly sharp, yet pleasurable.

While there are a variety of Roqueforts on the market, none are as exquisite as this artisanal version made by the renowned Jacques Carles, a persevering Frenchman in his nineties. His hometown, the dinky hamlet of Martrin, has more ewes than people, and Carles draws from several small sheep farms to produce a miniscule amount of cheese—a mere one percent of all the Roquefort produced in France.

By law, Roquefort must be made in southern France and aged in natural limestone caves along the Combalou Plateau. Carles lives just minutes from this labyrinthine edifice, where natural fissures in the rock draw in salty drafts of sea air that contribute to the cheese's taste and texture. At room temperature, Carles Roquefort turns velveteen. You'll want to sit down before you bite in: the flavors can last a good minute or more in the mouth, moving from sea-salty sweetness to minerals and milk, until your tongue blazes with heat. A cooling beverage, like Sauternes, is required as part of this baptism by fire, but you'll have a new appreciation for this highly sought-after delicacy once enjoyed by the Romans and, most especially, by King Charlemagne. After a taste, he requested cartloads delivered to his castle. Hopefully, your first bite will inspire such devotion and turn you away from blue cheese "crumbles" forever.

Good Matches: Ripe pears are the traditional pairing for Roquefort. A handful of walnuts bring out this cheese's earthiness. Really, though, it needs nothing. It's Roquefort! As the French gastronome Grimod de la Reynière once said, "Roquefort should be eaten on one's knees."

Wine/beer: Sauternes is the classic match. For something effervescent, try a wickedly hoppy IPA or Russian Imperial Stout.

CASATICA DI BUFALA

ITALY, BUFFALO MILK
PERSONALITY: An opera singer, supple and pitch-perfect, with bodacious curves.

Buffalo milk is known for its richness and its sweet, milky taste, both of which stand out in this luxurious loaf of pure white nougat. Casatica (rhymes with "erotica") gets her good looks from northern Italy, near Bergamo—an unlikely spot for a buffalo cheese since most herds are raised in the south and milked for mozzarella. No matter, the skill of two brothers, Alfio and Bruno Gritti, who replenished their father's cow dairy with water buffalo a decade ago, shines through, making this tender bomb a must-try.

Casatica has two layers: a fluffy rind that is slightly bitter—in the way that green bananas can be bitter—and a springy interior that is redolent of Brazil nuts and fresh yogurt. The total effect is a bit like chewing an unimaginably exotic bubblegum. Enjoy the complexity, and if you don't like the rind, simply remove it. There is plenty of zaftig interior.

Good matches: Around Di Bruno Bros., mongers like to use thick rounds of sopressatta as a landing pad for this cheese, in place of crackers. It's also good slathered onto baguette rounds.

Wine/beer: Try Prosecco, or better yet, demi sec, an off-dry dessert wine with more sweetness. A fruity lambic works well, too, as does a farmhouse-style saison with earthy, yeasty notes.

CONSTANT BLISS

UNITED STATES, COW'S MILK
PERSONALITY: Perfect in every way, just like a new infatuation.

Constant Bliss looks like a snow-covered muffin. It's just the right size to take to the movies or to eat in bed when you are exploring new realms of decadence with someone special in your life. Like so many laughably good advancements in the dairy sphere, Constant Bliss comes from Vermont. It's one of the first cheeses that the Kehler Brothers developed at their farm, Jasper Hill, in Greensboro—back when every American had a singular fixation with French cheese (they were attempting to recreate a cheese called Chaource, similar to Camembert, page 46). Today, the Kehlers make a variety of European styles, but Constant Bliss still embodies the simplicity and purity of their first efforts.

When this cheese is ripe, a beautiful creamline forms under the rind. Lemon flavors dominate, along with the fresh taste of Ayrshire cream and a trace of mushroom. Since this cheese ripens from the outside in, the center usually remains cakey, which makes for an interesting contrast in texture. Despite what you might think, this cheese isn't named after the euphoric feeling induced by eating it. Constant Bliss was a man, a Revolutionary War scout. He's been immortalized next to his buddy, Moses Sleeper (page 106), another sumptuous cheese that pairs well with summer picnics and new flames.

Good matches: Fresh berries or preserves work beautifully. Try sour cherry jam. For something decadent, slide a wedge of Constant Bliss under the first sautéed morels of spring. Good baguette is a must.

Wine/beer: Pick up some Champagne or, on the cheesemaker's recommendation: a citrusy wheat beer with plenty of effervescence.

All-American Bloomies

If you're a Brie-head, check out what's happening in the American triple crème scene. Within the last decade, there's been a flurry of great domestic bloomies made by American cheesemakers who have studied in France. If you like Constant Bliss, try its brother, Moses Sleeper (page 106), from the same maker in Vermont, then try Largo (page 104) from California—it's dense and cakey—or seek out Pennsylvania's Noble Road (page 106). For an interesting spin-off, seek out Jasper Hill's Harbison (page 96), a triple crème wrapped in spruce bark.

DÉLICE DE BOURGOGNE

FRANCE, COW'S MILK

PERSONALITY: A satin-shouldered temptress, the queen of French triple crèmes.

Délice has one thing on her mind, and that's a party. She's the kind of cheese that you can set out before or after dinner and, either way, she'll be the talk of the room. If you've grown weary of Brie, you'll be pleased with this strumpety sister. Give her cherries and bubbly, and you've got all you could ever want for breakfast or dessert.

You can tell a ripe Délice by its surface. If the rind is perfectly white, it's probably young; the interior will be rich and cheesecakey with a fresh, lemony taste. If you want something plusher, let this cheese sit in your crisper for a couple of days. When the rind has a stippled look—almost as if someone has drawn squiggles across it in pencil—the center will likely be gooey and the flavor will be more concentrated. This is a thick cake, much taller and moussier than Brie de Meaux (page 89), thanks to the addition of crème fraiche. It's sold in 4.5-pound wheels or in tiny muffin-sized portions, known as "mini Délice."

Good matches: For a classic Di Bruno Bros. pairing, serve Délice with Amarena cherries in syrup and spiced pecans. Duck prosciutto is an especially good addition. You can even wrap the duck prosciutto around half a cherry and a teaspoon or so of Délice for a ravishing bite before dinner.

Wine/beer: Go sparkly or pair with a Duvel. For something different, try a fruity lambic or gueuze.

HARBISON

UNITED STATES, COW'S MILK
PERSONALITY: A sexy librarian's cheese—all horn rims and whispers.

This cheese really is named after a librarian in Greensboro, Vermont, and it really is sexy: it's the consistency of cake batter. It comes in a bark-wrapped wheel about the size of a 7-inch record, and if you're lucky enough to snag one, you just might want to plunge a spoon into it on the spot. Harbison, from the much-loved Jasper Hill Farm in Vermont, is essentially Moses Sleeper (page 106) banded with pine bark. That means you get the sweet vanilla notes of a triple crème imbued with forest spice and an unusual fruity note that can only be described as the smell of someone sucking on a cherry cough drop, perhaps in the back stacks.

Harbison is the recent invention of cheesemaker Mateo Kehler, a great experimenter. When he wrapped some especially runny Brie-style cheeses with bark he'd collected from around his farm, he discovered that the flavors blended quite naturally. Thus, this new cheese was born. Jasper Hill is also famous for its spruce-girdled Winnimere (page 112), a funky cheese that's available from winter through late spring. Harbison is decidedly more summery, but it's available year-round.

Note: Make sure your wheel gives a little before you cut into it; the texture should be gooey. If the wheel feels firm, you may need to let it age in your crisper for a week or so, preferably in a sealed container, not in plastic wrap.

Good matches: Set out a jar of cherry preserves and some rustic bread, or use Harbison for dunking wild strawberries, pears, or black cherries. Because this cheese has notes of fruit and pine, it also pairs well with nut breads and rosemary crackers. For a strangely good pairing, try Harbison with Peach and Balsamic Compote (page 98)—the combination tastes like peach cobbler.

Wine/beer: Pair this with a berry lambic or a sparkling rosé. The cheesemaker recommends serving Saison Dupont.

PEACH BALSAMIC COMPOTE

Soft cheeses and stinkers love the acidic sweetness of peaches, especially when they've been cooked down. Whip up this compote during peach season to make a luscious pairing for Harbison (page 96) or Red Hawk (page 154), then use the leftovers to top waffles, crêpes, or French toast along with a spoonful of mascarpone (page 32) or ricotta (page 34).

MAKES 1½ CUPS

3 large ripe peaches (about 3 cups, chopped)

¼ cup granulated sugar

2 tablespoons aged balsamic vinegar (like Balsamico Suite)

¼ teaspoon salt

Mix the chopped peaches, sugar, vinegar, and salt in a small saucepan over medium-high heat. Simmer the mixture for about 5 minutes, stirring occasionally, until the fruit has softened. The sugar will melt as the peaches release their juices, so don't worry about the fact that you don't start off with any liquid. Remove the pan from the heat, and allow the compote to cool before ladling it into a jar or bowl. Refrigerated, this will keep for up to two weeks.

Note: Using a quality aged balsamic really makes a difference here. Ageing vinegar, like ageing wine, creates more flavor and a thicker, more viscous texture. Ask your cheesemonger to recommend a bottle. It will probably set you back twenty or thirty dollars, but you'll have it for years and you can always drizzle it on Parmigiano Reggiano (page 189) for a brilliant pairing.

HUMMINGBIRD

UNITED STATES, COW AND SHEEP'S MILK
PERSONALITY: A flutter of rich milk with electric flavor.

Like its namesake, Hummingbird is a bright, delicate cheese with a slightly avian shape—in fact, it may be the only cheese in America that's made in an oval format. At one week, it has the consistency of cheesecake with gentle citrus and vanilla notes; at three, it turns runny and pungent, like a well-ripened Robiola (page 107). Either way, it's a glorious summer cheese, perfect for toting to an outdoor concert with a baguette and some bubbly.

Cheesemaker Kristian Holbrook invented Hummingbird when he moved to Pennsylvania from Tennessee to make cheese at Doe Run Farm in Chester County. The rolling landscape and coastal plains of eastern Pennsylvania made him think of Lombardy, the seat of Robiola country, and he guessed that Philadelphia's Italian population might enjoy a taste of something homey. He was right. Hummingbird has been a big hit with the Italian Market crowd that shops at the original Di Bruno Bros. on 9th Street. In 2011, Hummingbird took home a gold medal from the American Cheese Society, a big honor for a little bird.

Good matches: Try pairing Hummingbird with flatbread or Semolina Crackers with Sea Salt (page 100) and Balsamic Poached Figs (page 182). Tart cherry preserves or sliced pears and honey also work beautifully.

Wine/beer: The cheesemaker recommends a dry hard cider. Prosecco is also lovely, as are wheat beers and Belgian ales, particularly Unibroue's La Fin du Monde.

SEMOLINA CRACKERS WITH SEA SALT

Inspired by a recipe that appeared on the blog 101 Cookbooks (101cookbooks.com), these crackers have become a favorite around the Di Bruno Bros. kitchen. The dough is easy to work with, and once baked, the crackers yield just the right amount of snap. I like to roll them out in long sheets and break them up once they've cooled, but you can also cut the dough into shapes before you bake these off. These are great crackers to serve with soft cheese, and their rustic look is especially nice alongside Hummingbird (page 99). Note: a sprinkle of fresh thyme, rosemary, or even saffron is a lovely touch before you put the dough in the oven.

SERVES 8 TO 10

1½ cup semolina flour
1½ cups all-purpose flour, plus more for dusting
1 teaspoon kosher salt
1 cup warm water
⅓ cup extra-virgin olive oil, plus ¼ cup for brushing
Sea salt and fresh herbs, for sprinkling

Combine the flours and kosher salt in the bowl of a stand mixer. (If you don't have a stand mixer, just use a wooden spoon.) In a separate mixing bowl, combine the warm water and ⅓ cup of extra-virgin olive oil. Add the wet ingredients to the dry and mix on medium-low speed. Use a dough hook attachment to knead the mixture for 5 to 7 minutes, or transfer the mixture to a well-floured surface and knead it by hand.

When the dough is pliable and no longer sticky, form it into a ball and cut it into four segments with a knife. Place the segments on a plate, rub the outsides lightly with olive oil, and cover them with plastic wrap. Refrigerate for 1 hour.

Dust a clean work surface with all-purpose flour. Place one segment of dough on the work surface and dust the top with flour. Flatten the dough as much as possible with the palm of your hand, then use a rolling pin to work the dough forward, then back. Rotate the dough

ninety degrees and repeat the rolling process. Continue rolling the dough, turning the dough ninety degrees every few rolls, until it is about ⅛ inch thick. The thinner, the better.

Transfer the dough to a lightly floured cookie sheet (on parchment paper if you wish). It helps to get two baking sheets going since you will have four flat rounds once you roll out all the dough. Brush the top of the dough with olive oil, and prick it with a fork every inch or so to prevent air bubbles. Then lightly sprinkle the tops of the crackers with sea salt and fresh herbs, if using.

Preheat the oven to 350°F. Bake the crackers on cookie sheets for approximately 10 minutes, then rotate the pan in the oven, and bake for another 10 minutes. Remove the crackers when they are just crispy and golden brown. Allow the crackers to cool completely, then break the sheets into pieces. Store in an airtight container for up to one week.

KUNIK

UNITED STATES, COW AND GOAT'S MILK
PERSONALITY: The Dorothy Parker of triple crèmes: biting but fashionable.

Nettle Meadow Farm in Thurman, New York, introduced this churlish smoothie a few years ago, and of course it became an instant phenom. *Esquire* deemed it one the sexiest cheeses in America, which probably prompted a lot of hulky types to run from their gyms straight to the cheese counter, antic-ipating a fey little puck without a lot of chutzpah. Think again, boys! Kunik (rhymes with tunic) is a hellraiser, tangy and saucy with a shock of black pepper that hits the back of your throat when this cheese is very ripe. Imagine a Robiola (page 107) with a horseradish vodka chaser.

Of course Kunik's strength is age-dependent. Young, this round of triple crème flirts with you, but leave it in the fridge for a week and this she-lion roars. Lorraine Lambiase and Sheila Flanagan make this cheese by hand at their 50-acre farm in the Adirondacks, using a combination of the farm's own goats' milk mixed with rich Jersey cream. If you like peppery Bries and Robiolas and you're not scared of a little "barnyard," you'll appreciate the complexity of this back-talkin' butter bomb. Few triple crèmes have this much flavor.

Good matches: Kunik pairs well with roasted beets and arugula; try using a slice to top a sum-mer salad. It can also handle exotic matches, like pickled garlic scapes or brandied cherries. An herby honey, like one touched with lavender, also pairs well.

Wine/beer: Go pink. Pick out a fruity rosé, or serve up a sparkly cocktail garnished with lavender or thyme. A Sauvignon Blanc can pal around with this, too, when it's on the young side; otherwise, lean on a New York Riesling. A wheat beer will be stellar, but only if you've got a young Kunik. A whacky lambic can take an aged round to the mat.

LA SERENA

SPAIN, RAW SHEEP'S MILK
PERSONALITY: A gutsy broad, slightly feral, with a lot of soul.

I like to think that if Dolly Parton were going to fall in love with a cheese, it would be this one. Why? Each round is bound in lace to hold its creamy center intact, and the flavor profile calls to mind, well, artichoke dip. I'm talking heavenly artichoke dip—the kind you pull out of the oven, bubbly on top and gooey within. There aren't many cheeses that combine feminine fashion with potlucky grace, and that's why I'm singing "Coat of Many Colors" to this one.

Be forewarned: this is a funky cheese, bold and pungent with a delicate vegetal hook. The vegetal taste comes from thistle rennet, which is used as a coagulant during the early stages of cheesemaking. The rennet is gathered from cardoons, thistle-like plants that grow in spiky patches across the rough-and-tumble Extremadura region of Spain.

Good matches: Scoop this onto rustic bread, along with strong-flavored sides like cornichons, olives, nuts, and cured meats. Try it with steamed or oil-cured artichokes, or see the party suggestion below in the Cheesemonger Note.

Wine/beer: This is a versatile cheese. The Spanish serve it with Cava or Oloroso sherry, but its slightly beefy nature begs for beer—try a saison. For something unexpected, go for a gin-based cocktail.

UNDERSTANDING SPANISH CHEESE

I like to think of most Spanish cheeses as chameleons. Very few of them stand out as open, proud, and ready to be consumed on their own. Most, like Manchego (page 51), Garrotxa (page 48) and Mahón (page 50), blend into a supporting cast for what Spain does best, which is all things cured pork. This is not a knock on Spanish cheese; the mentality there is that their cheeses should work in harmony with the rest of their epicurean delights.

One exception to the rule is La Serena. This raw sheep's milk cheese is soft and goopy, but it packs a powerful punch. Owing to its thistle rennet coagulation, there is a sour, savory sharpness not usually found in two-month-old cheeses. La Serena is a fabulous party cheese, especially if you buy the whole wheel. Cut off the top rind, throw in a spoon for smearing, and surround with slices of toasted bread and Vinho Verde. Watch your guests ooh and ahh.

-CHEESEMONGER HUNTER FIKE

LA TUR

ITALY, COW, GOAT, AND SHEEP'S MILK
PERSONALITY: A jetsetter who only sleeps in silk.

La Tur looks like a pillbox hat that Jackie O. might have worn. It's tiny, only two inches across, with a rippled, chenille-like surface the color of winter. It's a personal blizzard, all packed into a tote. Carry it on your next flight, or serve it to a traveling dignitary who has never experienced snow. Under its little shearling rind, La Tur holds the secret to three milks: cow, goat, and sheep. Cream from all three animals is blended into a decadent trifecta that expresses each type: grassy, tangy, nutty. It's utterly over-the-top.

Of course this luxury hails from the region of Piedmont, the home of so much good Italian wine and white truffles. La Tur is made by Caseificio Dell'Alta Langa, a company just outside the Italian town of Alba, a much-loved culinary center. The same company also produces luxe Robiola Bosina (page 107). If you don't see La Tur at a cheese counter, ask for its cousin, Rocchetta.

Good matches: Serve this accessible cheese at a party alongside berries or jam. It's also good with a drizzle of honey. Because La Tur has an ice-creamy quality, it's very good in place of dessert. Some of us have been known to eat it on graham crackers with a spoonful of Amarena cherries in syrup.

Wine/beer: This cheese calls for a sparkling Asti Spumante or an effervescent lambic, preferably one made from cherries or peaches.

LARGO

UNITED STATES, COW'S MILK
PERSONALITY: A geeky beauty that only listens to Chopin: highly coveted.

Like its name, Largo is a cheese that is both gentle and stately. If you find yourself in possession of it, consider yourself lucky. This rare creation from Napa is more likely to appear on a cheese board at the French Laundry than anywhere east of California. That's because Largo's maker, Soyoung Scanlan, was sought out by Thomas Keller, a chef who has made a career out of perfection. His cheese boards are notorious for their beauty and purity.

If you like the whipped quality of Délice de Bourgogne (page 95), you'll love the texture of this handmade version, which is pure alchemy. Scanlan is famous for drawing out every note in her milk and for bringing unparalleled artistry to the tradition of French-style cheesemaking. Her intensity is legendary; rumor has it, she sometimes sleeps in her cheese cave just to feel the humidity levels on her skin. Organic Jersey milk combined with crème fraîche makes this subtle stunner a conversation piece. For a superlative triple crème made from goat's milk, look for Andante Dairy's Minuet.

Good matches: Serve this with fresh apricots or berries. It needs little in the way of gewgaws to dress it up. In fact, you may not even need baguette.

Wine/beer: Go California all the way. Pick up a Sauvignon Blanc or something bubbly. For a stellar beer pairing, try Allagash Victoria, a Belgian ale that incorporates Chardonnay grapes into the mash.

SOYOUNG SCANLAN: CHEESEMAKER WITH SOUL

I am going to let you in on a little secret, one that is not known by many outside my circle of friends. I have a degree in Classical Music from the Peabody Conservatory, with a specialty in the Recorder. Yes, THE Recorder. The one and the same that you or your children were required to play for one year in elementary school, except that mine was handmade with rosewood in Holland. This does not embarrass me, but the truth is, I have a body like Cookie Monster, and the image of me dressed as a minstrel entertaining a king in sixteenth-century England makes it hard for people who learn this to stifle a laugh.

But one area where my degree proved to be an unquestioned advantage was when I learned of Soyoung Scanlan. Like me, she studied classical music through college, but has since dedicated her life to cheese. She purchases milk from two farms in Marin County, California, and from there the process is entirely a one-woman show. Equally adept at working with cow, goat, and sheep milk, Soyoung creates perfect little clouds of cheese, texturally otherworldly, each one the acme of their style. She makes cheese, crème fraîche, and butter for the French Laundry, which says all you need to know.

Through our shared love of classical music, I was able to convince Soyoung to send us one shipment of her highly sought-after cheeses. Now, we count ourselves as one of the handful of cheese shops that offer her incredible line.

–CHEESEMONGER HUNTER FIKE

MOSES SLEEPER

UNITED STATES, COW'S MILK
PERSONALITY: A handsome Vermonter with butter on the brain.

Ask any cheesemonger about his or her favorite American "bloomy"—a common term for downy-rinded cheeses—and you will probably hear about Moses Sleeper. If you don't, raise your brow and look disappointed. Moses Sleeper is probably the most revered Brie-style cheese coming out of the United States. It's everything you could want in a French cheese except that it's not from around Paris; it's from Greensboro, Vermont.

Expert cheesemaker Mateo Kehler, the heartthrob of the American dairy scene, created Moses Sleeper a few years ago, using milk from his pasture-raised Ayrshire cows. The result is a lush, sweet, palate-coating experience. Young, this cheese tastes like butter and hay; as it ripens, you may detect traces of walnuts and steamed cauliflower, which are typical in Camembert-style cheeses. Note the delicate rind—it's not a bath mat; it's a thin veneer of mold that yields easily between your teeth. This is the mark of a great bloomy cheese.

Good matches: Pair Moses Sleeper with brandied cherries or blackberry jam, or swing savory with sautéed mushrooms. For a beguiling appetizer, toast some baguette rounds, top them with pear slices and hunks of Moses Sleeper, then broil them for a minute or two before adding a drizzle of honey.

Wine/beer: Champagne or a light Beaujolais work well here, and so do Belgian Tripels and saisons. Norman cider works nicely with especially ripe wheels.

NOBLE ROAD

UNITED STATES, COW'S MILK
PERSONALITY: The Pearl of the Poconos.

If you want to taste France in Pennsylvania, Noble Road is the most direct dairy route. This beautiful "Brie" from Calkins Creamery is made by Emily Bryant Montgomery, a woman who knows how to draw sweet, vegetal notes out of her Wayne County Holstein milk. Until recently, Montgomery used raw milk for these wheels, making them a much sought-after delicacy across the East Coast, but fear of an FDA crackdown has caused her to shift to pasteurization. No matter: her cheeses still reflect quality craftsmanship and delicious flavor.

Noble Road is like a feast packed inside a little trousseau. The texture is sumptuous with distinct notes of lemon and mushrooms. You might as well be on a spring picnic—you can practically taste clover, chive blossoms, burbling brooks, and bees buzzing around the hooves of Holsteins. You can taste the field. No wonder this cheese is named Noble Road, after the path that runs past the Bryant's farm. What a way to celebrate land that's been in the family for five generations.

Good matches: Start with a great baguette. If you need anything to supplement the experience, serve a little honey and sliced pears or apples. The vegetal notes in this cheese also pair well with sautéed mushrooms, artichokes, and asparagus. Try folding Noble Road into an omelet along with any of these items—be sure to top it with fresh chives and a squeeze of lemon.

Wine/beer: Pour a glass of Champagne or a Duvel. Like the best of Bries, it needs bubbly to cleanse the palate and offset the lush texture. For something interesting, try a pint of Saranac Pomegranate Wheat.

ROBIOLA BOSINA

ITALY, SHEEP AND COW'S MILK
PERSONALITY: The middle child between Brie and Taleggio: an adult cupcake.

Robiola, also known as *Due Latte* (two milks), is a good excuse to travel to Italy. This luscious beast from the northern climes is soft and runny-creamy with a wrinkled surface that looks like a brain—cheeses with this sort of appearance are often labeled "brainy." Now you know why. If you like Taleggio (page 158), you'll find this slightly more lady-like cousin friendly and compatible as long as it's not too ripe. Like a good Brie, the aroma of Robiola should be mushroomy and pleasant, without any bulldoggish odors or traces of ammonia.

Cheese aficionado and writer Janet Fletcher says the taste of Robiola reminds her of "rice pudding," simple and direct. This is an excellent cheese for entertaining; its paper wrapper looks like a crinoline hoop skirt, and its chenille-like surface intrigues the eye. For a Lombardy party, pair this off with a round of La Tur (page 104), which is made by the same dairy, and you will have guests weeping into hankies and kissing in doorways. You may never serve plain ol' Brie again.

Good matches: Understated pairings serve this cheese best: a few berries, some almonds, a spot of honey. For a festive first course, serve Robiola on toasted baguette rounds with a tuft of tart cherry preserves and a crank of black pepper.

Wine/beer: Prosecco all the way; otherwise, pour a pilsner or wheat beer.

SAINT MARCELLIN

FRANCE, COW'S MILK
PERSONALITY: **Anna Pavlova in a little crock.**

This is the perfect cheese for one. Okay, two. It's the size of a small pastry and so fragile, so very fragile, it comes packed in its own little crock. The surface is netting-thin, the center silky and supple. Really, this cheese is a tiny tutu in a box. Pack it for a picnic or, better yet, wrap it in a hanky and take it to the ballet. It would be fantastic during intermission.

Mild and slightly mushroomy, Saint Marcellin is similar to Banon (page 88), sans chestnut leaves. A large format version is sold as Saint Felicien, but then you don't get the crock, and it's quite elegant—great for serving olives or almonds in later. Take care to ask about the ripeness of this cheese. It gets bolder and softer as it ages, so you'll want to know what to expect, especially if you plan on pairing it with wine.

Good matches: Try this on a cheese plate with apple slices and toasted baguette or brioche rounds. In Lyon, Saint Marcellin is a ubiquitous cheese often served on top of salads. Try it in place of a poached egg on top of salad Lyonnaise. All you need is a little frisée, some bitter greens, lardons or thick-cut bacon, a light vinaigrette, and some buttery croutons.

Wine/beer: Lean toward a Rhône red, a Gewürztraminer, or a sparkling French wine. An effervescent abbey beer works well, too.

SEAL BAY

AUSTRALIA, COW'S MILK
PERSONALITY: **A minx, utterly buttery and impudent.**

Compared to many other triple crèmes, Seal Bay is a yacht amid a sea of flotation devices. It comes in a thickish log, about the size and shape of a woman's arm. Add kid gloves and you get the visual: this is a downy log of sexy sexiness with an absolutely supple texture and a flavor that can only be described as "Champagne-ready."

If you flinch at mushroomy Bries, you've got a friend in Seal Bay. Nothing offends; everything is pleasant and pearlescent. You can strike words like "bite" or "tang" from your triple crème lexicon because this cheese doesn't have even one freaky quality. To add to the glamour, it's made on a remote island situated between Australia and Tasmania where designer cows eat designer grass, or something like that. King Island's lush pastures make this cheese what it is. Go ahead, run a fingertip through it like frosting.

Good matches: Seal Bay pairs nicely with berries and preserves. Try a thin layer of apricot, peach, or cherry jam. It's so rich that you could easily serve it for dessert with thin slices of pound cake or very thin gingersnaps.

Wine/beer: Offer flutes of champagne or sparkling cocktails (try a Kir Royale or Bellini). For something different, fill champagne glasses with sour cherry kriek, a wonderful Belgian fruit beer.

SOTTOCENERE

ITALY, COW'S MILK
PERSONALITY: Like truffle bubblegum, with ash.

If you ever need to beg someone for forgiveness or repent for a petty deed, take a sartorial hunk of Sottocenere. It's great for bargaining with the heart of a jilted lover. Few who see it can refuse a taste, let alone look away. That's because Sottocenere (pronounced so-toe-chen-NAY-ray) comes dusted with a thin layer of toasted cinnamon, nutmeg, coriander, and licorice. Its name literally means "under ash." Those might sound like bold flavors, but they are a mere caress in the dark; what you really taste here is sweet milk and black truffles. Don't hold back. Put your face down next to this one and breathe it in. Then whisper, "Forgive me."

Sottocenere is made in Italy's Veneto region, a lushly agrarian area that encompasses two romantic cities, Venice and Verona. It's also the seat of romantic cuisine: steamy polenta, fruity Asiago, salty prosciutto, and this butterball of a cheese stuffed with truffley bits. Other truffle cheeses exist, but this one brings the wild pigs out of the woodwork. No one can refuse its bread-doughy softness, its dapper rind.

Good matches: A porch swing, a hot tub—you can and should eat this one anywhere and everywhere. Make sure you've got a good baguette to go with it, and if you want to get fancy, serve slices of musky melon. Sottocenere is also dreamy tossed into polenta, scrambled eggs, or risotto.

Wine/beer: Reach for bubbly or Barbera. A yeasty beer with soft tones, like a wheat beer, also works.

The Sottocenere Cheesesteak

Next time you're looking to dress up a Philly cheesesteak, take a cue from Good Dog Bar and Restaurant, where the menu includes truffley cheesesteak empanadas made with Sottocenere. All you need is a decent hoagie roll and a thick slab of this cheese to slip under your chopped beef and fried onions. Trust us, you won't miss the "Whiz" when you see how well this melts and you taste that little bit of unearthly mushroom; it's like the Italians made Sottocenere for South Philly. Amen.

TICKLEMORE

ENGLAND, GOAT'S MILK
PERSONALITY: A doughy heartbreaker with
a rugged shell.

One glance at Ticklemore through the window
of a cheese shop, and you might think you are
gazing at a crustacean. The exterior looks like a
bumpy whelk with fine caramel-colored stria-
tions, but cut into the paste and you'll find a
nougaty softness that gives off the warm smell
of yeast doughnuts. The flavor is delicate, mildly
sweet, doughy, and a touch lemony and herbaceous. Look for a wedge that's fudgy under the
rind, a sign of ripeness.

Debbie Mumford and Mark Sharman
make Ticklemore at Sharpham Creamery in
Devon with milk from a nearby farmer who
lets his ladies roam the Dartmoor plains. Their
heath-healthy diet of grasses and hedgerows
infuses the milk with a wild range of flavors,
making Ticklemore one of the most sublimely
nuanced goat cheeses anywhere. You won't taste
any sketchy tang, just supple herbs and petals.
Once you try it, you'll understand why Di
Bruno Bros. can barely keep it in stock.

Good matches: This cheese needs nothing to
accompany it, but if you want to play off its herbal
undertones, serve it with lavender honey and a
walnut scone or some thyme-flecked biscuits.

Wine/beer: Try Beaujolais or dry Riesling. A
wheat beer with plenty of citrus snap works
well, and so does a saison.

TRUFFLE TREMOR

UNITED STATES, GOAT'S MILK
PERSONALITY: The Victoria's Secret model
of goat cheese, a tantric truffle experience.

Few cheeses have arrived on the American
cheese scene to such fanfare. When Mary
Keehn of Cypress Grove Dairy released this
soft-ripened goat cheese studded with black
truffles in 2009, it raked in awards at major food
shows around the world. For a while, it was
impossible to find. People hoarded every toothsome crumb, holding private Truffle Tremor
parties behind closed doors. Imagine rooms full
of quaking cheese fiends, sipping from Champagne flutes and smiling truffled smiles.

This is a velvety, earthy cheese—aromatic
and elegant. The whisker-like truffle bits are
subtle enough to let the milk sing. The rind
looks very much like the downy coat of a Brie
or a wheel of Humboldt Fog (page 74)
Keehn's other famous cheese. Notice that as
Truffle Tremor ages, a creamline forms just
below the rind while the center remains
smooth and slightly chalky. These contrasting
textures make for a gorgeous cheese-eating
experience. Serve this at a party, and you will
have friends for life.

Good matches: All this needs is some really
good baguette, a handful of dark grapes, and
maybe a dish of walnuts or toasted hazelnuts.

Wine/beer: A yeasty Champagne is the only
way to go here, unless you favor an effervescent
saison.

WEYBRIDGE

UNITED STATES, COW'S MILK
PERSONALITY: The baby of the family, diminutive and gentle.

Weybridge is a small medallion of organic double crème made from the cheesemakers' special herd of heritage Dutch Belted cows, a breed with a prominent white stripe around the middle. Patty and Roger Scholten make this cheese with their four children in Middlebury, Vermont, then pass it on to the state's premier ageing facility, The Caves at Jasper Hill, for finishing. The Scholtens are very focused cheesemakers; they funnel all of their energy into producing this single disc, named after their tiny hometown.

Young Weybridge is dense and fudgy, but it turns molten as it matures. It's known for its small format—one 3-ounce round serves two to three people—and for its dense, luxurious texture. Although it's only a double crème, it's very rich. The Scholtens like to serve Weybridge for breakfast since the flavor is mild with a slightly toasty quality along the rind.

Good matches: Weybridge's slightly tart flavor makes it a good fit for jam. Set out a basket of berries and some fresh bread. For a Vermont-themed cheese plate, add a hunk of Tarentaise (page 132), a wedge of Reading Raclette (page 129), and a bluesy slab of Bayley Hazen (page 227).

Wine/beer: Pick a grassy Grüner Veltliner or a glass of Champagne. A farmhouse-style saison works perfectly.

WINNIMERE

UNITED STATES, RAW COW'S MILK
PERSONALITY: **The craft brewer's fave, a lambic-inspired hipster.**

Few cheeses are celebrated with the kind of fanfare that Winnimere receives when these spruce-bound wheels are released each winter. The reason for this hoopla is twofold: Winnimere comes from a pair of highly respected cheesemaking brothers at Jasper Hill Farm in Vermont, and it's a cheese that pairs well with craft beer. In fact, when the Kehler brothers began making this cheese, they washed it in their own lambic brewed from wild yeast that was harvested in their cheese cave. Cheeses don't get much geekier than this.

Today, the Kehlers use a brine wash, but they still experiment with bathing small batches of Winnimere in suds from around the country, which makes for an interesting twist on "local." For cheese geeks, these arranged marriages offer a chance to taste just how a boozy wash can affect the taste of an American cheese. On the whole, Winnimere smacks of bacon, spruce bark, caramelized onions, and toasted hazelnuts. It's lumberjacky. The recipe is based on Vacherin Mont d'Or (page 136), a seasonal mindbender from the Swiss Alps. If Winnimere boggles your brain, seek out Rush Creek Reserve (page 132), another American Vacherin-style cheese, this time from Wisconsin. They're both incredible.

Good matches: It's criminal to eat Winnimere without a spoon. Bring your wheel to room temperature, peel back the rind like a sardine can, and scoop the soupy insides onto bread. A jar of really good marmalade makes for a stunning pairing. Toast some walnuts alongside.

Wine/beer: You can go with a Gewürztraminer, by all means, but this is such a stunning cheese to pair with beer you'd be remiss not to grab a few brews. Try a lambic, gueuze, or saison. Better yet, pick up all three and notice how each bottle brings out different notes in this cheese.

Behind-the-Counter Winnimere Dip

When the first wheels of Winnimere arrive from Jasper Hill in late fall, the holiday rush is usually full on at Di Bruno Bros. Busy cheesemongers have been known to skip lunch and snack on Winnimere with potato chips. The combination is strangely alluring, especially if you use salt-and-vinegar potato chips—cheesemonger Rocco Rainone calls these "the poor man's cornichons." Try serving Winnimere as a dip for potato chips at a party, but only in the company of your most laid-back friends. Some will no doubt find the thought of Winnimere and lowbrow snack food appalling.

CHEESE BOARD: An Evening in Paris

Now that you're mingling with Vixens, it's time to pop the Champagne, pull out the silver, and break out the fresh berries. The following knockouts from France are selected with the purist in mind. You could easily prepare a similar board, just as stunning, with American-made craft cheeses (I said *craft*, not *Kraft*, dah-hhlink), but it wouldn't quell the lusty Francophile in quite the same way.

With this cheese board, Jacques Brel and Edith Piaf, preferably on vinyl, are essential pairings for the ears. Wear mules, satin robes.

Valençay (page 82)
Délice de Bourgogne (page 95)
Comté (page 121)
Morbier (page 151)
Carles Roquefort (page 92)

Suggested accompaniments: blackberries, strawberries, pears, cherry preserves, caramelized pecans, ginger thins, a whopping good baguette.

CHEESE 101: How Cheese is Made

If you wake up tomorrow and decide to become a cheesemaker (and this happens more often than you might think), here is a general sense of what you'd need to get started:

Learn about animals.

At its most basic, cheese is fresh milk that's been curdled, drained, pressed, and usually aged. The key ingredient, my friend, is milk—really good milk. So, what breed are you going to select for your fields? Let's say you want to make a Brie-style cheese. Are you going to use Jersey milk? Jersey cows are small and friendly, and they're known for their rich, buttery milk. Then again, Holsteins are good producers, and Ayrshires have gained favor in Vermont. Looks like you better taste some cheeses made from different breeds. Or maybe you should just go to France, the seat of bloomy cheese, and gaze across the Parisian basin for divine inspiration.

Figure out what to feed them.

Once you've determined which animals are best for your style of cheese, you'll need to plant crops. You've probably heard that pasture-raised cows make the best burger. Well, they also produce some of the best cheese. You can opt for corn silage, which is the cheapest way to bulk up your girls (you do know that only heifers give milk, right?), but if you want to produce extraordinary cheese, you'll want to let them loose on the range. As you drink their milk, you'll notice that the flavor changes through the seasons. In spring, it's floral from tender greens and wildflowers; in fall, it's nuttier from winter grasses.

Set up a "make room."

Now that you're milking twice a day, it's time to get a curd vat, which looks like a giant cauldron. You'll also need to get a pasteurizer if you're making young cheese, like Brie. While you're at it, order some good rubber boots, a bunch of cheese forms to create uniform wheels, some rennet (a coagulant), and plenty of starter culture. You're now in the fermentation business. Make sure you've got your license. Now you can begin making cheese—pull out your recipe and get ready to stir.

Cheese is made from three basic ingredients: fresh milk, rennet, and microbes that acidify and flavor the milk. Traditionally, rennet was extracted from the stomach lining of an animal. Today, most cheesemakers buy synthetic rennet in tablet or liquid form, but the hardcore still use the traditional stuff.

Build a cave.

Once you're ready to age your cheese, you'll need to find an *affineur*—someone who is trained in cheese maturation—to handle the ageing of your wheels, or you can build a cheese cave and teach yourself. Caves don't have to be built from stone. Some are just temperature-controlled rooms with carefully maintained humidity. Make sure you've got shelves that allow plenty of air to circulate. Fresh cheeses, like ricotta and mozzarella, don't undergo any ageing at all, while hard cheeses like Cheddar or Pecorino can be aged for years. During ageing, cheeses don't just sit in a cave developing lovely personalities. They require daily attention. On a small farm, cheesemakers handle this themselves. At a big operation, affineurs move about like nurses, often in white smocks, caring for the cheese. Some wheels need baths to keep them moist, while others require daily flipping or rubbing to achieve particular flavors and textures. The process can be very labor-intensive.

Now you just need to hang out and make sure your little beauties ripen properly. You may want to rub them every day so that the mold on the surface doesn't grow too wild.

Find a market.

When you and your cheese are ready for a grand debut, you can buy a card table and set up at a farmers' market, or you can arrange to meet with some local cheesemongers for a tasting. If they like what you've got, you're in business. Now, all you have to do is head home to keep milking cows twice a day and planting fields and making cheese and nursing the wheels in the cave. Somehow, you'll manage to sleep.

Women and the Artisan Cheese Revival

Until the Industrial Revolution, many cheeses were made by women. Farm wives kept copper kettles in their kitchens to cook excess milk, and with a clever mix of bacterial cultures—often exchanged between neighbors—they produced delicious cheeses, which they put up during winter months. In the United States, the first industrial cheese plant, built in Rome, New York, in 1851, set the course for change. World wars and food rationing wiped out nearly all small-scale producers, and consumers grew accustomed to block Cheddar and, yes, cellophane-wrapped Singles.

In the sixties and seventies, "artisan cheese" began making a comeback in the United States, led by a small group of women working in different parts of the country. In California, Mary Keehn began raising goats; in Vermont, Allison Hooper followed suit; Judy Schad introduced chèvre to Indiana. Today, their companies are thriving (Cypress Grove, Vermont Butter & Cheese Company, Capriole Farm), and all three women are considered pioneers—not just for reviving European recipes in the United States, but also for building on those recipes to create hand-crafted uniquely American products. Many of their original creations appeared in these last two chapters, including Truffle Tremor (page 110), Old Kentucky Tomme (page 78), and Bijou (page 66), just to name a few.

CHAPTER V

MOUNTAIN MEN

(bold, Alpine)

These cheeses are your hiking buddies. They pack well, share well, and they rival any deli cheese when it comes to a sandwich. Plus, they know how to party with red wine, dark beer, and wild spirits.

Appenzeller | Ascutney Mountain | Beaufort | Challerhocker | Lavender Mustard | Comté | Emmentaler | Swiss Fondue | Fontina Val d'Aosta | Gruyère | Old Man Highlander | Pleasant Ridge Reserve | Raclette | Reading Raclette | The Incredible Bulk | Rush Creek Reserve | Tarentaise | Tomme Crayeuse | Tomme de Savoie | Vacherin Mont d'Or | Cheese Board: Monastic Traditions | Cheese 101: How to Taste Cheese

117

APPENZELLER

SWITZERLAND, RAW COW'S MILK
PERSONALITY: A whiffy hiking buddy with a sharp, herb-driven intensity.

This bold cheese is part of the Alpine Trifecta that the Swiss often use in fondue (see recipe, page 126), along with with Gruyère and Emmentaler. Like those other mountain mamas, this is a great melter. It's also a good table cheese, especially for a crowd since a little goes a long way. Stronger than Gruyère, it packs a nutty wallop with a long finish of fruit peel and herbs.

Appenzeller originated as a monastery cheese with the St. Gallen monks of northeastern Switzerland. Centuries later, this popular style is now produced by seventy-five different cooperatives, and each one uses a slightly different brine solution to wash the wheels as they age. The recipes for this potion are carefully guarded secrets, but most contain some combination of wine or hard cider mixed with herbs. For an artisanal American rendition, try Ascutney Mountain, from Vermont.

Good matches: Melt Appenzeller on homemade pizza or toss it into a gratin. As a snack, serve it with cured meats, cornichons, spiced nuts, mustard, or onion jam.

Wine/beer: Pair this with a blood-red Burgundy or a spicy Gewürztraminer. A big malty fella like a Doppelbock or an Oktoberfest works well. Pack some schnapps if you take this cheese on the slopes.

ASCUTNEY MOUNTAIN

UNITED STATES, RAW COW'S MILK
PERSONALITY: A spring sparrow—vegetal with a hint of sweet pea.

Every now and again, a cheese comes along with a flavor so unique it haunts you. Ascutney Mountain is one such cheese—it fills your mouth with the taste of sugar snap peas and sweet cream. Think of risotto. Although the texture is firm, the mouthfeel is creamy, thanks to the rich milk of Jersey cows. The paste is golden with tiny "eyes," or holes made from air bubbles. (Cheese without holes is called "blind cheese.")

Ascutney Mountain is made at Cobb Hill, an intentional community in Hartland, Vermont. There, a gypsy band of resident cheesemakers produce this beautiful Alpine offshoot using the Swiss recipe for Appenzeller. Only fifty wheels of Ascutney are produced each week, making this a true small-batch cheese. The wheels are matured for eight to ten months at nearby Jasper Hill, one of the premier ageing caves in the United States. A well-aged wheel can pack a wallop, so always ask for a sample if you plan on pairing this cheese with wine.

Good matches: Make this cheese part of a spring supper of fresh greens, sautéed morels or ramps, and toasted bread. On a hike, pack Ascutney Mountain with a handful of almonds or hazelnuts.

Wine/beer: Serve a lush white or an easygoing lager.

BEAUFORT

FRANCE, RAW COW'S MILK
PERSONALITY: The Paul Revere of
Gruyères, an inspiring figure.

Beaufort is a mystical experience. This mountain cheese from the Savoie has a creamy complexity that stirs both the taste buds and the imagination. Are you really tasting wildflowers? Yes. Are those honey-covered almonds dancing in the background? But of course. Several cheese luminaries attribute their livelihoods to a single revelatory Beaufort encounter: cheese expert Patricia Michelson opened a London cheese shop after tasting Beaufort, and renowned Wisconsin cheesemaker Mike Gingrich created Pleasant Ridge Reserve (page 128) in Beaufort's image. (Above Gingrich's door at Uplands Creamery, a moonish photo of Beaufort hangs like a talisman.)

What makes this cheese so spectacular? Alpine milk from an ancient breed of Beaufort cows, my friend. Wheels made in spring and summer are prized for their richness and flavor. This is a moist, supple beauty—firm but pliable, with a natural rind that is brined twice a week for a full year as it ages. Beware, a single bite may change your life.

Good matches: On a cheese board, pair this with toasted walnuts, a mild-flavored salami, dried cranberries, and honey. Beaufort is also an excellent melter.

Wine/beer: Try a Chardonnay, Rhône red, or a malty bock beer.

CHALLERHOCKER

SWITZERLAND, RAW COW'S MILK
PERSONALITY: A goth version of Gruyère
whose name means "Sitting in the Cellar."

Of all the Alpine cheeses sold at Di Bruno Bros., this one just might be the favorite stepchild. Challerhocker (pronounced "HOLLer-hocker") is new to the scene, but it's gained a cult following among cheese heads for its meaty, caramelized flavor and its immodestly silky texture. It's the cheese equivalent to roasted bone marrow—earthy, herby, buttery, bearish.

Challerhocker is made at a small creamery near Zürich by the cheesemaker Walter Rass. He washes the wheels with a potion of wine, herbs, and spices, then cellars them for ten months or more. If you like Gruyère, you'll notice that the paste here is smoother, less grainy. If you're an Appenzeller fan, you'll find Challerhocker less waxy and very creamy. If you don't know what we're talking about, just trust our enthusiasm. This is a strong-cheese lover's dream. Some customers travel across the state for it.

Good matches: Rent a cabin in the mountains and eat this by the fire, along with walnuts or almonds and dates or dried figs. It's also wonderful with toasted bread and roasted whole garlic cloves.

Wine/beer: Play off the herbiness with a brambly Syrah, or explore the caramelized notes with a Madeira or sherry. Flying Fish Brewery's Exit 4, a Belgian-style Trippel with clove notes, is a favorite Di Bruno pairing.

CHALLERHOCKER

COMTÉ

FRANCE, RAW COW'S MILK
PERSONALITY: The French ambassador of beauty and wholesomeness.

A bite of Comté lights up your mouth, filling it with salty toffee, buttered toast, and just a whiff of fresh-cut hay. If you need to impress a date, expand your circle of friends, or blow the minds of the uninitiated, set out a wedge of Comté. Just remember, it rhymes with *enchanté*.

Marcel Petit Comté is the best you can buy—ask any cheesemonger. Petit's ageing facility in the Franche-Comté region is sometimes referred to as the "cathedral of Comté." The wheels are aged in an old stone military fort, and the attention given to maturation is unparalleled. A team of five tasters oversees the cave, sampling 300 cheeses per day to determine how long each wheel should be aged and at what temperature. Check YouTube for videos of this process—you'll be transported to another era.

Good matches: Roast some garlic, toast some hazelnuts, and make this cheese a centerpiece before dinner. For dessert, try serving Comté with walnut bread or biscotti and dried fruit. If you can find Armenian pickled walnuts, grab a jar; the pairing is magical.

Wine/beer: Seek out a minerally Chardonnay, an Alsatian Pinot Noir, or a dry sherry. Dogfish Head's Punkin Ale is a favorite Di Bruno Bros. pairing, but you could also try a caramel-rich dopplebock or fruity lambic.

EMMENTALER

SWITZERLAND, RAW COW'S MILK
PERSONALITY: A strapping Swiss with a buttery smile and big eyes (meaning holes).

When you buy "Swiss cheese" at the deli counter, you're essentially purchasing faux Emmentaler—a hugely flavorful mountain cheese that was developed in western Switzerland during the thirteenth century. Why settle for the plastic knock-off when many cheese shops carry the real deal? The difference in quality is startling, not unlike the obvious difference between Swiss chocolate and Hershey's. Look for these two words stamped along the rind: "Emmental" and "Switzerland."

Low in salt and fat, Emmentaler makes a great snack. It's sweet and savory with a sharp note on the finish, much like the classic Alpine cheeses Gruyère (page 127) and Comté. Two details make it visibly distinct: golf ball–sized holes and formidable girth. Wheels of Emmentaler average 200 pounds, making it one of the heftiest "lite" cheeses around.

Good matches: Make a primo grilled cheese sandwich on sourdough bread, or serve this as a table cheese, alongside ham, pickles, crudités, and fresh fruit. Truffle mustard (page 122) elevates this to new levels.

Wine/beer: Serve this with a spicy white or a light- to medium-bodied red. Try a bock beer, dark lager, or Oktoberfest beer.

LAVENDER MUSTARD

Something amazing happens when you dab this mustard onto charcuterie and bold Alpine cheeses, like Challerhocker (page 119) and Emmentaler (page 121). It adds a layer of herbaceous flavor and cleanses your palate. Try it on sandwiches or on a cheese board of hearty salamis, pickles, and dense cheeses. It's also a wonderful base for vinaigrette.

MAKES 1 CUP

2 tablespoons dried lavender buds
   (organic and unsprayed)
2 tablespoons dry white wine, like
   Sauvignon Blanc
2 tablespoons honey
6 ounces smooth Dijon mustard
2 tablespoons crème fraîche or sour cream
Salt and white pepper

Place the lavender buds in a small saucepan over low heat and toast them gently for about 30 seconds, just until you can smell the floral aroma over the pan. Add the wine and allow it to cook down until the pan is almost completely dry, being careful not to burn the lavender. Remove the pan from the heat and add the honey to the "bloomed" lavender. Transfer the contents to a serving dish and whisk in the Dijon mustard and the crème fraiche or sour cream. Add white pepper (about six to eight good cranks should do) and a pinch of salt, to taste. Well-sealed and refrigerated, this will keep for up to two weeks.

Note: Lavender buds can be found at spice stores or farmers' markets.

Variation: Truffle Mustard
For a variation on this recipe, add 4 tablespoons of black truffle cream (available at specialty stores) in place of crème fraiche and omit the lavender and white wine. Truffle mustard also pairs well with Alpine cheeses, charcuterie, and roast beef.

FONTINA VAL D'AOSTA

ITALY, RAW COW'S MILK

PERSONALITY: Big, smooth, and a little brutish—like Lawrence Olivier with a rind.

From the Italian Alps, this mild-mannered relative of Raclette (page 129) is much loved for its buttery, full-flavored woodsiness. It won't stink up the house, but it will make its presence known on a cheese plate. If you like classic hunks, this is a great cheese to include amid a selection of Italian showstoppers, somewhere between your fresh mozzarella and your hard Pecorinos. Of course, it melts beautifully.

Fontina Val d'Aosta is made by a number of producers in Piedmont. Make sure you get the authentic stuff, not the sliced imitations wrapped in red wax. Real Fontina is made with the raw milk of Valdostana cattle that live and graze in the shadow of Mont Fontin. You can practically taste the lush foothills and the rows of Nebbiolo grapes ripening nearby.

Good matches: Melt this on pizza or panini, or serve it on a charcuterie board with pickled onions, gherkins, and cured Italian meats. Try grating Fontina into scrambled eggs or omelets, along with diced ham and sautéed onions or mushrooms.

Wine/beer: Pick a Barbera, Chianti, or a white wine from northern Italy. Many beers pair with Fontina, from crisp pilsner to nutty brown ales.

SWISS FONDUE

Making fondue is a great way to use up extra cheese that's lying around—you don't have to stick strictly to Emmentaler and Gruyère. Just be sure to use firm cheeses, and take the time to stir the pot slowly. It helps to have a glass of wine and a second pair of hands in the kitchen. If you add the cheese all at once it will separate, so slow, careful stirring—*in figure eights!* as my Swiss grandmother always insisted—is essential.

SERVES 4 TO 6

½ pound Emmentaler, grated
½ pound Gruyère, grated
1 teaspoon all-purpose flour
1 garlic clove, halved
1¼ cups dry white wine
Dash ground pepper
Dash nutmeg
3 tablespoons brandy or kirsch
2 crusty baguettes, cubed

Toss the grated Emmentaler and Gruyère with the flour in a large mixing bowl so that all of the cheese is lightly dusted. Then, rub the inside of your fondue pot with the halved garlic.

Place the fondue pot on the stove and add the white wine. Bring it to a boil over medium heat, then lower the heat and begin adding pinches of grated cheese, stirring in each addition and making sure it melts before you add the next bit. You'll need to stir the mixture constantly. Figure eights!

When all of the cheese has been incorporated, move the fondue pot from the stove to a heating element on the table. Add a dash of pepper, nutmeg, and the brandy or kirsch.

Serve with a lightly dressed salad, cornichons, and the cubed bread. Remember, if you lose a piece of bread in the pot, you have to kiss the person who fishes it out for you.

THE MANY USES OF GRUYÈRE

Whenever I want to bring a piece of cheese home but do not want to spend over $20 per pound, I reach for Gruyère. Along with Taleggio (page 158) and Parmigiano Reggiano (page 189), Gruyère offers more bang for your buck than any other cheese, and it is so versatile! It pairs beautifully with several varieties of beer and wine, or you can knock off a hunk and tear into some hearty bread. Better yet, try it in grilled cheese sandwiches, fondue, macaroni and cheese, or scalloped potatoes. Gruyère shines brightest when it is melted.

-CHEESEMONGER HUNTER FIKE

GRUYÈRE

SWITZERLAND, COW'S MILK
PERSONALITY: A wild child with breath like warm onion bagels.

This classic Alpine from the canton of Fribourg is the cheese that most Americans associate with French onion soup, but for the Swiss, this is the ultimate fondue cheese (opposite page 126). Its character is smooth, assertive, savory: think of caramelized onions, herbs. The flavors meld beautifully with ham and mustard, so if you crave sharp cheese on a sandwich, this ought to be your steady.

Many makers produce Gruyère, both abroad and in the United States, so the quality varies. Look for a cave-aged variety. If you'd like to try a similar Alpine cheese with some sweetness, check out French Comté Gruyère (referred to simply as Comté, page 121). The two are similar, but Swiss Gruyère tends to be more piquant and herbaceous. Both cheeses date back to the thirteenth century.

Good matches: On a cheese board, serve Gruyère with toasted hazelnuts, thinly sliced ham, cornichons, mustard, and onion jam. Try a dark bread, like pumpernickel.

Wine/beer: Grab a Grenache or Alsatian Pinot Gris. This is one cheese that can stand up to a smoked beer (*rauchbier*, in German).

OLD MAN HIGHLANDER

UNITED STATES, RAW COW'S MILK
PERSONALITY: If Robert Redford were a cheese, he'd be this one. Rugged but gentle.

Calkins Creamery in Honesdale, Pennsylvania, produces this young, Gouda-style heartthrob with a nutty swagger. Like Redford, this old man has a leathery exterior, offset by a creamy center that's exceptionally smooth. You'll taste walnuts and sweet cream, thanks to the Bryant family's lovingly raised, grass-fed Holsteins.

Emily Bryant Montgomery runs her cheesemaking operation on the family's 250-year-old farm in rural Wayne County, the heart of the Poconos. Here, Old Man Highlander ages for nine months in an underground cave, alongside other original cheeses like Cowtipper, Noble Road (page 106), and Vampire Slayer. Bryant uses morning and evening milk to produce this signature, natural-rinded superstar. You'll find it at restaurants and farmers' markets across the East Coast. Bryant also makes a similar cheese called Daisy.

Good matches: This rustic cheese begs for hearty bread, stone fruit, and a handful of almonds. It's also good just for snacking. On a cheese board, try serving it with a butterscotchy aged Gouda, like L'Amuse (page 216) for an interesting pairing of young meets old.

Wine/beer: Pair this with a bottle of Syrah or a nut brown ale.

PLEASANT RIDGE RESERVE

UNITED STATES, RAW COW'S MILK
PERSONALITY: A titan of American cheese, most likely to become president.

Pleasant Ridge Reserve deserves a drumroll; it's the only three-time Best of Show winner at the American Cheese Society (ACS) Awards, an annual showcase of the best United States cheeses. Wisconsin cheesemaker Mike Gingrich devoted years to developing this recipe after tasting a sweetly complex bite of Beaufort (page 119) in France. He returned to America, sowed the lushest fields possible, and bred special cows to achieve a buttery, golden dream wheel that lasts as long in your mouth as a thrilling French wine. In a case full of American cheeses, Pleasant Ridge Reserve shines like the resurrection.

You'll taste pineapple pound cake, toffee, nuts, wildflowers, straw. Gingrich's careful attention to each wheel means that you never get a bland bite, though batches vary depending on the season. Gingrich and his collaborator, Andy Hatch, pasture their cows and only use the best milk from May through October, just like traditional French makers of Beaufort. For an outlandishly good nibble, look for their release of Pleasant Ridge Reserve "Extra Aged" in late fall and winter. After a year or more of ageing, these wheels offer a complexity that's unparalleled—not just in America but pretty much anywhere.

Good matches: Taste this cheese by itself, then add simple accompaniments—a few dried cranberries or walnuts, perhaps? For a simple but stunning dessert, serve this with a glass of Muscato and some very thin nut-studded biscotti, the way legendary Wisconsin chef Odessa Piper used to serve this native cheese at her Madison restaurant, L'Etoile.

Wine/Beer: Mike Gingrich favors a Manhattan. Otherwise, try a glass of fruity Shiraz or a pint of nut brown ale.

RACLETTE

SWITZERLAND AND FRANCE, COW'S MILK
PERSONALITY: A stocky Swiss funkmeister
with plenty of cologne.

In winter, there's nothing better than this rich, supple stinker melted over boiled potatoes. The Swiss have perfected this national dish by serving it with cornichons and cured meats, along with plenty of libations. Traditionally, a large wedge of this cheese was heated over a fire, then scraped—as it melted—onto potatoes, hence the name Raclette, from the French word *racler*, "to scrape." Today, electric Raclette ovens function much like tabletop hibachis; they make for a cozy evening as each diner gets his or her own little melting pan.

Be forewarned: A ripe Raclette will stink up your fridge, but it's well worth it. As the cheese melts, the flavor mellows. If you visit Switzerland or the French Savoie around the holidays, chances are someone will make you a Raclette dinner. Never refuse it, especially if you happen to be in a mountain chalet. The experience lasts all evening, and it's a great way to stay warm and well-sated.

Good matches: For a Raclette party, ask each guest to bring a pickled item. An assemblage of cornichons, cocktail onions, and other vinegary bits helps to cut through the heaviness of the meal. Boil plenty of red potatoes, set out the pepper grinder, and enjoy a long dinner. Prosciutto or any thinly sliced ham pairs well. Plan on one pound of cheese for every four guests.

Wine/beer: The Swiss like to drink beer (something light-colored) or kirsch with this meal, but a fruity Grenache or off-dry Riesling is also lovely.

READING RACLETTE

UNITED STATES, RAW COW'S MILK
PERSONALITY: An idealist of a cheese with
strong flavor and a sense of mission.

Some cheeses have soul. Reading Raclette has both heart and soul. It's not just a stunning Alpine in the style of European Raclette, it's also part of a nonprofit that brings city kids out to Spring Brook Farm in Reading, Vermont. Each time you buy a wedge, you help fund a potential young farmer or cheesemaker. Behind the scenes, this cheese is sometimes called "Righteous Raclette."

Reading Raclette became a sensation when it appeared on the scene in 2010. It's bold without being stinky, and it's loaded with rich Jersey milk from pasture-raised cows so the texture is creamy and the taste nuanced. Herbs, wild onions, nuts, and hints of caramel coat the tongue. Proprietors Jim and Karli Hagedorn developed this cheese with the help of a French cheesemaking consultant. Together, with cheesemaker Jeremy Stephenson, they produce this glorious beast the old-fashioned way, using copper vats to stir the curd and forming each wheel by hand.

Good matches: Throw a Raclette party and melt this cheese over potatoes, or make the best ever open-faced sandwich by broiling this cheese on a baguette with a layer of speck (or prosciutto) and minced purple onion underneath. Top each gooey round with half a cornichon for a spectacular appetizer.

Wine/beer: Pair this with a Pinot Noir, Syrah, or a dry Riesling. Need a brew? Try a brown ale.

THE INCREDIBLE BULK

Philadelphians are big on their hoagies, and this one, inspired by mustachioed monger Adam Balkovic, has become a store favorite. It calls for Reading Raclette (page 129), but you can use any big, bold cheese. Eat this belly-filler hot or cold, and note that it's especially good "cured" in the fridge overnight so that all the spices and juices co-mingle. Try packing it for a picnic or long car trip.

SERVES 1

1 hoagie roll or olive roll

2 to 3 tablespoons pesto

5 slices mortadella

5 slices sandwich pepperoni or salami

¼ pound Reading Raclette, sliced

4 green olives, coarsely chopped

6 fire-roasted or sundried tomatoes, coarsely chopped

Slice the roll open and slather pesto along the inside. Arrange the ingredients on the roll starting with the mortadella, then the pepperoni, Raclette, olives, and tomatoes and wrap the sandwich tightly in foil. Let the sandwich sit for 20 minutes to allow the flavors to meld, or heat it in your oven for 15 minutes at 350°F. The cheese will become wonderfully gooey.

RUSH CREEK RESERVE

UNITED STATES, RAW COW'S MILK
PERSONALITY: The Brigitte Bardot of
Wisconsin cheese—sensuous, otherworldly.

This glowing moon of perfect Wisconsin milk is
made in the style of Vacherin Mont d'Or (page
136), a custardy Alpine cheese that's only available in winter. At Uplands Cheese Company,
where Rush Creek Reserve was developed,
cheesemaker Andy Hatch wanted to create a
washed-rind cheese out of autumn milk when
his cows transition off pasture onto straw and
grain. (He uses spring and summer milk to
make Pleasant Ridge Reserve, page 128, one of
the most stunning cheeses in America.)

The result is ethereal, a pudding-like creation bound in spruce bark that tastes like nuts
and spring onions. The rind is delicate enough
to pierce with a spoon, so you can ladle the soft
center onto bread. When this cheese debuted in
2010, the *New York Times* ran a rave and it
became the cheese of the moment. Waiting lists
still precede Rush Creek around the holidays.

Good Matches: With warm baguette and a
plate of crudité, you've got an elegant appetizer
no one will forget. Peel back the top rind, and
this wheel becomes heavenly dip.

Wine/beer: A Riesling is perfect. Otherwise,
try a malty Belgian or a cherry lambic.

TARENTAISE

UNITED STATES, RAW COW'S MILK
PERSONALITY: A rebel Gruyère made in the
U.S.: big and beautiful.

Although many people have the impression that
the best cheese comes from France, when they
try Tarentaise they experience a revelation. Made
in Vermont, this stunning Alpine-style cheese is
arguably better than its European counterpart,
Abondance. The flavors are bold without being
sharp, and the sweet-savory notes play off one
another like a young couple at a barn dance.
You'll taste ripe fruit, hazelnuts, and toasted
bread. It's a picnic lunch wrapped in a rind.

Tarentaise originated in North Pomfret,
where a pair of corporate evacuees, John and
Janine Putnam, shacked up to make a new life.
They were so successful with this cheese that
they enlisted the help of a neighbor to keep up
with supply. Now, both farms—Thistle Hill and
Spring Brook—produce this ravishing beauty.
It's a great example of what an American
cheese can be when makers start with quality
organic milk, a copper cauldron, and enough
patience to age their cheeses slowly and grace-
fully. Tarentaise is made by hand every step of
the way.

Good matches: Use this as you would
Gruyère, served atop French onion soup or
tucked into a sandwich. To showcase its flavors,
pair it with date cake, a pressed delicacy made
of dates and almonds.

Wine/beer: Choose a fruity red, like a Pinot
Noir or Grenache. A dark, malty beverage also
works well. Try a doppelbock.

TOMME CRAYEUSE

FRANCE, COW'S MILK
PERSONALITY: A home-schooled hitchhiker with psychedelic fur.

Crayeuse, which means "chalky," defines the character of this unusual cheese from the Savoie. It's powdery on the outside, with two layers of filling inside: one that's intensely creamy and another that's damp and clayey. Together, they create a gorgeous cheese, both visually and texturally. Prepare your palate for an equally interesting range of flavors: damp earth, wood mushrooms, and wild yeast. It's a head rush of truffle-y soft pretzel.

Tomme Crayeuse was created in 1997 by the well-known affineur, Max Schmidhauser. For fans of Tomme de Savoie (page 135), this is a pleasant departure. Anyone who has rind issues will do well to cut off the exterior, which tends to develop pollen-yellow splotches. Cheese geeks find this one enchanting, but newbies will beg for mercy. As a conversation-piece, this cheese is totally worth exploring.

Good matches: Hunt this one down for a garden party or a rustic French cheese plate. Serve it with raspberries, toasted walnuts, or a salad of fresh herbs and mushrooms. Of course, it's bliss with nothing more than fresh bread and jam.

Wine/beer: This is a great before-dinner cheese, especially with a buttery Chardonnay or a smooth Pinot Noir. You can also swing bubbly, with Champagne. Try a wheat beer.

TOMME DE SAVOIE

FRANCE, RAW COW'S MILK

PERSONALITY: The ultimate Boy Scout—full of character, the size of a canteen.

Tomme de Savoie looks like the kind of cheese you'd find in a mountain village if you landed in the rustic kitchen of an apron-wearing *bonne maman*. Small and round, it's a semi-firm cheese with tiny eyes (holes) and a surface dotted with colorful molds. Think of a suede handbag or a felt canteen. If you fear cheese with fur, just remember you can always cut off the rind. Inside, the paste is pristine, full of earthy flavors: mushrooms, lichen, and hazelnuts.

As its name suggests, this cheese is a specialty of the Haute-Savoie, a region of France that nuzzles against Switzerland. "Tomme" simply refers to any small wheel of cheese that ranges from three to twelve pounds. All tommes tend to look rustic; they're essentially peasant cheeses. In the United States, several makers use this term for their handmade, mountain-style mini wheels. Try Andante Dairy's Tomme Dolce for a shining example (page 174).

Good matches: Add this to a French country cheese plate with plenty of stone fruit, nuts, cornichons, charcuterie, and pâté. All you need is a checkered tablecloth and a little Edith Piaf playing in the background.

Wine/beer: Most whites will purr. Look for one with plenty of fruit, like an Alsatian Riesling. Beaujolais can also be lovely. Choose a beer with some nutty sweetness, like a Belgian Dubbel or an Extra Special Bitter (ESB).

VACHERIN MONT D'OR

SWITZERLAND, COW'S MILK
PERSONALITY: A silky gem. Think "fondue party in a box."

The British food writer Patricia Michelson once compared the texture of Vacherin to "the folds of a satin peignoir." If you watched *Mad Men*, you know what a peignoir is: a nightie. Vacherin might as well be sexy sleepwear. It's pudding-soft and ultra silky. Depending on ripeness, the taste can vary from delicately complex to rich and oniony.

Traditionally, Vacherin is served warm, in its spruce box, with the top rind removed so you can dip bread or potatoes into the liquid center. Since Vacherin is seasonal, you will only find it in winter and spring, so grab it if you see it. It's hard to find but absolutely exquisite.

Good Matches: For a sensuous supper, boil up some new potatoes—the smallest you can find— and dip them into a wheel of slightly warmed Vacherin, using fondue forks or toothpicks. Serve an array of pickled vegetables alongside. Tender greens dressed with a light vinaigrette are a perfect accompaniment.

Wine/beer: Pick a hefty Alsatian white with some spice, like a Gewürztraminer. For beer lovers, a Belgian Trappist ale, like Orval, works like a dream.

Vacherin Fondue

To warm Vacherin, remove any plastic and wrap the entire cheese box in foil— this is to prevent any goodness from oozing out. Bake at 300°F for 20 minutes. If you start with cold Vacherin from the fridge, you may need closer to 30 minutes. Remember, you want to serve this cheese warm, not piping hot, so keep an eye on it. When the center is soft to the touch, remove it from the oven, and use a butter knife to peel back the top rind. Then stir a tablespoon of white wine into the center. Serve immediately.

CHEESE AND SEASONALITY

Many foodies get excited when November and December roll around, knowing that with the conclusion of the calendar year comes the first wave of fresh truffles from Italy. But hardcore caseophiles pine for this season because it means Vacherin Mont d'Or is on the way.

In the Swiss Alps, as the winter storms come rolling in, herds of cattle are moved indoors and fed hay and silage in the absence of fresh grass. This diet has a higher fat content than their typical summer grazing, and the resulting milk cannot be used for big, aged cheeses like Gruyère. Instead, Vacherin Mont d'Or is produced. The smaller, younger wheels are goopy goodness, like melted Gruyère that won't congeal at room temperature.

In the United States, several producers abide by this seasonal approach to cheese making, but two stand apart as astonishingly excellent examples of Vacherin: Winnimere (page 112) and Rush Creek Reserve (page 132). Winnimere, from Jasper Hill, is a sixty-day-old, spruce bark-bound, beer-washed puddle aching to be released from its striking, orange rind. Cut into it, let it run, scoop it up with bread and savor its pronounced nuances: sour cherries, bacon fat, smoke, mustard—it's a flavor bomb!

Upland's Rush Creek Reserve, like Winnimere, is raw milk, bound in spruce and aged for two months. But instead of the beer washing, it is bathed in a more traditional brine, which allows for the savory, sylvan notes of the wood to shine. Like all brine-washed cheeses, there is a distinct beefiness that makes eating it on bread feel like a complete meal.

–CHEESEMONGER HUNTER FIKE

CHEESE BOARD: Monastic Traditions

The early religious orders of Europe are famous for washing cheese with spirits. The process adds color to the rind—usually a twinge of moonish orange—and dials up bold flavors. Washed-rind cheeses, as these are called, are often a bit "beefy" or "brothy" in taste. In other words, they're robust. It's thought that monks, who lived modestly—often without eating meat—developed this style of cheese to satisfy their hankering for beef.

This cheese board needs some Gregorian chants and big Trappist ales. If you can't find one of the selections below, substitute authentic Munster (page 152), which is a corruption of the word "monastery," or Hooligan (page 148), a Trappist-style stinker from Cato Corner Farm in Connecticut. Pecorino di Fossa (page 190), a fermented cheese with religious significance, is also a great addition.

Abbaye de Belloc (page 40)
Frumage Baladin (page 169)
Epoisses (page 143)
Appenzeller (page 118)

Suggested accompaniments: Serve this board with grapes, fig jam, caramelized onions, speck (cured ham), coarse mustard, baguette, and walnut bread.

CHEESE 101: How to Taste Cheese

Great cheese, like great wine, has what's often called "terroir"—the taste of its birthplace. To develop your palate, it's fun to employ a couple basic techniques that cheesemongers use to evaluate wheels. Here are a few things you can try at home:

Give a sniff.

Eighty to ninety percent of your taste perception comes from smell. Before you sink your teeth into a gooey wedge, take a deep inhale first. Try to identify scents that are familiar to you: Hay? Mushrooms? Butterscotch? The barnyardy smell of a farm? Be sure you start with room-temperature cheese: flavor notes are released as the cheese warms.

Hint: Professional judges break off a small piece of cheese, warm it between their fingers, then inhale deeply before tasting. Warming the cheese in this way releases its scent. Note that once cheese has been exposed to air for long periods or to plastic wrap, it loses some of its flavor, so break off an unadulterated corner before you begin studious consideration.

Try to taste "The Journey."

Great cheese tends to have layers of flavor, or what some people call "the journey." The first bite of a Cheddar, for example, can taste citrusy, then turn sweetly nutty before it finishes on a slightly bitter hook or sharp swell. Many commercially-produced cheeses are "one note:" their journeys should only end in a sandwich.

Hint: It helps to set a piece of cheese on your tongue, then inhale a breath over it, and exhale through your nose before you begin chewing. If you try this, you'll be amazed how much more you can taste.

Identify the dominant flavor.

Some cheese educators advise their students to play "Animal, Vegetable, or Mineral" when they taste a new cheese. Surprisingly, this works pretty well as a starting point. You can detect "animal" when you encounter washed-rind cheeses; many of them smell barnyardy and taste "stewy" or "beefy." For an example of a "vegetable"-like cheese, try anything that looks like Brie; chances are you'll smell and taste mushrooms. Mineral-like qualities are often found in fresh goat cheeses or cheeses that have been aged in limestone caves, like Roquefort.

Hint: Cheese educator and importer Daphne Zepos used to say that when she tasted a new cheese, she tried to associate it with a particular place—like a pasture, a market, or the smell of a friend's kitchen. Picturing that place as she ate helped her recall the flavor profile later when she needed to describe the cheese to customers.

Keep a cheese notebook.

If you find yourself geeking out, keep a record of the cheeses you taste. When you break out a new wedge, jot down notes about its appearance, texture, smell, and flavors. These notes can come in handy at the cheese counter, or in bed—they sound very seductive when read in a baritone voice.

A Beginner's Cheese Lexicon

These are some common descriptors used by tasting pros. They're also great terms for composing haiku, especially on party napkins after a few drinks.

Grassy | Herby | Mushroomy | Woodsy | Citrusy | Tangy | Fruity | Toasty | Nutty | Sweet | Butterscotchy | Buttery | Milky | Muttony/Lanoliny | Beefy | Brothy | Oniony | Barnyardy | Earthy | Cavey

CHAPTER VI

STINKERS

(whiffy, boozy)

These are the beefcakes your mother warned you about. They can get a little whiffy, but that's only because they like to skip showers and sleep in the hayloft. Fill a growler and break out the whiskey—it's bonfire time.

Ardrahan | Epoisses | Fat Cat | Grayson | Gubbeen | Hooligan | Hudson Red | Limburger | Limburger Mac 'n' Cheese | Mont Saint Francis | Morbier | Munster | Quadrello di Bufala | Grilled Peaches with Quadrello di Bufala | Red Hawk | Saint Nectaire | Scharfe Maxx | Scharfe Maxx S'mores | Taleggio | Cheese Board: Pinochle with Grandpa | Cheese 101: How to Store Cheese

ARDRAHAN

IRELAND, COW'S MILK

PERSONALITY: Feisty but comforting, like the perfect mother-in-law.

If there were a "cozy" category for cheese, Ardrahan might rock top placement. It is, in a word, plump. Picture a round cushion of cheese with rouged cheeks. The texture is satiny, and like all great washed-rind cheeses, the aroma is homey as long as you don't mind a little cow barn mixed in with your soup-on-the-stove flavor profile. Most folks who shy away from champion stinkers like Epoisses (page 143) or Limburger (page 149) find Ardrahan to be a ladylike entrée into the sweetly whiffy category of cheeses. If you like sautéed mushrooms and sourdough bread, you won't have any trouble devouring this cheese over the course of an evening.

Ardrahan hails from county Cork, where it's made by the enterprising cheesemaker Mary Burns. She's lauded for reviving artisanal cheese in Ireland and for creating a superior product with the milk of her family's grass-fed Friesians. Mary's website offers a selection of recipes, including "The Ardrahan Breakfast" which involves warm rolls, tomato slices, and melted Ardrahan topped with chutney and black pepper.

Good matches: Try Ardrahan with sautéed mushrooms on toast or alongside a warm mushroom salad topped with walnuts and fresh chives. On a cheese board, play off the peanutty notes in this cheese with a dish of roasted nuts and some dried fruit.

Wine/beer: Monastery beers love this little beast, but a pint of Guinness is more in keeping to its true faith. Try a bold, earthy red or a Gewürztraminer.

EPOISSES

FRANCE, COW'S MILK

PERSONALITY: A French granny—cozy but fierce, especially on a hot day.

To enjoy Epoisses you have to put yourself at the end of a long dirt road, walking toward a farm-house with the scent of pot roast wafting through the windows. There is something comforting, even familiar, about the smell, even though Epoisses hails from Burgundy where sixteenth-century monks developed this unusual brandy-washed cheese to fortify their mostly vegetarian diet. If you can imagine a cheese that tastes like beef stew, well, this is it. Take a whiff; it's like inhaling sautéed onions inside a dank kitchen. The texture, however, is supple, almost liquid, which is why each wheel comes in a balsa wood box that protects its fragile interior.

The smell of Epoisses is notorious, even in France, where it's been banned on trains. Don't let that scare you, however. Only über ripe wheels are wildly pungent; a young Epoisses smells of gently braised onions. Like all washed-rind cheeses, these wheels look a little bit like orange pincushions—round and plump. Because they're brined, a salty, slightly gritty layer may form along the crust—harmless, authentic.

Good Matches: Epoisses is a great cheese to serve before a holiday meal, like Thanksgiving, when guests are ravenous and the smell of roasting meat hangs heavy in the air. Simply peel back the top rind and dip celery sticks or baguette rounds into the creamy center, fondue-style. For an unusual and stunning snack, serve Epoisses with bitter marmalade and a nip of Scotch.

Wine/beer: White Burgundy makes for a fantastic pairing, especially if you want to play off terroir (Burgundy grapes grow in the same region where Epoisses is made). Beer drinkers, pick a Belgian Tripel.

WHY EPOISSES TASTES LIKE BEEF

Like most cheesemongers, I list Epoisses in my top ten cheeses. Along with Roquefort, foie gras, and Champagne, it represents the height of French decadence, which is ironic given its humble beginnings. Epoisses was originally created by Trappist monks who were attempting to develop a meat substitute during the Lenten season.

They succeeded. Epoisses is big and beefy, packed with umami sensation and a powerful wallop of flavor. When slathered on bread with a glass of Trappist ale (a dubbel or tripel), it would leave the most ravenous carnivore fully sated.

-CHEESEMONGER HUNTER FIKE

EPOISSES

FAT CAT

UNITED STATES, RAW COW'S MILK
PERSONALITY: **A Chester County beefcake with a gentle purr.**

Fat Cat is a great gateway cheese for anyone who likes the mouthfeel of a triple crème but wants to explore stronger, earthier flavors. Young, this cheese tastes mushroomy with a lovely yeasty aroma that calls to mind freshly baked bread. As it ages, it grows beefier and takes on the smell of sautéed onions. For a similar cheese with more kick, look for Red Cat, a variation on this cheese washed in beer.

In Philadelphia, Fat Cat is much loved by locals who appreciate the hard work of Sue Miller and her family, who make this cheese at their dairy farm in Chester County. The Millers use raw milk from their own pastured Holsteins—a small herd of about eighty—and hand-make cheese in small batches three times a week. This is an excellent cheese for a wintery supper or a country picnic.

Good Matches: Grab a loaf of rustic bread or walnut rolls, and serve this cheese alongside stew or a dish that features sautéed mushrooms. Fat Cat is also good with apricot jam and cured meats.

Wine/beer: Pick up a bottle of Chardonnay, or try serving this with Smuttynose Old Brown Dog Ale or another full-bodied, hoppy brown ale.

GRAYSON

UNITED STATES, RAW COW'S MILK
PERSONALITY: **A grizzly fellow from Virginia with an Italian temperament.**

Taleggio heads, give me your attention. Next time you get the urge to worship at the feet of a beefy master, ask for Grayson. From Galax, Virginia, this pudgy dawg has all the trappings of an Italian Taleggio (page 158)—the same prawn-colored rind, the same mattress-like feel (think Memory Foam), and a similarly arresting shtink. Since it's made from raw milk, and most imported Taleggio ain't, Grayson is arguably a New School cheese with Old World flavor. You're not going to find more nuanced barnyard beefiness on American soil than this, unless you toss your shirt off and jump on some Hooligan (page 148).

Rick and Helen Feete make this cheese at Meadow Creek, where their Jerseys graze, rotating among pastures. The Feetes are full-on dairy nerds, and last we heard, they still lived in a trailer. Liz Thorpe, who writes about her visit to their farm in *The Cheese Chronicles,* compares Grayson's texture to a plump burlesque dancer and puts the flavor "somewhere between ballpark peanuts and coarse pâté." Tell me you aren't left breathless.

Good matches: Grayson is panini-ready; try it on a grilled cheese sandwich with bread-and-butter pickles à la Saxelby Cheese in Manhattan. Dark bread, bacon, and cornichons pair well, too. If you want to offset the funk, try a tomatoey jam or chutney.

Wine/beer: Pick a Belgian Tripel or a barrel-aged funkster. A big beer is essential to counteract this cheese's largesse. If you're a wino, you'll need a red with thunder thighs, like a full-bodied Zin, or a spicy Gewürztraminer. For the hardcore: bourbon.

GUBBEEN

IRELAND, COW'S MILK

PERSONALITY: An Irish rose, lovably smelly and hardy.

In the kingdom of stinkers, two prize rounds come from lady cheesemakers in County Cork: Mary Burns who makes Ardrahan (page 142) and Giana Ferguson, who produces this pinky butter cake. With its rose-colored rind, Gubbeen (pronounced *goo-BEAN*) is one more sweet-smelling reason that you should explore luxuriant washed-rind cheeses. Take a bite and let your mind wander back to the moment you first rode a bike without training wheels. Gubbeen has that thrilling rubber-on-pavement aftertaste that comes with some brine-washed cheeses, a flavor that's a bit wild but also sentimental. Folded into the background, you'll notice hints of peat, sautéed mushrooms, toasted hazelnuts, and mustard greens.

Ferguson is a cheese maven, having been at it since 1979, and together she and her husband Tom nurture a "cheesemaker's herd," as they call it: an amalgam of breeds. Theirs includes Jerseys, Shorthorns, British Friesians, and the Kerry Cow—Ireland's only native bovine. Milk from each breed contributes something special to Gubbeen; one breed might deliver a rousing wallop of butterfat while another delivers sweetness. Playing with milks at this level is the mark of a plum cheesemaker. Ferguson's children, Fingal and Clovisse, are also food artisans; they run a smokehouse and an organic garden that supplies local restaurants.

Good matches: Think of Gubbeen as the sticky toffee pudding of cheeses and pair it with nuts and honey, along with rum-soaked raisins. Or, serve it for an appetizer with just-picked baby vegetables, like carrots, breakfast radishes, and wee zucchini. Highly recommended: stuff squash blossoms with Gubbeen—just give them a quick dip in egg batter, then fry. It's a perfect way to express a cheese named after the Gaelic word *gobin*, or "small mouthful."

Wine/beer: Pair this with a Zinfandel or a Burgundy, or seek out a fruity brown ale or IPA.

HOOLIGAN

UNITED STATES, RAW COW'S MILK
PERSONALITY: A rural princess with a
potty mouth.

Put on your Daisy Dukes and crank up the
jukebox. Cato Corner Farm's Hooligan, as its
name suggests, is full of wild, fatty-licious stink.
Prepare yourself for the smell of boiled peanuts,
pick-up truck exhaust, and bare feet. Mark and
Elizabeth MacAlister, the mother-and-son team
that makes this little beast in Colchester, Connecticut, are famous for cutting some seriously
stinky cheese and naming their wheels appropriately. If you like Hooligan, look for Drunken
Hooligan or the famed Dairyaire.

Like Epoisses, Hooligan is a washed-rind
cheese. Twice a week, it's bathed in brine and
buttermilk to develop an orange crust, which is
edible despite the fact that it begins to resemble
a poisonous mushroom. Inside, Hooligan turns
lush and creamy, with notes of steak and
sautéed onions. The combination is glorious.
Both Slow Food and *Saveur* magazine have recognized this as one of the best cheeses being
made in the United States. Just don't be surprised if feral cats come out of the woods while
you're eating it and try to lick your breath.

Good matches: Break out the moonshine
and the Johnny Cash. All you need is some
good bread and some county fair kettle corn.

Wine/beer: A cheese this bold needs a Belgian blonde. For a striking match, try Russian
River Temptation. An old world red wine may
do the job, but it needs to be husky and, ideally,
French.

HUDSON RED

UNITED STATES, RAW COW'S MILK
PERSONALITY: A happy hipster with a light
aroma of hay and bike rides.

Made in the style of Alsatian Munster (page
152), this treat from Ghent, New York has
become a washed-rind darling of the cheese
counter. It's lush and meaty with a hint of Brussels sprouts, but the boldness is dialed back
compared to other stinkers in this class. Crack
the windows, but don't fret: you won't need to
air out the house. This isn't as brutally funky as
Munster or Limburger (page 149).

Hudson Red comes from Twin Maple
Farm, a hub for Hudson Valley cheese promo-
tion. The owners started off with an umbrella
business called The Pampered Cow, which they
launched to promote local cheeses from their
area. Soon after, they retrofitted a barn to create
a cheese-making facility. Using milk from their
neighbor's Jersey herd, they experimented with
making cheese, to great success. In 2011, Hudson Red won a gold medal from the North
American Jersey Awards.

Good matches: Grab some pickled Brussels
sprouts and a loaf of pumpernickel bread. For a
fall cheese board, add caramelized onions or
roasted veggies and some cured meat, like speck
or bresaola, along with sliced apples and toasted
walnuts.

Wine/beer: Pick a Riesling from the Finger
Lakes, or choose a beer from the Big Apple, like
Local 2 from Brooklyn Brewery—a malty Belgian Strong Ale with plenty of fruit and a hint of
hops. For something interesting, try a tart Flem-
ish sour or a snifter of Cognac.

LIMBURGER

GERMANY, COW'S MILK

PERSONALITY: The equivalent to absinthe in the cheese world—toxically strong but strangely appealing.

The nice thing about mentioning the word "Limburger" in a crowded room is that it's easy to evacuate the amateurs. Limburger smells gory, but it's actually a lot mellower than most people think; if you can stand to eat raw onion on a burger, then you're not going to be traumatized by a brick of Limburger. Take it out on the porch with a couple cans of beer and some good rye or pumpernickel bread, and you've got the fixings for a decent Euchre tournament or, at the very least, some dominoes. Add sardines and onions, and it's likely you'll attract old guys in loafers and black socks.

Limburger has its roots in Belgium (thank the Trappists), but today it's mostly associated with the Germans who export it in rich, unctuous blocks. When German immigrants settled in the States, they brought the recipe for Limburger with them and built factories throughout Wisconsin. Today, there is only one surviving Limburger maker on American soil: Myron Olson of Chalet Cheese Cooperative in Monroe, Wisconsin. He still starts his mornings with a slice of rye toast slathered with Limburger and strawberry jam. If you want to meet other Limburger heads, travel to Florida, which has the highest per capita Limburger consumption in the United States. Those snow birds need to peck at something.

Good matches: Try Limburger on a grilled cheese sandwich, or make like cheesemonger Dan Black and whip up a Limburger lamb burger. Because it's a powerhouse, Limburger works perfectly in mac 'n' cheese (see recipe, page 150).

Wine/beer: Find an assertive red with big barnyard notes, or go for a Belgian Strong Dark Ale, especially one with some fruit. An icy bock beer works, too. Keep that in mind for Oktoberfest.

LIMBURGER MAC 'N' CHEESE

Don't hate on Limburger until you've tried this recipe. Its fierce flavor gets subdued when you blend it into a creamy sauce, and if you don't tell those persnickety friends of yours what cheese you used, they'll never know. Shhh. . . let's keep it a secret. I first published a version of this recipe on the 30 Days 30 Ways Macaroni & Cheese blog (30days30waysmacandcheese.com), and it's become a favorite around our house. The pumpernickel croutons on top really make this dish, so make sure you don't leave them out. Feel free to add crumbled bacon or cubed ham.

SERVES 4

3 tablespoons unsalted butter, plus extra
    for buttering the pan
4 slices stale pumpernickel bread
1 large yellow onion, diced
2 to 3 tablespoons olive oil
2 cups dry macaroni (8 ounces)
¼ cup all-purpose flour

2 cups whole milk, warmed
1 (8-ounce) brick Limburger cheese, cubed
    (with rind)
1 tablespoon brown mustard
1 teaspoon salt
¼ teaspoon black pepper
½ cup grated Parmigiano Reggiano

Preheat the oven to 350°F and butter a 1.5-quart casserole dish or 8 x 8-inch square pan.

While the oven is preheating, set the pumpernickel bread on your oven rack (you can use a cookie sheet, but it's not necessary) to dry it out. If the bread is already very stale, just give it a good toast.

In a skillet, sauté the chopped onion in olive oil over high heat. Once the edges turn brown, after about 5 minutes, set the onions aside in a bowl.

Remove the pumpernickel toasts from the oven, and cube them. Then use the skillet from the onions to sauté the bread cubes until very crisp, about 10 minutes..You may need to add a little more oil.

In a stockpot, bring 2 quarts of water to a boil, and add the dry macaroni. Follow the cooking instructions on the package, but cook it about 2 minutes less than required so that the pasta is just approaching al dente; check it after 5 minutes—it should stick to your teeth. Drain the pasta.

To make the cheese sauce, melt 3 tablespoons of butter in a medium saucepan. Once the butter melts, turn down the heat and whisk in the flour. This will create a thick paste for a roux. Stir constantly for 1 to 2 minutes as the raw flour taste cooks off: it should smell toasty.

Gradually add the warm milk, whisking constantly to prevent lumps from forming. Stir the mixture over medium heat for 10 to 12 minutes, or until the sauce has thickened and coats the back of a wooden spoon. Remove the sauce from heat and stir in the Limburger, brown mustard, sautéed onions, salt, and the black pepper.

Pour the sauce over the macaroni and spread the mixture into a prepared casserole dish. Top with a layer of grated Parmigiano, followed by the pumpernickel croutons.

Bake for 30 minutes or until the sauce around the edges bubbles. Serve with crisp beer and pickles.

MONT SAINT FRANCIS

UNITED STATES, RAW GOAT'S MILK
PERSONALITY: **A tough girl who likes
hiking boots and bourbon.**

A washed-rind cheese made from goat's milk? You won't see this whiffy broad around very often since most washed rinds are made from cow's milk. That makes Mont Saint Francis something of a legend, a Yeti of the cheese world. Although it's categorized as a "stinker," this ruby round doesn't have the same gusto as an Epoisses (page 143) or a Hooligan (page 148). Its aroma is less barnyardy, its flavors more subdued, though you will still taste beef and onions. Let's just say you won't detect as much roasty char—we're talking slow-cooked pot roast with pearl onions.

Judy Schad makes Mont Saint Francis at Capriole Farm in southern Indiana. Considered one of America's goat-cheese pioneers, Schad has devoted the last thirty years of her life to raising a healthy herd of 500 nannies and keeping her farm afloat in a county where she runs the last working dairy. Her passion for cheese, and for sustainable farming, extends beyond the barn. She's a founder of the Raw Milk Cheesemaker's Association and an active member of Slow Food. Try her other gorgeous creations: Wabash Cannonball (page 83) and Old Kentucky Tomme (page 78).

Good matches: Try serving this cheese with grilled peaches that have been kissed with bourbon and brown sugar—a recommendation from the cheesemaker. On a cheese plate, pair this with other iconic American goat cheeses, like Humboldt Fog (page 74) and Bijou (page 66).

Wine/beer: Offer a round of Kentucky bourbon, or serve this monastic-style cheese with an abbey beer. If you choose wine, select a spicy Pinot Noir or a late-harvest Zinfandel.

MORBIER

FRANCE, COW'S MILK
PERSONALITY: **A muscle-y type with an
easily identifiable mohawk of ash.**

Morbier is one of the most striking cheeses. It has a pale orange rind and a layer of ash that snakes across its middle. Originally, the ash was used to separate evening milk from morning milk; the ash kept the flies away and prevented the curds from drying out when cheesemakers had leftover milk from the night before. Today, the layer of ash is merely decorative, but it gives Morbier a distinct look—kind of like the fins on an old Buick.

A good Morbier should be gently beefy, not bland. The aroma should be yeasty, the center pudgy, almost gooey. Lots of blah Morbier skulks in grocery cases, so always ask for a taste. The best wheels bulge a bit when cut and have a golden, creamy interior.

Good matches: Serve Morbier on a cheese plate with green grapes, walnuts, cured meat, and an array of other French cheeses, like its cousin Comté (page 121). It's also wonderful melted over potatoes, or toasted on an open-face ham sandwich.

Wine/beer: Go for a fruity red Beaujolais or a rich Pinot Gris, or select a Belgian ale or lager.

MUNSTER

FRANCE, COW'S MILK
PERSONALITY: **A member of The Addams Family, milky and macabre.**

The "Muenster" sold at deli counters is nothing like the real thing invented by medieval French monks. True German Munster is a granny killer—smelly, fiercely flavored, and menacingly orange, at least on the surface. The hue comes from washing the rind with salt water, which adds moisture and encourages bacteria to behave like vampires, breaking down the curds into liquid silk.

Munster is the patriarch of the washed-rind cheese family, a brood that includes whiffy wheels like Epoisses (page 143). The French have perfected this style of cheese making, thanks to their early religious orders. The name "Munster" actually means "monastery." It's still made in Alsace; a nearly identical version, called Géromé, is made in Lorraine. In 1978, Munster and Géromé were married when the government decided to recognize them as a single style of heritage cheese. Look for Munster-Géromé. Anything else is a copycat.

Good matches: Make like the French and melt Munster over boiled potatoes, then add a pinch of toasted cumin seeds. For an interesting twist, take the suggestion of food innovator François Chartier, who suggests stuffing chopped rosemary into the center of some Munster and allowing it to macerate for several days before serving it with an Alsatian Gewürztraminer. The strong floral note in rosemary is a good match for Munster vapors.

Wine/beer: Pick a spicy Gewürztraminer or Alsatian Pinot Gris. A big abbey beer will work well. Consider Allagash Tripel.

QUADRELLO DI BUFALA

ITALY, BUFFALO'S MILK
PERSONALITY: **A Taleggio with more luxurious clothes.**

Ultra rich cream sandwiched between tender crusts of woodsy rind? Please! The look and feel of this cheese, which resembles a square-shaped panini, has inspired what cheesemongers around Di Bruno Bros. call "cheese on cheese." It involves using a bready, heady cheese like this one in place of a baguette and stacking meats or other cheeses on top of it. That's right: total decadence. But if you're in search of a gluten-free bread substitute, well, an idea like this comes in handy.

Quadrello di Bufala is Lombardy's gift to Taleggio fans. It's supple and fudgy with a milkier profile than Taleggio (page 158) and not quite as much funk. The makers, a pair of brothers, raise their own water buffalo and operate a cheese plant that now makes twenty-five different kinds of buffalo-milk cheese. If you like this one, try their Blu di Bufala (page 229) and Casatica di Bufala (page 93). They're wonderful.

Good matches: For a wicked little appetizer, try Grilled Peaches with Quadrello di Bufala (page 153). On a cheese plate, try the "cheese on cheese" phenomenon described above by using Quadrello as a base layer for cured meats or stronger, funkier cheeses. Red Cat (the beer-bathed sibling cheese of Fat Cat, page 146) is a favorite pairing for this cheese because of its mushroomy, scalliony profile that snuggles right up next to Quadrello's mild, milky sweetness.

Wine/beer: Try an earthy Italian red, like a Barbera, or a funky beer with plenty of yeasty citrus notes.

GRILLED PEACHES with
QUADRELLO DI BUFALA

Cheesemonger Adam Balkovic likes how the pleasant sweet-tart quality in buffalo-milk cheese plays off the acidity in fresh peaches to create a sultry appetizer. If you can't find Quadrello di Bufala, a rich version of Taleggio, seek out mozzarella di bufala (page 34) or use Casatica di Bufala (page 93). Bresaola—thinly sliced, air-cured beef from Lombardy—adds a dark swath of purple here, and a lovely burst of salt.

SERVES 6

Arugula, for garnish
3 ripe peaches, halved and pitted
2 tablespoons melted unsalted butter
½ pound Quadrello di Bufala, cut into
    quarter-inch slabs
2 ounces Bresaola, sliced into ribbons

Preheat the grill to medium heat, then prepare six small plates with a handful of arugula. Brush the peaches with butter on all sides.

Grill the peaches cut-side down for 5 to 8 minutes, or until grill marks form, then flip the halves and grill them for another 5 minutes, or until the peaches are softened.

Place a hot peach half onto each salad plate and drape a slab of Quadrello di Bufala on top so that it melts. Garnish with bresaola ribbons. Serve immediately.

Note: if you want to get fancy, add a swoosh of aged balsamic to this dish as a final flourish.

RED HAWK

UNITED STATES, COW'S MILK
PERSONALITY: A roller derby girl, after a long night on the rink.

This beautiful rebel from Cowgirl Creamery is an example of one of the best washed-rind cheeses coming out of the United States. In 2003, Red Hawk won "Best in Show" at the American Cheese Society (ACS) Awards, an honor that sets it apart from many of the other toughs in the case. It's fudgy and dense with a lot of sass up front and a lingering peanutty taste that makes it unique. It's also a triple crème, which makes it extra alluring, especially for those who have not yet been initiated into the family of washed rinds. Tell them it's the Lady Gaga of cheese.

Red Hawk is made by Sue Conley and Peggy Smith, who started making cheese together in 1997. Today they run a successful business with three fabulous cheese counters: in San Francisco, Washington D.C., and Point Reyes Station (their home base). In the dairy world, they're considered leaders not just in the artisanal movement but also in promoting sustainable agriculture. They produce 3,000 pounds of cheese per week, using organic milk from their neighbors, the Strauses.

Good matches: Try serving this with roasted peanuts and dried peaches. It's also good with caramelized onions, marmalade or peach jam, and rye toast.

Wine/beer: For a grown-up Snickers Bar, serve Red Hawk with Rogue Chocolate Stout. A Pinot Noir or Alsatian Riesling also works well.

SAINT NECTAIRE

FRANCE, COW'S MILK
PERSONALITY: A brooding tween, funky but still too young to wear high heels.

Let me put it nicely: Saint Nectaire is for people who secretly want to like stinky cheeses but don't have the palate for it yet. So, consider it "training wheels" for funkier stuff; if you want to work your way up to Epoisses (page 143) and Hooligan (page 148), those elegant Everests, Saint Nectaire is a very respectable place to start. It's deeply creamy, like Brie, but the rind is washed in brine, giving it a gentle tangerine glow. The flavor profile veers toward buttered vegetables, but there's a whole garden here, earth and all. "Humid cellar" has been used to describe the smell. I prefer to think of it as "root cellar." When ripe, the finish on this cheese calls to mind dandelion greens. If the taste is too bitter, remove the rind.

Saint Nectaire has a rich history in the Auvergne. It was served to Louis XIV, who fell to his knees for it, and it's been cherry-picked by the French government for special status as a name-controlled cheese, an honor given to few regional specialties. In France, Saint Nectaire is made with unpasteurized milk, but import laws forbid raw cheeses this young to come into the United States. Still, the makers have managed to create a soulful disk for export. Try this when you're ready for an oh-so-tiny risk.

Good matches: Serve this with sautéed leeks or mushrooms on a burger. On a cheese plate, grapefruit marmalade or chutney pair well. For a stunning sandwich, load this onto a baguette or a panini with onions, arugula, and fig jam.

Wine/beer: Serve a glass of Pinot Noir or Beaujolais—something fruity but not too sparky. A hoppy saison, like Thiriez Extra, works magic.

SCHARFE MAXX

SWITZERLAND, RAW COW'S MILK

PERSONALITY: Wild, feral, and frisky; this one wears leather pants.

Two brothers from Studer Dairy in Thurgau recently developed Scharfe Maxx as a way to expand their line of strong cheeses (the dairy also makes Appenzeller, page 118) and since its appearance on the scene, The Maxx has become the red hot stinker on every cheesemonger's list. As far as Alpine cheeses go, this one trumps most on the whiffy factor, as its name suggests. The red bull on the label precedes the gore.

Scharfe Maxx is made from milk that has been thermalized, a process that involves heating milk just to the point before pasteurization. Purists frown on this, but you'll see that, even with this high-tech twist, Scharfe Maxx is richly complex with the taste of milk, herbs, and onions. The texture is smooth, almost fudgy, but it doesn't turn oozy the way other Stinkers do as they age. If you like bold Alpine cheeses like Emmentaler (page 121) and Gruyère (page 127), chances are that you'll love this to pieces.

Good matches: Make a knockout French onion soup with broiled Scharfe Maxx on top, or take a wedge on a picnic with a crusty loaf and some speck. For a simple dinner, melt Scharfe Maxx over home fries or roasted veggies.

Wine/beer: This is a great cheese for brown ale; otherwise, soften the stink with a sweet talking Riesling or a racy Pinot Gris.

SCHARFE MAXX S'MORES

Here's a wild pairing that cheesemonger Matt Shankle debuted at a recent in-house competition: it's a sandwich cookie made of Scharfe Maxx (page 155), dark chocolate, and nougaty torrone. (If you've never had torrone, think of it as a high-class marshmallow studded with almonds.) Serve these at room temperature, after dinner, alongside coffee stout.

SERVES 4 TO 6

1 (3-ounce) dark chocolate bar
3 ounces soft almond torrone
¼ pound Scharfe Maxx, sliced into four
   ¼-inch slabs

You can assemble these s'mores in advance, or you can set out the ingredients and invite guests to make their own. Simply stack chocolate and slices of torrone between slabs of Scharfe Maxx. The exact ratio isn't a science.

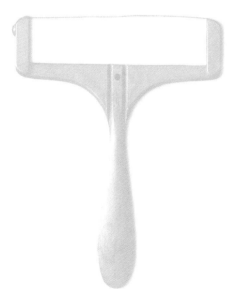

TALEGGIO

ITALY, COW'S MILK
PERSONALITY: A linebacker—formidable, aromatic, and absolutely awesome.

Taleggio is the all-time great gateway stinker. It can be a bit whiffy, but mostly it's just a bulging cushion of mushroomy lushness encased in a thin orange crust. The Italians have popularized this washed-rind cheese in a way that no other culture has dared. While the Germans have Limburger and the French have Epoisses, both of these robust cheeses tend to freak out the American palate; leave it to the Italians to popularize their tricksy little beefcake. You can enter any city supermarket now and find yourself a cuddly wedge of Taleggio, and at most parties, you'll receive a few fist bumps from those in the know.

Lombardy is Taleggio country. The same area produces mascarpone (page 32), Gorgonzola (page 213), and Grana Padano (page 184)—all stunning. If you like the blissfully sumptuous textures of mascarpone and Gorgonzola, take a chance on Taleggio. Cheese expert Max MacCalman sums it up best when he calls it "a comfort food cheese to the max." He compares Taleggio to eating mashed potatoes.

Good matches: Spread a fat hunk on some ciabatta bread or toasted sourdough. For a rustic meal, lay a slab of Taleggio over a bowl of piping-hot polenta, along with some sautéed mushrooms or a garlicky grilled sausage.

Wine/beer: Any big Italian bombshell will do: Barbaresco, Barolo, Brunello. A buttery Chardonnay with apple or pear notes also works well. Iron Hill Pilsner is magical.

Taleggio and Salami Ravioli

Here's a simple appetizer that's become popular at cheesemonger parties: scoop a teaspoon or so of ripe Taleggio onto a thin slice of salami, then fold it in half. Seal the edges by running your finger along it and applying light pressure. Boom, you've got a half moon of salty meat that oozes soft cheese when you bite in. Ninth Street cheesemongers love to serve these puppies after hours with beer.

WHAT TO DO WITH ENDS

I'm always disappointed when customers tell me they threw away some cheese that had been hanging out in their fridge a little too long. Please, people, never let a fleck of mold, or even a solid coating of it, deter you from using your cheese. While it might not be prime, there are still plenty of good uses for leftover cheese.

Scrape the mold off with a knife (or, if ample, remove the outer half-centimeter of the cheese), and shred it with your grater. Take the pile of tasty remnants and try one of the following:

Grilled Cheese: While there are certain cheeses that label themselves "melting cheese," all cheese will melt if shredded and heated. Pick just one leftover, or mix a few together, and create a concoction that will be different, but delicious, every time.

Mac and Cheese: It doesn't have to be Gruyère or Cheddar. Any cheese can be used. It might be different every time, but so long as you are using quality cheeses, it will always be tasty.

Fromage Fort: Why this hasn't caught on in America is beyond me. The French will take all of their ends, melt them together in a pan, and mix in some wine and garlic. Spruce it up with some dried herbs if you like. Take the blend, smear it on some bread with the same wine, and enjoy.

–CHEESEMONGER HUNTER FIKE

CHEESE BOARD: Pinochle with Grandpa

Some nights, you just want to stay in and eat strong cheese for the sake of nostalgia. This cheese board is a mix of old school and new school, but all of the cheeses are friendly with peanuts, pretzels, and Paul Anka on the hi-fi. Break out the canned beers or hit the liquor cabinet. And for goodness sake, burn a little incense. This is one stinky cheese plate. Consider it a rite of passage.

Gorwydd Caerphilly (page 170)
Hooligan (page 148) or Munster (page 152)
Scharfe Maxx (page 155)
Challerhocker (page 119)
Stichelton (page 174)

Suggested Accompaniments: Spiced nuts, popcorn, pumpernickel bread, marmalade, salami, sliced red onion, lavender mustard (see recipe, page 122).

CHEESE 101: How to Store Cheese

Treat cheese like a new puppy. Put down paper, silly, not plastic. Cheese needs to breathe. Waxed paper or parchment paper work well. Avoid Saran or shrink wrap; they suffocate all the living enzymes. If you buy a cheese in plastic, it's a good idea to change its dressing when you get home. Then refrigerate it in the coldest part of your refrigerator: the vegetable drawer. Here are some suggestions for maximizing your purchase:

Hard cheese

Your Parms and Pecorinos will last almost indefinitely if you wrap them in waxed paper (a cloth napkin works exceptionally well, too), then drop them into a roomy Zip-lock bag. If a little mold forms, simply remove it with a vegetable peeler.

Soft cheese

Any gooey, runny, downy little thing should be stored naked in a glass or plastic container. Air it out every two to three days. If you notice it getting damp, wipe its brow.

Blue cheese

Blue cheeses can be vexing. They like to spread their blueness. Store them apart from other cheeses. Wrap them in a layer of waxed paper, followed by a loose cloak of tinfoil. They'll thank you by remaining soft and crumbly.

Buying Tip: Cheese tastes best when it's cut from the wheel and cared for properly by its handlers. Because cheese is a sensitive creature, its flavors can deteriorate the longer it sits in the fridge. Buy it fresh and eat it within a few days.

Reviving Cheese: If your cheese dries out in the fridge, dampen a cloth with some white wine or warm water and moisten its surface.

CHAPTER VII

ROCKSTARS

(rare, revered)

Everybody has an idol. These cheeses are worshipped for their complexity, for their craftsmanship, for the quality of the ingredients that go into them. If you're a Cheddar fan, consider this list your British Invasion. All but a few of them are made (or at least inspired) by the Queen's minions.

Avonlea | Beecher's Flagship Reserve | Cabot Clothbound Cheddar | Cheddar Ale Soup | Zeke's Maple Bacon Grilled Cheese | Fiscalini Bandaged Cheddar | Frumage Baladin | Gorwydd Caerphilly | Isle of Mull Cheddar | Keen's Cheddar | Lincolnshire Poacher | Montgomery's Cheddar | Ogleshield | Sparkenhoe Red Leicester | Stichelton | Tomme Dolce | Vermont Shepherd | Cheese Board: Craft Beers and Artisan All-Stars | Cheese 101: How to Pair Beer and Cheese

163

AVONLEA

CANADA, RAW COW'S MILK
PERSONALITY: British Cheddar meets *Anne of Green Gables*—earnest and earthy.

Amid the Cheddar set, Avonlea is something of an anomaly. It was developed on Prince Edward Island by an enterprising ice cream shop-owner named Scott Linkletter who got bitten by the cheese-making bug in Britain. Rumor has it he got so excited by his first taste of real Cheddar that he arranged to study with a pair of Cheddar masters in Somerset (namely George Keen and James Montgomery) before launching his own business. Later, Linkletter worked with Canadian cheesemaker Armand Bernard to develop a special recipe, and in 2011 the two caused a sensation at the American Cheese Society (ACS) Awards when Avonlea won Best Clothbound Cheddar.

Avonlea is notable for its briny, buttery taste and gentle tang. Sometimes it has a hint of baked potato. Like other clothbound cheeses, Avonlea can be a twinge musty around the rind. Cut off the muslin and eat the sweet, crumbly center. Few Canadian cheeses make it into the States, so this is a rare treat. Linkletter claims he named this cheese "Avonlea" because this is how Cheddar would have tasted at the turn of the century when *Anne of Green Gables* was written.

Good matches: Apples, nuts, and chutney always work well with crumbly bums like this one. Try melting it on raisin-walnut bread with a layer of coarse-ground mustard.

Wine/beer: Pick a dry, red Bordeaux or a hoppy IPA.

BEECHER'S FLAGSHIP RESERVE

UNITED STATES, COW'S MILK
PERSONALITY: The Ivy League grunge rocker of the Cheddar-sphere—earthy but sophisticated.

In the world of Cheddars, Beecher's is a newcomer. Created in 2002, it's the invention of Seattle food pioneer Kurt Beecher Dammeier, who wanted to add brewpub appeal to the world of cheesemaking. When he opened Beecher's Handmade Cheese in Seattle's Pike Place Market, it became an instant phenomenon, and Dammeier has since gone on to open a giant retail-plex in Manhattan, complete with a cheesemaking room and restaurant. Despite the Disney-esque grandeur of his vision, Dammeier produces excellent cheese under the watchful eye of cheesemaker Brad Sinko.

Beecher's Flagship Reserve looks like a clothbound Cheddar, but it contains starter cultures traditionally found in Alpine cheeses. This contributes to BFR's superior meltability and rich nuttiness, a trait that often lurks in the low notes of wonderful Cheddars. For something extraordinary, try Beecher's Marco Polo Reserve, which is studded with green and black peppercorns—it's a salami lover's paradise.

Good matches: Make this into a grilled cheese sandwich at once!

Wine/beer: Try this with a glass of Syrah or a brown ale.

CABOT CLOTHBOUND CHEDDAR

UNITED STATES, COW'S MILK

PERSONALITY: This is the "labradoodle" of Cheddars—it's got so many flavors going on that it's a breed unto itself.

Before block Cheddar existed in big yellow lumps, the British perfected a cave-aged cheese that was wrapped in cloth. Clothbound Cheddar, or "bandaged Cheddar" as it's also called, is the original Cheddar cheese. A few American makers have revived this process because it produces a beautiful, sharp, slightly crumbly Cheddar: just like the kind the Queen eats.

Cabot Clothbound is Vermont's answer to British Cheddar. It's remarkably sweet with distinct notes of brown butter and toasted pine nuts. You may even detect notes of Gruyère or Parmigiano. If you don't love the earthy robustness of traditional British Cheddars like Keen's (page 171) and Montgomery's (page 172), give this one a try. It's caramely and buttery without a musty edge. Note that this is a pasteurized cheese and yet the depth of flavor is remarkable—one reason this cheese is a rockstar.

Good matches: This is a great autumn cheese, especially alongside Honeycrisp apples. It's also remarkably good with condiments like apple-pepper jelly or stone-ground mustard. With a dish of salted almonds or pretzels, you've got an instant snack.

Wine/beer: For a red, try a Pinot Noir or a cigar-boxy Rioja. For a white: Chardonnay, moderately oaked. Cabot Clothbound also works well with dry cider, pale ales, and nut brown ales. Dogfish Head's 90-Minute Imperial IPA is an inspired pairing.

CHEDDAR ALE SOUP

In fall and winter, this is a cozy recipe to serve with dark bread and just-picked apples. Look for a local sharp Cheddar in your area or try one from Cabot Creamery in Vermont, always a reliable source. The cheese is on display here, so the better the Cheddar, the deeper the flavor. Soft pretzels are an excellent side; so are blue corn chips. Try garnishing this soup with bacon and chopped scallions. For a party, pour this soup into shot glasses and pass them around as shooters.

SERVES 6 TO 8

4 ounces (1 stick) unsalted butter
1 small yellow onion, diced
$\frac{1}{3}$ cup diced green bell pepper
$\frac{1}{3}$ cup diced red bell pepper
$\frac{1}{3}$ cup diced yellow bell pepper
1 cup all-purpose flour
1 cup dark beer
3 cups chicken stock, heated
$\frac{1}{2}$ cup heavy cream
1 pound sharp Cheddar, grated (roughly
   6 cups)
Salt and freshly ground pepper
Sliced green onions, for garnish (optional)
Chopped crisp bacon, for garnish
   (optional)

Melt the butter in a medium stock pot over medium-low heat. Add the onions and peppers and cook, stirring occasionally, about 5 minutes. The onions should soften and turn translucent.

Whisk in the flour and stir vigorously until the mixture is well combined and begins to smell nutty, about 1 minute. It will be the consistency of thick paste, but don't fret.

Reduce the heat to low and slowly whisk in the beer, followed by half-cup increments of the warm stock. Mix well with each addition, taking care that the mixture does not become lumpy.

Add the heavy cream, and turn the heat up to bring the mixture to a low boil. As soon as bubbles appear, reduce the heat to low and allow the pot to simmer for 10 minutes, stirring regularly. The soup should thicken and coat the back of a wooden spoon.

Drop in the grated cheese, a handful at a time, being sure to mix well after each addition. Add salt and pepper to taste. Garnish with green onions and bacon if you wish.

Note: Be sure to reheat this soup slowly to avoid it breaking.

ZEKE'S BACON MAPLE GRILLED CHEESE

This sandwich is named in honor of Ezekial Ferguson, who was a fixture behind the counter at 9th Street for many years before he left Di Bruno Bros. to work for a small-batch cheese-maker. Zeke loved Cheddar, bacon, and maple syrup. He created a version of this sandwich behind the counter one day after he returned from a Vermont road trip. This is a bold grilled cheese with a fried egg on top: think of it as Cheesemonger French Toast.

SERVES 1

2 tablespoons unsalted butter, softened
    and divided
2 large slices ciabatta or crusty white
    bread
3 ounces Cabot Clothbound Cheddar,
    thinly sliced or grated
1 slice purple onion, separated into rings
3 slices bacon, cooked until crispy
    (try Vermont Smoke and Cure)
2 to 3 teaspoons Jed's Maple Jelly
    (or substitute maple syrup)
1 large egg

Note: For a crowd, make these into open-faced sandwiches and toast them under the broiler. Add a sunny-side up egg to each one at the end. For best results, start with toasted bread; top it with bacon, onion, then cheese. Broil it until the cheese bubbles, then remove the pan from the broiler. Plate each sandwich, then add a spoonful of maple jelly, followed by a fried egg.

Warm a skillet on low heat. Butter one side of each bread slice. Flip one over and layer cheese, onion, and bacon on top. Place it in the skillet, butter-side down.

Flip over the other slice of buttered bread and spoon maple jelly onto it. Set it on top of the open-faced sandwich in the skillet, jelly side down.

The secret to a good grilled cheese is cooking it on low so that the cheese melts, so don't rush things. After about 8 minutes, when the cheese is melted, flip the sandwich over. Don't worry if some of the cheese crumbles fall out. They'll crispen the edges of the bread.

Start a second skillet, a small one, over medium heat. Put the remaining butter into it, and when it melts, crack the egg into the pan. Cook it on medium heat for about 3 minutes for a sunny-side up egg. Flip it if you want to fry it completely.

Plate the grilled cheese and top it with the fried egg. If you want to pick up the sandwich with your hands, slide the egg inside.

FISCALINI BANDAGED CHEDDAR

UNITED STATES, RAW COW'S MILK
PERSONALITY: The Dick Dale of Cheddars, full of surf punk.

Cheddars, like guitars, can have different tones. This star from Modesto, California, is decidedly electric. It's full-flavored and creamy on the tongue with a dynamite horseradishy finish. If you like Vermont's Cabot Clothbound (page 165) or Montgomery's Cheddar (page 172), try this for an eye-opening experience. It's like a cheese and a jam session all in one.

Fiscalini is a collaboration between Vermont-trained cheesemaker Mariano Gonzalez and California dairy farmer John Fiscalini. Both are committed to their Holsteins and to land stewardship; the creamery uses farm waste to generate electricity, thereby reducing greenhouse gases. This is truly a cutting-edge Cheddar, and the quality is on par with the great British clothbounds of Somerset.

Good matches: Grate this into grits, layer it on top of burgers, or put Fiscalini out on a cheese board with some apple butter, toasted walnuts, and brown bread. This cheese can also stand up to a variety of sweet pickles or tangy chutney.

Wine/beer: Pair this with a California Cabernet or a West Coast IPA, like Stone Brewing's Arrogant Bastard Ale.

FRUMAGE BALADIN

ITALY, RAW COW'S MILK
PERSONALITY: The home brewer's cheese of choice, flecked with spent barley.

From Piedmont, this creamy disk studded with spent barley from Le Baladin brewery packs two great flavors together under one rind: beer and cheese. You'll smell yeasty goodness when you peel back the wrapper, and you'll taste plenty of toasty malt on the finish. There are lots of beer-washed cheeses on the market, but it's rare to find one that contains actual remnants of the fermentation process. The addition of spent barley in the paste and along the exterior lends a nutty taste to an otherwise earthy, subtle cheese—you may even think you're eating almond butter.

Frumage Baladin also gets its taste from cardoons, a wild thistle that can be used as a coagulant in place of animal rennet. The flavor of cardoons is decidedly vegetal, much like an artichoke, but in this cheese the taste plays second fiddle to the yeasty barley. Frumage Baladin is handmade at a solar-powered cheese company called Le Fattorie Fiandino, a family business that dates back to the 1700s.

Good matches: On a cheese plate, pair this with sweet Coppa salami, almonds, dried apricots, grapes, and whole wheat or sourdough bread.

Wine/beer: A barleywine or Trappist ale are ideal pairings, since this is a beer-centric cheese. If you prefer wine, pick a light white with vegetal notes.

GORWYDD CAERPHILLY

WALES, RAW COW'S MILK
PERSONALITY: An underground legend marked by earthy, low-fi notes.

Gorwydd Caerphilly (GOR-with care-PHILLY) is the turducken of cheese. It has three distinct layers: a mushroomy rind, a subcutaneous streak marked by cauliflower notes, and a chalky center that's full of lemony tang. Try each layer separately, then together, for a taste of masterful cheesemaking. Caerphilly originated in the 1800s as a Welsh miner's cheese. Rumor has it that wives used to wrap Caerphilly in cabbage leaves and send it off to the mines in their husbands' lunches. The thick rind made it easy to transport, and the earthy qualities were believed to offset the dangers of inhaling coal dust.

Today this exceptional cheese is made by the Trethowan family. They bear the distinction of being trained by the last maker of original Caerphilly, Chris Duckett. Like so many British cheeses, this one nearly died out during World War II when cheese was rationed and cheesemakers were required to support the war effort by producing government Cheddar. Neal's Yard Dairy in London ages Gorwydd Caerphilly for several months, or until the rind turns velveteen.

Good matches: In summer, set out a hunk of this rustic cheese alongside steamed farmers' market vegetables. It's especially good with asparagus. In winter, serve it with cabbage soup, stew, or shepherd's pie.

Wine/beer: Try a Pinot Noir or a spicy Alsatian white, but the best pairing is probably hard cider or a yeasty wheat beer. Golden Monkey, a Belgian-style Tripel, is a cheesemonger favorite.

ISLE OF MULL CHEDDAR

SCOTLAND, RAW COW'S MILK
PERSONALITY: A happy drunk with a thick Scottish brogue.

Take a whiff of this curious cheese from the Inner Hebrides and you'll smell a malty distillery. That's because the cows at Sgriob-rudh (Gaelic for "red furrow") Farm are fed the spent barley from whiskey production at the local Tobermory Distillery. Oh happy day, a clothbound Cheddar that tastes like a Scotch!

This sweet, peaty cheese is made on a small farm run by husband-and-wife team Chris and Ian Reade and their sons. The Reades raise their own animals and are very particular about their milk, which is evident in each rugged-looking wheel. The color of the paste varies depending on the season (in winter, this cheese is white; in summer, golden), and sometimes you'll find a lightning bolt of greenish spores. No worries, that's just a little ambient blue mold sneaking into a fissure. The Reade family encourages such rebellious streaks.

Good matches: Put out the mustard, the pretzels, the apple butter, and key up the player piano. This cheese will make you want to roll back the rug and dance jigs.

Wine/beer: Skip the wine and go right for the Scotch (Tobermory, if possible). A smoked beer or cask-aged barleywine makes for a ravishing side.

KEEN'S CHEDDAR

ENGLAND, RAW COW'S MILK
PERSONALITY: A salty granny from
Somerset with a pocket flask of vinegar.

In the world of traditional Cheddar, there are two reigning British monarchs: Montgomery's (page 172) and Keen's. Both hail from Somerset and are made by hand, then smeared with lard, and wrapped in cloth. Every cheesemonger secretly roots for one or the other, and yet ripping on either would be a sacrilege. Make like the Pepsi Challenge, and ask to taste both Keen's and Montgomery's side by side. You'll see why they've won so many British Cheese Awards and received a special demarcation from the heritage organization, Slow Food.

The best way to distinguish Keen's? Think salt 'n' vinegar potato chips. Look for a whiff of vinegar on the nose that turns sharp and salty as it unfolds on your tongue. Keen's is not your sweet, earthy charmer, which is how you might characterize Montgomery's; it's a barracuda, full of acidic succulence and teeth! If you want the sharpest British Cheddar on the block, Keen's is your baby. It's made by George and Stephen Keen, who carry on the cheesemaking tradition established by their Great-Aunt Jane in 1898.

Good matches: Grab some rustic bread, a jar of coarsely ground mustard, a crisp apple, and some bread and butter pickles. Done.

Wine/beer: Open a Pinot Noir or Cabernet; few things are better, however, than Cheddar and IPA.

LINCOLNSHIRE POACHER

ENGLAND, RAW COW'S MILK
PERSONALITY: A deep, thoughtful Cheddary
sort with a slightly smoky aura.

If you're a fan of British Cheddar, this variation is especially interesting, in part because it's made on the east coast of England where the soil is chalky—much different from the lush pastures of Somerset where most Cheddars are birthed. You can taste the different climate in this cheese's nutty, herby undertones; it's almost as if there's a Gruyère tiptoeing in the background. The texture is dry, bordering on brittle, but it softens quickly on the tongue.

Lincolnshire Poacher is considered one of the all-time great British cheeses. It's produced at Ulceby Grange in Alford under the watch of two young brothers, Simon and Tim Jones, who have fully embraced traditional British cheesemaking on their family's fourth-generation farm. The Jones brothers have figured out how to sustainably raise crops and run a dairy in an area where few farms exist. Although Lincolnshire Poacher is a fairly new cheese, it's won many awards, including Best British Cheese at the World Cheese Awards in 2001.

Good matches: Figs, apples, chutney, and toasted or smoked nuts are always welcome when serving this cheese. For something a little different, try dried mango or dried pineapple.

Wine/beer: This cheese loves dark beer, bourbon, or a Cab blend. A Chardonnay also works well.

MONTGOMERY'S CHEDDAR

ENGLAND, RAW COW'S MILK

PERSONALITY: The Henry Rollins of Cheddar: artful, big, a well-rounded performer.

Many cheeses have groupies, but Montgomery's Cheddar has fanatics. This clothbound cheese made by Jamie Montgomery of Somerset is made by hand, using a traditional peg mill to break down the curds—a process that was used in "cheddaring" prior to World War II. Montgomery's is not just one of the best Cheddars in the world; it's really one of the best cheeses in existence. The taste is sublime: round, complex, and yet subtle. The folks at Neal's Yard Dairy who age this cheese have compared the flavor to caramelized crackling "on a Sunday roast."

If you've been raised on block Cheddar, consider this your awakening. Montgomery's Cheddar isn't aged in plastic like so much American cheese; it's smeared with lard, bound in cloth, then tucked away in an ageing cave for a year or more. The process lends a unique taste to the cheese, especially near the rind. If that earthiness is unappealing to you, simply dig in closer to the center of the wheel where the paste is sweet and fruity.

Good matches: Eat this cheese alone in your room. If you offer some to friends, don't fuss with too many accompaniments. Perhaps a handful of nuts, some sliced apples.

Wine/beer: Pour a glass of jammy Zin or Cabernet, or seek out an English Bitter or crisp British Pale Ale.

VISITING JAMES MONTGOMERY

I had the pleasure of visiting Manor Farm in March of 2007. This is an impressive place, with gleeful, grazing cattle, green pastures, and an enormous farmhouse packed with maturing Cheddars. But what stood out to me had nothing to do with cheese. It was James Montgomery's office.

It looked like a tornado had recently blown through. Awards, certificates, and other verifications of excellence were strewn about in random piles on his desk and chair and falling from the shelves. Jason, my guide and Neal's Yard correspondent, prodded him a bit about whether he planned to hang the awards, and Montgomery acknowledged, "Yeah...I have to get to that someday."

He then urged us to follow him into a room where set wheels of Cheddar were being larded and bound in cloth. "I want to show you something," he said, grinning. He led us to a stainless steel table with a space beneath it so hot water could warm the cheese as it was prepared for ageing—it was an invention he had been working on for the last couple years. The warm surface kept the lard soft as the wheel was enrobed in cloth. "This gives it a tighter seal, and will do a better job of keeping out the mites," he said proudly.

I remember turning back toward the office, staring at the mountains of awards he had won. Worldwide acclaim lay all around on his desk, yet he was indifferent. He only sought opportunities for improvement. It was this commitment to excellence that inspired me to give my son the middle name "Montgomery." What better example could I set for my child?

—CHEESEMONGER HUNTER FIKE

OGLESHIELD

ENGLAND, RAW COW'S MILK
PERSONALITY: A rogue melter, otherwise
known as "West Country Raclette."

If you go to London's Borough Market, one of
the highlights for any eater is an Ogleshield
sandwich made on rye bread with red onions.
Melted, this rough-and-tumble British stinker
turns into sumptuous goo. If you have a thing
for Raclette (page 129), you will turn into an
Ogleshield worshipper. At room temp, this is a
fudgy golden wedge with tiny eyes (holes) and
an orange rind. The smell is pungent and, as
with many washed-rind cheeses, a tad peanutty.

Ogleshield is made by the great Cheddar
master James Montgomery of Somerset, who
named this cheese after a battle shield found on
his land (his farm is thought to be the original
Camelot). He sent a trial batch to William
Oglethorpe, head of the cave at Neal's Yard
Dairy, who improved upon this cheese by washing its rind. The collaboration resulted in a new
name that reflected both parents: Ogleshield. Its
creamy appeal comes, in part, from Jersey milk,
rather than Friesian-Holstein milk, which
Montgomery uses to make his famous Cheddar.

Good matches: Drape slices of Ogleshield
over warm potatoes, grilled leeks, French onion
soup, or a flame-licked burger.

Wine/beer: A roasty, malty beer is the best
partner. Otherwise, pour a glass of Pinot Noir.

SPARKENHOE RED LEICESTER

ENGLAND, RAW COW'S MILK
PERSONALITY: A gentle giant named after a
bull, worshipped by those in the know.

Sparkenhoe Red Leicester (pronounced
"lester") is famous in the cheese world for its
gentle complexity. It was invented by an English
farmer in 1745 to honor his prize bull,
Sparkenhoe, and over time it became wildly
popular as a Cheshire County cheese. Like all
great inventions, it was copied, warped, then
abandoned, until a recent pair of British cheesemakers named David and Jo Clarke decided to
resurrect the original recipe in its native region.

You can see the care that goes into this
rare beauty, which is handmade and bound in
cloth. The Clarkes pasture-raise their cows,
which means you can practically taste the
British countryside. Don't be turned off by the
gonzo orange color—it's natural, from the
annatto plant, which produces a russet dye. The
texture is dry, perfect for shaving over a fall
salad for a splash of color. The taste is faintly
sweet, nutty, and toasty with just a slight tang.

Good matches: Serve this with smoked ham,
caramelized pecans, and dried cherries for a
lovely snack plate. It's also good toasted on an
open-faced sandwich dressed with onion or
tomato jam.

Wine/beer: Pick an IPA or a proper British
ale. Avoid intense red wines, unless you veer
toward nutty and dry, like Amontillado or
sherry.

STICHELTON

ENGLAND, RAW COW'S MILK
PERSONALITY: **A rambunctious blue fox,
rare and beguiling.**

If you're a fan of Stilton (page 234), this is the
Holy Grail. It's the only raw-milk Stilton on the
market, and yet it cannot, by law, be called Stilton.
The story behind Stichelton is this: back in 1989,
Stilton became a name-protected cheese in the
U.K., a designation that is supposed to assure
quality and prevent cheese recipes from being
diluted or copied by cheesemakers near and far.
Today, only dairies in three shires can make Stilton, and the wheels must conform to certain
specifications.

   When this law was written, all Stilton was
made with pasteurized milk, and so this element became a federal requirement. Lovers of
traditional cheese frowned on this stipulation,
since Stilton originated in the early 1700s as a
raw-milk cheese—long before pasteurization
existed. Enter two cheese devotees, Joe Schnei-
der and Randolph Hodgson, who decided to
resurrect raw-milk Stilton on a small farm in
Nottinghamshire. By law, they couldn't call this
raw-milk classic "Stilton" any more, so they
made up the name "Stichelton." The result is a
spicy, savory, ultra rich cheese that boasts hints
of walnuts, chocolate, and wet leather.

Good Matches: Play up Stichelton's toasty
notes by serving it with a dish of hazelnuts,
preferably broiled for a moment and tossed
with a pinch of sea salt. Figs, dates, and candied
bacon pair beautifully, too.

Wine/beer: Tawny port is perfect, but you
might also experiment with barleywine or
chocolate stout.

TOMME DOLCE

UNITED STATES, RAW COW'S MILK
PERSONALITY: **A virtuosic cherub who
feeds on Schubert and jam.**

This special cheese comes from Andante Dairy,
a one-woman operation in Petaluma, California.
You can taste the quality of the milk in this
firm, tomme-style cheese, and you can't help
admiring the creativity that goes into the rind.
It's rubbed down with a mixture of plum
brandy mixed with local jam from June Taylor,
the cheesemaker's neighbor and a vendor at the
Ferry Plaza market in San Francisco. The flavor
of plums pervades this cheese, along with notes
of raw almond and salt caramel.

   Cheesemaker Soyoung Scanlan works in
such small batches that wheels of Tomme Dolce
are rarely sold outside of the Bay Area. This is
an especially unusual selection from her reper-
toire because it's an aged cheese; most of her
releases are young, like Largo (page 104). If you
can find this toothsome wonder, set aside some
time to taste it alone in a room with nothing
but classical music to distract you. You may be
able to sense that this cheesemaker is a classi-
cally trained pianist: each note is pitch-perfect.
That's why she's a rockstar. Few venues outside
of The French Laundry and Di Bruno Bros.
offer her masterpieces.

Good matches: Serve Tomme Dolce naked
or with a dish of whole blanched almonds.

Wine/beer: Play off the Basque influences in
this cheese with a Spanish white, or go for a
light Riesling. Fruity wheat beers and lambics
work well, but beware of anything too zesty or
overpowering.

VERMONT SHEPHERD

UNITED STATES, RAW SHEEP'S MILK
PERSONALITY: Rustic and sensuous—a rogue hermit with mutton chops and wild herbs stuck to his beard.

If you enjoy firm sheep's milk cheeses from the Basque region, you'll be interested in this award-winning version from a pioneering maker in Putney, Vermont. In the United States, Vermont Shepherd bears the distinction of being one of the oldest and best-known aged sheep's milk cheeses on the market. David Major and his family began production in the nineties after studying French cheesemaking in the Pyrénées. Today, they milk 250 pasture-raised ewes and make cheese during the spring and summer months. Wheels become available in November and are sold through April, or until the supply runs out. If you get your mits on a wedge, consider yourself lucky.

Vermont Shepherd has the look of a large Brazil nut pressed into the shape of a flying saucer. The rind is husky-looking from cave ageing, and the paste is ivory and waxen. Each wheel varies in flavor with the season, but the dominant tastes are of almonds and herbs. The finish is sweet, almost fruity.

Good Matches: Serve this cheese with honey and dried figs or cherry preserves—a classic French Pyrénées match.

Wine/beer: This versatile cheese goes well with an earthy red or a buttery Chardonnay. You could also try a lager or a sweet, malty dopplebock.

CHEESE BOARD: Craft Beers and Artisan All-Stars

The last decade has brought on a beer and cheese renaissance, with microbreweries and small-batch cheesemakers reviving two ancient arts. This cheese board highlights a few favorite craft-made combinations, culled from many Di Bruno Bros. tasting nights over the years. Gather your friends and put them in charge of foraging for these treasures.

Flying Fish Belgian Abbey Dubbel and Largo (page 104)

This clean, almondy beer brings intrigue and effervescence to a handmade triple-crème that coats your mouth with perfect California milk. If you can't find this rare beauty, try a local triple crème from your area.

Victory Golden Monkey and Gorwydd Caerphilly (page 170)

This Belgian Tripel offers some hunky Trappist spice to a very funky cheese. The combination is like a wonderful cauliflower gratin: earthy and creamy with a twinge of coriander and clove. This is a pairing for the hardcore: monastic beer meets the cheese of Welsh miners.

Yards India Pale Ale and Isle of Mull Cheddar (page 170)

Cheddar and IPA are a classic combination—bitter plays off bitter to create balance. Here, the floral aroma and citrus-forward taste of a favorite Philadelphia beer underscore the scotchy sweetness of a small-batch Cheddar made from the milk of cows fed on spent barley. You've got two distilleries in one here. What could be better?

Duck-Rabbit Milk Stout and Point Reyes Original Blue (page 239)

The milk sugar in this toasty stout from North Carolina mingles sweetly with Point Reyes Original Blue, a sea-salt rich cheese from California. The makers claim that Point Reyes Original Blue has three ingredients: raw grass-fed milk, coastal fog, and briny Pacific air.

Rogue Imperial India Pale Ale and Rogue River Blue (page 218)

For comparison's sake: a second pale ale and a second raw-milk blue. We're playing off sweet notes here. Oregon's Rogue River Blue comes wrapped in brandy-soaked grape leaves, which lend an earthy, raisiny vibe. Try this cheese with the stout, too. You'll probably discover that the Imperial India Pale Ale, which is radically hopped, overpowers the other cheeses.

Accompaniments: Serve with baguette, sourdough bread, apple butter or chutney, toasted almonds or walnuts, and pears. Follow it up with a warming stew or rustic game dinner.

CHEESE 101: How to Pair Beer and Cheese

For decades, people have viewed cheese and wine as soul mates, but with craft breweries popping up around the country and easy access to great imports, many cheese geeks are undergoing a change of heart. Beer likes cheese, and cheese likes beer back. Ask a room full of cheesemongers which fermented bevvie they prefer, and you'll probably find an equal number in each camp.

On a hot day, nothing beats a wheat beer with goat cheese. On a cold night, a stout or porter can bring toasty notes to a heavy blue. Here are a few pairing basics to guide you, thanks to a little help from our friend Dean Browne of Philadelphia Brewing Company. These pairings are guaranteed to sway even the stodgiest wine noodge.

Mellow Beer Likes Mellow Cheese

Think of your fresh chèvres and mild goat cheeses. These delicate, young things are easily trampled by strong flavors. Play off their bright, citrusy notes with a like-minded beer. Anything lemony and herby makes these cheeses sing their daffodil hearts out.
EXAMPLE: Philadelphia Brewing Company's Walt Wit and Humboldt Fog (page 74)

Bitter Beer Likes Bitter Cheese

Ever notice how bitter grouches attract other bitter grouches? The same principle can be applied to beer and cheese. For example, aged Cheddars often have a characteristic bitter finish: it's not unpleasant, but it gets you in the back of your throat. Next time you've got a sharp Cheddar on your hands, introduce it to an IPA. The grapefruity hook, common in this style of beer, mellows when you let it nuzzle against a sharp cheese. In fact, this pairing has been known to make IPA-haters swoon.
EXAMPLE: Dogfish Head 60-minute IPA and Cabot Clothbound Cheddar (page 165)

Funky Cheese Likes "Monk-y" Beer

Monks started the tradition of washing cheese in beer, a technique that yields pungent wheels with distinctive orange rinds. The French classic is Epoisses. Many American makers have followed suit, creating winners like Red Hawk (page 154) and Hudson Red (page 148). The flavor profile of these cheeses is often described as "beefy" and "oniony," so just imagine what kind of pint you'd drink alongside beef stew. Something robust, right? Maybe a Belgian Dubbel or a Trappist Chimay?
EXAMPLE: Chimay Grand Reserve and Epoisses (page 143)

Sweet Stouts Like Salty Hunks

Consider the chocolate-covered pretzel. The success of this flavor pairing can be used to create a beer-cheese algorithm. Take a big salty blue, and give it a chocolate turn-down. Wow. You won't be able to stop eating that wedge of Colston Bassett Stilton (page 234). If you find a really briny blue, like Strathdon (page 240), which carries hints of sea salt from its birthplace on the Scottish coast, you can blow young minds by pairing it with an oyster stout. Blues and stouts are really fun to play with. So are blues and barleywines.
EXAMPLE: Flying Fish Exit 1 Bayshore Oyster Stout and Strathdon Blue (page 240)

CHAPTER VIII

WISE GUYS

(old school, hard)

You don't get to be old and crusty without a good story. Most of these characters have been around for centuries; they're the ancient cheeses your Italian Grandpops grew up gnawing. They pack a punch, and they'll never spoil. Break them out over a game of dominoes, or serve them with cocktails.

Asiago d'Allevo Stravecchio | Cacio di Bosca al Tartufo | Caciocavallo | Fiore Sardo | Balsamic Poached Figs | Sicilian Olive and Smoked Almond Tapenade | Foja de Noce | Grana Padano | Basil and Pine Nut Pesto | Juni | Laguiole | Moliterno | Montasio | Paški Sir | Parmigiano Reggiano | Piave | Pecorino di Fossa | Pecorino Ginepro | Pecorino di Pienza (a.k.a. Grand Old Man) | A Pecorino-Perfect Martini | Pecorino Romano | Pecorino Toscano | Pepato | Provolone | Ragusano | Remeker | Roncal | Scamorza | Testun al Barolo | Trugole | Tomato and Pancetta Strata | Tuma Persa | Ubriaco | Cheese Board: Emilio's Ultimate Tailgate Hamper | Cheese 101: Charcuterie Demystified

ASIAGO D'ALLEVO STRAVECCHIO

ITALY, RAW COW'S MILK
PERSONALITY: A big, rugged fellow with lots of fruit and spice.

Sweet prickle. That's what you should feel on your tongue when you taste this traditional hard cheese from Trentino, the northern-most province of Italy. The region is known for its superior milk, which comes from a special breed of Bruna Alpa cattle that graze in the shadow of the Dolomites. Imagine spring-fed rivers, lush pastures.

Be sure to select Asiago *d'Allevo*, meaning "raised" or "matured." Another style of Asiago, known as *pressato,* is the mass-market version. Both are controlled by the Italian government to ensure quality, but the craftsmanship varies. Pick a hunk of Asiago that's aged at least nine months (designated as *Stravecchio)*, and your mouth will be flooded with the taste of pineapple.

Good matches: Northern Italians eat Asiago as a snack. Set out a wedge with some rustic salami. You can also create little flavor torpedoes in a salad or pasta dish by tossing in cubes of Asiago. Delish!

Wine/beer: A nice white from Trentino is always a safe bet; go for a red if your hunk is well aged. Beer is an easy partner, especially Pilsners and lagers.

CACIO DI BOSCA AL TARTUFO

ITALY, SHEEP'S MILK
PERSONALITY: The mushroom hunter's friend, abundantly truffle-y.

Truffles in cheese can be overpowering, especially if the maker uses truffle flavoring, which imparts a synthetic taste. When you see the dark swaths of truffle in this cheese, you'll know it's the real deal. Once cut, the wheels look like vanilla ice cream loaded with chocolate bark, and they're just as decadent. Sheep's milk is rich, so even though this is a firm cheese, the mouthfeel is buttery, and the aroma of sweet cream and truffles will make you swoon on the spot.

Cacio di Bosca attracts "truffle groupies," as cheesemongers at Di Bruno Bros. like to say. Once someone serves this cheese at a party, the rest of the neighborhood flocks over to bankroll the import of more wheels. Who can blame them? Tuscany knows how to take an already gorgeous wheel of Pecorino and spin it into something unearthly. Just approach the counter with a faraway look in your eyes and whisper the word "Tartufo." Anyone who works at Di Bruno Bros. will know which cheese you mean.

Good matches: Set this out for a pool party in summer, or serve it before a big holiday meal to whet people's appetites. You can also shave it over pasta or risotto for amazing effect. For an insane twist, use this cheese to top Oysters Rockefeller.

Wine/beer: Pick an earthy red wine, or explore one of cheesemonger Hunter Fike's favorite beer pairings: Saison Dupont. As he explains, "The saison starts out bright and lemony but gets barnyardy, and the cheese starts out a little barnyardy, then turns bright. It's miraculous."

CACIOCAVALLO

ITALY, COW'S MILK
PERSONALITY: The cowboy's friend, a potent old-timer who rides with a lasso.

"Cheese on horseback" is the direct translation of this bulbous, aged cheese from southern Italy. You'll recognize it by its shape, which resembles an engorged water balloon. Back in the day, these were hung to dry in pairs from either end of a rope so that they could be easily draped over a saddle and trotted into town. If you've ever had Scamorza (page 199), a similarly shaped cheese, just remember that this is the stronger version.

Caciocavallo begins as a *pasta filata* cheese, meaning that the curds are spun—just like mozzarella. You'll notice that the taste is similar to sharp provolone, but there is something else: a sweet, toasty quality that calls to mind Parmigiano. A mere three months of ageing turns this initially mellow fellow into something robust with just a bit of grit to the texture. Toss a Caciocavallo over your shoulder like a canteen and head for the woods or the beach.

Good matches: Pack this cheese on a road trip or take it surfing. A tub of olives or sun-dried tomatoes and a link or two of Sicilian pepperoni are all you'll need. At home, try swapping it into a Caprese salad in place of fresh mozzarella. Mark Vetri, one of Philly's most notable chefs, serves Caciocavallo with octopus.

Wine/beer: Seek out a spicy southern Italian red, or nab an IPA.

FIORE SARDO

ITALY, SHEEP'S MILK
PERSONALITY: A deity in the world of ancient cheeses, smoky and bright.

This beauty from the Bronze Age is not a household name, but it should be. Say it with me: *fee-OR-a SAR-doh*. It tastes like preserved lemons—like citrus, olive oil, and salt— mixed with smoked almonds. That's because it's brined, then slowly smoked over balsa wood. If you like Pecorinos, school yourself on this ancient recipe that predates the Romans. It will make you feel like Zeus. At least one Di Bruno cheesemonger has an image of Fiore Sardo emblazoned across his chest.

Production of Fiore Sardo, which means "Sardinian flower," is carefully guarded by the Italians, and even Slow Food, a group that advocates for preserving food traditions, has singled out this cheese for a special honor. Why? Shepherds still make some Fiore Sardo in mountain huts, called *pinette*. Before the shepherds smoke the cheeses over open fires, they rub down the wheels with lard and olive oil, just as tradition dictates. Put down that *Patagonia* catalog and eat your way into the rugged climes!

Good matches: At Di Bruno Bros., Emilio Mignucci loves to serve this cheese on a snack plate (see Emilio's Ultimate Tailgate Hamper, page 205). "Fiorde Sardo is what I want for each and any game that I watch," he says. "It can be sharp, but the smoke is light and delicate. And it finishes a little buttery." Try using it in pesto or as a grating cheese in place of Pecorino Romano.

Wine/beer: Pair this with a take-charge red, like Chianti or Primitivo; after dinner, Moscato is an elegant accompaniment. Porters and strong ales love this to pieces.

RECIPE

BALSAMIC POACHED FIGS

Keep a jar of these savory figs in your fridge door around the holidays. They're great paired with blue cheese, tossed into stuffing, or puréed and spread on the base of a crackery goat cheese pizza. They're especially good with firm sheep's milk cheeses, like Fiore Sardo (page 181).

MAKES 2 CUPS

1 pound dried Calmyrna figs
   (about 2 cups)
1 cup amber honey
1½ cups white balsamic vinegar
2 sprigs fresh thyme
1 small bay leaf
1 pinch kosher salt

Combine the figs, honey, vinegar, thyme, bay leaf, salt and 1½ cups water in a two-quart stock pot, and bring the mixture to a boil. Reduce the heat and keep it on a low simmer for approximately one hour, until the liquid reduces by half and becomes syrupy.

Transfer the figs to a storage container and allow them to cool thoroughly in the liquid. Store the figs in syrup for up to a month in the refrigerator.

SICILIAN OLIVE and
SMOKED ALMOND TAPENADE

Tapenade, a sexy little olive spread that originated in Provence, is a great way to use up hard cheeses that are rattling around in the back of your fridge. In this recipe, smoked almonds and honey play off the sultry-sweet notes in rustic Foja de Noce (page 184), but you don't have to tell anyone if you change out the cheeses. Use any hard Pecorino or Parmigiano, and play around with the lemon and honey to keep the salty notes in check. Serve this with baguette rounds or pita chips, or slip it into a sandwich for a riveting surprise.

MAKES 1 CUP

¼ pound Foja de Noce, grated
⅓ cup smoked almonds
⅓ cup dry-cured Sicilian olives, pitted
1 small garlic clove
2 tablespoons lemon juice
2 tablespoons honey (preferably light-colored)
3 tablespoons extra-virgin olive oil

Place all of the ingredients in a food processor and purée until the mixture is finely chopped, about the consistency of pesto. You may need to add a couple tablespoons of water if the paste is too thick. If you don't have a food processor, try dicing the ingredients, then use a mortar and pestle to create a paste.

Covered, this tapenade will keep in the refrigerator for up to two weeks.

FOJA DE NOCE

ITALY, SHEEP'S MILK
PERSONALITY: A gentleman dandy in a
tweed suit, thoughtfully Proustian.

If you were going to eat a cheese in Central
Park, it should probably be Foja de Noce.
Wrapped in walnut leaves and aged in mountain caves, it's the sort of cheese you want
everyone to see that you're eating. The moist
paste is halo-gold, the rind bark-like. You will
certainly attract the attention of squirrels and
probably a few candy-colored ladies who have
been to Le Marche.

Foja de Noce is a Pecorino, so it has all the
primal whomp of a nutty, aged sheep's milk
cheese, and yet there is so much more going
on: a lazy kind of sweetness, a buttery stealth
that lingers, a dreamy, woodsy depth. You can't
help but lean back on your elbows and stare at
all of the people talking over smoke rings, without wondering, "Why, world, are you eating
hotdogs and popsicles when you could be eating Foja de Noce?"

Good matches: Set out a wedge of Foja de
Noce with a small jar of truffle honey and some
nuts. Then, forget about everything. If you need
to appear more personable, prepare Sicilian Olive
and Smoked Almond Tapenade (page 183).

Wine/beer: Drink a glass of Barolo, or pour a
pint of amber or Scotch ale. Roasty notes and
maltiness are encouraged here. Mead would also
be appropriate.

GRANA PADANO

ITALY, RAW COW'S MILK
PERSONALITY: Parmigiano's understudy—
lovely, but less celebrated.

The recipe for Grana Padano predates Parmigiano, and yet it's considered a less-refined substitute. That's because this mild, fruity cheese
from Emilia-Romagna has fewer regulations
placed on its production, so it's usually younger
when it leaves the ageing caves—usually around
six months, whereas Parm is required to mature
for at least eighteen. Sample them side-by-side,
and you'll notice that they taste pretty similar,
but if Parm is an acrobat, Grana Padano is a
waify gymnast. This cheese just can't perform as
many tricks, flavor-wise.

In Italy, Grana Padano is a household
cheese, used in recipes and for snacking. In the
United States, it became known as a cheaper
alternative to Parm, but increased demand has
changed that, alas. The best wheels hail from
Trentino, and when it's well-aged, this Grana is
magnificent. Seek it out, and like Boccaccio,
you may find yourself envisioning a mountain
of grated cheese for a *Decameron*-esque feast of
ravioli boiled in capon's broth. *Grana*, it should
be noted, refers to any "granular" hard cheese
that can be grated; Padano refers to the Po
River region, where this cheese originated.

Good matches: Grate Grana Padano over
pasta, or stir it into risotto. For a snack, try
breaking off chunks of this cheese and dipping
them into aged balsamic. For pesto, this is an
excellent choice.

Wine/beer: You can't go wrong with Prosecco or a rough 'n' tumble Chianti or Barolo—
choose the latter if you're also serving cured
meats. Otherwise, grab an amber lager. For
something special, try Dogfish Head's Aprihop,
a cheesemonger favorite.

BASIL AND PINE NUT PESTO

There are probably as many recipes for pesto in the world as there are kinds of cheese. If you don't already have a favorite, try this one, which is heavy on the cheese and basil. Toss this with pasta, spread it on grilled bread, or stir it into soup, scrambled eggs, or even salad dressings for great effect.

MAKES 1 CUP

2 cups loosely packed basil leaves
2 small garlic cloves
½ cup pine nuts
1 cup grated Grana Padano
4 to 6 tablespoons extra-virgin olive oil

For a smooth pesto, combine the basil, garlic, pine nuts, and cheese in a food processor or blender to form a paste, then gradually add the olive oil. For a more rustic version, use a mortar and pestle or a mezzaluna (a curved blade with a handle built for rocking) and chop the first four ingredients together in small amounts before transferring the mixture to a bowl and adding the olive oil. Pesto tastes best the day it's made, but it also freezes well.

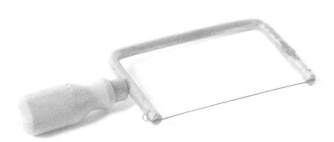

JUNI

ITALY, RAW COW'S MILK

PERSONALITY: The mixologist's friend, a juniper-laced cheese that pairs well with gin.

Break out the Bocce balls, and start slinging the drinks. Juni, a newcomer to the cheese world, is a pungent little tuffet that slices like cheesecake and smacks of a stiff gin drink. That's because native juniper berries harvested from Piedmont are dropped into the curds when this little beefcake is in formation. As this cheese ages over a period of sixty days, it takes on other whiffs and flavors: mushroom, damp stone, butter, pine. Is it cologne or is it cheese? You decide, preferably over a gimlet or dirty martini.

Juni is made by a longstanding creamery that sources milk from a very rare breed of red cattle, known as the Pezzata Rosa d'Aropa. For more than a century, the Rosso family has made cheese, but this new gem is one of their most distinct offerings. This style of cheese is called "toma brusca," which essentially means "acid cheese." Don't let this turn you off. Fresh milk is simply soured so that the curds form naturally. This very traditional method of cheesemaking contributes to Juni's flavor profile, particularly its ebullient tang.

Good matches: Juni pairs well with herb and licorice flavors. Try it with a salad laced with dill and thyme, or shave it over thinly-sliced fennel and watercress tossed with a little lemon juice and olive oil. It's very good with cocktails. On a plate, add smoked almonds, green olives, and some shaved speck or fennel-spiked Finnochiona (a terrific Tuscan salami).

Wine/beer: Pair Juni with gin and tonics, or a mineral-heavy red. For beer, seek out an oddball, like a barrel-aged concoction with a juniper accent. Otherwise, try a saison.

Cocktails and Cheese

Ignore people who tell you that cheese doesn't pair with cocktails. Gin, with its herbal aroma and taste, is excellent for taming salty sheep's milk cheeses (see the **Pecorino-Perfect Martini**, page 192). Cheeses wrapped in leaves, like **Banon** (page 88), also pair well with gin. For a bright little number, like **Pantaleo** (page 56), or a soft goat cheese, like **Leonora** (page 76), try a Hendricks 'n' Tonic with a cucumber garnish instead of lime.

Here is a cocktail cheese sampler for your next gin smash: **Carre du Berry** (page 69), **La Serena** (page 103), **Juni** (page 186) or **Pecorino Ginepro** (page 191), **Pecorino di Pienza** (page 191) or **Moliterno** (page 187), **Bleu des Basques** (page 229) or the white-chocolate taser that is **Cabrales** (page 233).

For whiskey-based cocktails, serve aged Cheddars, aged Goudas, or **Stilton** (page 234).

LAGUIOLE

FRANCE, RAW COW'S MILK
PERSONALITY: A buttery, tarty sort with fall-apart-on-the-tongue appeal.

Laguiole (pronounced LAY-ohl) is a firm cheese that takes its name from a town in south-central France. If you're familiar with Cantal (page 48), this is essentially a raw-milk version. Although only a single producer kicks out this mouth-watering stunner, it was once widely produced across the countryside; in fact, "burons," or cheesemaking huts, were built solely for the production of this labor-intensive specialty first developed by monks.

Like Cheddar, this is a milled cheese—a process rarely seen in French cheesemaking. Curds are literally passed through a grinder to form pellets that are then pressed together and molded. The resulting texture is nubby. A bite of Laguiole breaks apart like stars. Moist and delicate, it will fill your mouth with a tart tingling and set your head swimming with Van Gogh paintings.

Good matches: Set out a basket of pears and a plate of prosciutto, then lean back and stare at the sky. If possible, slice off hunks with one of the famed knives from Laguiole; this cheese was made for slicing with an elegant pocketknife.

Wine/beer: Dig out a dreamy Merlot or trot off across the hills with a six-pack of IPA.

MOLITERNO

ITALY, SHEEP'S MILK
PERSONALITY: The perfect first-date cheese when you're having red wine.

The first thing you'll notice about this Pecorino-style cheese is its scarred-looking rind. It looks like something you might see at a tattoo convention. The pattern actually comes from baskets, or *canestrati*, which the Sardinians use in shaping this rugged sheep's milk cheese. Once the wheels are formed, they're rubbed down with olive oil and aged for several months until they turn hard but moist.

Moliterno's paste is oat-colored, the texture crumbly. Remember that Sardinia is a brambly island, loaded with rocks and sheep. You'll taste these things when you bite off a piece—think toasted nuts, olives, wet rock, woodfire. There's a craggy beauty to the flavor, a taste of camping trips and arrowhead hunts, which is to say that this is a cheese of nostalgia. When you leave Moliterno out on the counter, it will bead fat, so only set out as much as you plan to eat.

Good matches: Serve Moliterno to a new flame with sopressata and hot pepper jelly. If your date is sweet rather than saucy, offer Marcona almonds and truffle honey.

Wine/beer: Pick up a table wine, preferably a powerhouse Italian red. It's no sin to serve this with a gin drink, either.

MONTASIO

ITALY, RAW COW'S MILK
PERSONALITY: Like Sylvester Stallone: strong and sturdy but sweet inside.

This is the ultimate working man's cheese of northern Italy. It's not as pineapple-y as Asiago (page 180), but it's still sweet with a butterscotchy earthiness that's hard to pass up. Montasio is made in the Alpine region of Friuli where it's officially recognized by the Italian government as a specialty of the region. This honor, called a "Protected Designation of Origin," took cheesemakers thirty years to earn, though this cheese has been made in the Italian Alps since the 1200s. The recipe was originally developed by a group of mountain-dwelling monks at the Moggio Abbey.

Today, Montasio is used all over Italy for *frico*, a lacy crisp made of toasted grated cheese. Italians tend to eat Montasio when it's young, but the American palate leans toward sharper, sweeter flavors. Aged Montasio gains a lactic, or milky, sweetness that's almost like candy.

Good Matches: Pack a working man's lunch with a hunk of Montasio, some cured meat, olives, and a wedge of crusty bread. On a cheese board, try Montasio with sliced red pears.

Wine/beer: Pick a simple white, preferably from Northern Italy; a Sauvignon Blanc or Pinot Grigio also works well. For something more robust, try a Valpolicella. A lager or pilsner work, too.

PAŠKI SIR

CROATIA, SHEEP'S MILK
PERSONALITY: An obscure cheese from a remote island—a wildling.

The Croatian island of Pag is a rocky, windswept place known for two things: delicate lacework and this fascinating cheese the color of driftwood. On the nose, it smells like acorns and pine. On the tongue, it tastes surprisingly bright, like citrus and salted herbs. This is a cheese that cries out for desert camping and vision quests; it is a cheese of extremes, an ideal snack for the parched renegade. One can imagine the photographer Ansel Adams carrying a roughhewn nub in his pocket through Yosemite.

Paški Sir is made with the milk of small, lean, indigenous sheep. They munch salty grasses where they can, since much of the island is rock. Each one produces less than half a liter of milk each day, due to the conditions, which means that creating a single wheel of this crystalline delicacy requires diligence and good herd management. Although this is a new import to the United States, Paški Sir has garnered raves from every cheesemonger we know. It's a great gift for foodies.

Good matches: Try sage honey and salted anchovies, a combination favored by Croatians. Truffle honey pairs well, too, as do quince paste and fig jam. For a twist on traditional pesto, blend this cheese with pistachios and olive oil, or just shave curls of Paški Sir over steamed veggies.

Wine/beer: Try a Riesling or South American Malbec. Otherwise, try a Pilsner or an IPA, depending on the age of the cheese.

PARMIGIANO REGGIANO

ITALY, RAW COW'S MILK

PERSONALITY: **A laugh riot of flavor, the Jim Henson of hard cheeses.**

Authentic Parmigiano is a Muppet movie in your mouth. It's so good, so full of bright tasting joy—pineapple, sea salt, toasted almonds, vanilla—you may erupt in crazy laughter, or even whinny. We've all seen it happen, when the forces of umami (the sweet-salty taste commonly associated with Parm, or some Asian cuisine) wake a person from Parm-shaker slumber. Once you taste real Parm, you will never go back to the green can. . . unless you don't really care for the company you are serving. Anything labeled "Parmesan" from America is an imposter.

Real Parmigiano is splurgey because it's a labor-intensive cheese. For example, authentic Parm can only be made in certain "zones" of Emilia-Romagna between April 15 and November 11, when the cows are eating the lushest grass. Each wheel must then be stamped with its birth date to ensure that it's properly aged a full eighteen months before it's released on the market. For the finest Parm, Di Bruno Bros. looks to master ager Giorgio Cravero, a fifth-generation cheese man who selects and matures the finest wheels at his cave in Bra. Each wheel is routinely cleaned, flipped, and even tapped with a small mallet to detect the pitch of ripeness. Ahh, that must be some sweet jazz.

Good matches: Break off chunks of Parm and dip them into truffle honey or aged balsamic for an earth-shattering experience.

Wine/beer: Giorgio Cravero serves his authentic Parm with Prosecco. For something more robust, try a glass of Valpolicella. Don't be embarrassed to try it with a Lambrusco either, a sparkling red from the same area. As for beer, lagers always work well; so do amber ales.

Save Your Parm Rinds for Soup

In Italy, Parm rinds are used like bay leaves. Instead of throwing out the hard ends, toss them into a broth-to-be. As it simmers for hours, the ends will soften, releasing sweet-salty flavor. This is a great way to add depth to vegetarian recipes, in particular. Before you serve the soup, remove the ends. Chop them into "croutons" if you want, then toss them back in. Soft and chewy, these little nuggets add great texture, and the letters stamped into the rind will remind you of alphabet soup.

THE PERFECT DUO: PARM AND BALSAMIC

I have never been much of a dessert guy. At a restaurant, I am apt to order a second appetizer after the entrée while my wife enjoys her pots de crème. But at home, a few nuggets of Parmigiano Reggiano drizzled with syrupy aged balsamic suffice every time.

This is to Italians what peanut butter and jelly is to Americans: a comforting pairing, beloved nationwide and available in almost every household. There is no wonder why. Parmigiano is nutty, crunchy and earthy against the sweetness and viscosity of the balsamic. Together they are the perfect end to a meal: enough complexity to leave you wanting for nothing, and just enough sweetness to close off the palate.

—CHEESEMONGER HUNTER FIKE

PIAVE

ITALY, COW'S MILK
PERSONALITY: The Mars Bar of the cheese world, it's all almonds and nougat.

If you want a less salty and less expensive version of Parm, Piave (pronounced pee-AH-vay) is your new stalwart. It's got the same crumbly, crystalline texture, but it's a tad sweeter. Think butterscotch and a whiff of almonds.

Piave is named after a river in the Veneto, an Alpine region of northern Italy where native cows, the Bruna Alpa, are raised for their rich milk. The complex flavor notes in this cheese come from their food source, mostly wild grasses and mineral springs. Note that Piave is sold in three categories depending on its age. Look for one that's aged six months or more, known as Piave *Stagionato* or "Red Label."

Good matches: This is a great table cheese. Serve it before or after dinner with a swoosh of good balsamic and a dish of almonds or walnuts. It's also stellar stirred into risotto. For something unusual but delicious, try a nibble with dried mango.

Wine/beer: Pair this hard sweetie with raisiny reds, Zinfandel, or Riesling. A brown ale or malty Belgian Dubbel also works well.

PECORINO DI FOSSA

ITALY, SHEEP'S MILK
PERSONALITY: A rare "buried" gem, steeped in ancient tradition.

There are Pecorinos. . . and then there are Pecorinos. This is a special cheese, and once you try it, you'll understand why. Like most Pecs, it's made from sheep's milk, the richest of milks, but it's aged in an unusual way: in the ground. That's right, since Roman times, cheesemakers have followed a ritual of carrying this cheese into the Umbrian hills, wrapping it in cloth, lowering it into a hollow, packing it in wild herbs (juniper, wild thyme, rosemary), then burying it. The tradition harkens back to an age when ancient cultures were often raided, and cheesemakers were forced to hide their wares from roving bands of Saracen pirates.

Tucked away, this cheese ferments, becoming pleasantly sweet and almost boozy. After ninety days, it's unearthed on the Feast Day of Saint Catherine and served around the winter holidays. The flavor is rich and earthy—imagine buttered popcorn served at a backyard bonfire. Although this is a hard cheese and not very pretty-looking, it dissolves on your tongue like a good piece of fudge.

Good matches: This makes an impressive fireside appetizer alongside martinis. Try serving it in a rustic dish, cubed or broken into shards. After dinner, pair it with chestnut honey, dried fruit, and dessert wine.

Wine/beer: This salty character needs a glass of port or sherry, though martinis are an especially fine touch. You could also play around with sparkling wine or a hard cider.

PECORINO GINEPRO

ITALY, RAW SHEEP'S MILK
PERSONALITY: Picture a handsome wood-cutter with juniper cologne.

Ginepro is a bright, woodsy cheese that is bathed in balsamic vinegar and packed in juniper berries. Notice the deep mahogany coloring around the rind, a striking contrast to the white glow of the paste. This semi-hard sheep's milk cheese is a Pecorino, although it's nothing like its more popular cousin, Romano. Ginepro is usually sold on the young side so that its center is soft and citrusy, not yet compact and crystalline.

In the province of Emilia-Romagna, Ginepro is used as a table cheese, but it's also a great cheese for cocktail parties, since it's fatty and forceful enough to stand up to surly drinks. On a cheese board, its black rind causes double takes.

Good matches: Pick up a loaf of olive bread, some walnuts, and a bitey Italian salami. This is a good cheese to eat alongside soups or to filch from the fridge as you suck down a martini.

Wine/beer: Try a citrusy wheat beer, a bottle of Chianti, or a licorice-scented white. For something different: a briny cocktail with a twist of lemon, preferably one made with gin.

PECORINO DI PIENZA (A.K.A. GRAND OLD MAN)

ITALY, SHEEP'S MILK
PERSONALITY: A gentleman's cheese, best served with olives and a martini.

When the characters on *Mad Men* were slinging back drinks, they should have reached for a Pecorino chaser. This one, nicknamed "Grand Old Man" after the cheesemaker's grandfather, is fit for the jet set. It's the Armani of Pecorinos, the luxury liner of hard grating cheeses that are too good to grate. Reserve this one for retirement parties, cocktail soirees, and evenings of bachelor-to-bachelor banter. No cigars, please; you'll ruin your palate.

Grand Old Man is distinguished by a year-long maturation period (most Pecorinos fly off the shelf after three months) and incomparable taste. Notes of almond and olive ring like bells, but there's no sharp clang or rough, muttony taste. The recipe for this Tuscan godfather extends back a millennium, making it one of the oldest Pecorinos in existence. When you break off a hunk, you're touching tradition—it's Homeric. Look to *The Odyssey* for references.

Good matches: Truffle honey and Tuscan-style bread create the ultimate trifecta here. For an interesting variation, try it with plum *membrillo*, a variation on the Spanish fruit paste that is typically made from quinces. To serve, break this cheese into chunks using a sturdy knife, and set it out in a dish as you would almonds. Each bite should be savored like candy.

Wine/beer: This is an excellent cocktail cheese, particularly for a gin drink or something Champagne-based. A spicy Italian red is ideal, too. Beer is not the best pairing here, but it would be perfect with that rare Scotch lingering in the back of your liquor cabinet.

A PECORINO-PERFECT MARTINI

Winston Churchill never used any vermouth in his martinis. Franklin D. Roosevelt made his with plenty (four parts gin to one part vermouth). My friend Gerard, a former Benedictine monk, swears by eight to one, and I've found this ratio creates a splendidly bright and briny martini, ideal for serving alongside a hunk of room temperature Pecorino and a dish of almonds. At 5 p.m. on a Friday, few things are this satisfying.

SERVES 2

8 ounces Plymouth gin (about 4 shots), cold

1 ounce Noilly Pratt Vermouth (½ shot), cold

4 Sicilian olives, skewered onto a pair of toothpicks

Pour the gin and vermouth into a cold shaker filled with ice. Shake well, about 20 seconds, then pour into chilled martini glasses. Add olive skewers and serve immediately.

Note: Store your bottles of gin and vermouth in the refrigerator so that they're cold to begin with. Keep a shaker and a set of martini glasses in the door of your freezer. When you make martinis, the drinks will get cold quickly without requiring much shaking. It also prevents the ice from melting and watering down your cocktails.

PECORINO ROMANO

ITALY, RAW SHEEP'S MILK
PERSONALITY: Salty as hell, like an old fighter with a rugged face.

If your kids are acting up, give 'em a hunk of Pecorino Romano. If you need to add some flavor to a soup, give it some Pecorino Romano. If you haven't guessed it, PR has attitude. It's so salty it makes your tongue buzz. Cheesemonger Ezekial Ferguson calls it a "big punch to the mouth." Keep a hunk in your cheese drawer, and you can serve it as punishment or add flavor to anything—soups, stews, sauces.

A word on Pecorinos: In southern Italy, there are as many kinds as there are basilicas. Most of them are table cheeses, sold at a young age. They're simple, meant to go with wine. This one is not a snacker. The aggressive salinity is too much for most palates, unless you've got a thing for 50-pound salt licks. The best imported PRs come from two major producers, Locatelli and Fulvi (see note below); the latter is the most authentic in terms of flavor, but both companies embrace tradition. Where does that salty flavor come from? Why, from master salters, of course, who rub new wheels in dry salt before sending them off to *caciare,* or ageing rooms.

Good matches: Grate this cheese over anything and it will add bedrock flavor. Try it on pastas, sautéed broccoli rabe, roasted veggies, salads, and pizzas. For a waker-upper, serve it in tiny cubes on a plate of antipasti.

Wine/beer: Go for Chianti. Alas, beer is a poor match because this is such an intense, fatty ol' dog.

DEMYSTIFYING PECORINO

One of the most confusing bits of terminology in our profession is the difference between "Pecorino," "Romano," and "Locatelli." In our Italian Market location, the three are often used interchangeably, but they should not be confused.

Of the three, the broadest term is Pecorino, which refers to any and all Italian sheep milk cheeses (the root of the word, pecora. means "sheep" in Italian). Every region of Italy produces Pecorino of all varieties, young and old, flavored with pepper or truffles, wrapped in leaves or buried in ash. But the most popular variety of Pecorino is Pecorino Romano. Romano is hard and salty, and is generally used as a grating cheese, although some of our, shall we say "heartier," customers swear it is the best snacking cheese around.

Locatelli is the most popular brand name of Pecorino Romano. Ironically, Locatelli, as well as most other producers, now make their cheese in Sardinia. In 1954, the governing agency controlling Pecorino Romano allowed milk from Sardinia to be used, owing to its high quality and low cost. There are currently three producers of Romano still working out of Rome. One of them, Fulvi, has been a store favorite for decades, and serves as the principal rival of Locatelli. Stop on in and taste them side by side!

-CHEESEMONGER HUNTER FIKE

PECORINO TOSCANO

ITALY, SHEEP'S MILK
PERSONALITY: Big and buttery, like a good bodyworker.

If Pecorino Romano (page 194) is the ultimate grating cheese, Pecorino Toscano is the quintessential table cheese. Unlike its cousin from Rome, Toscano is not a salty slayer. It's got just the right balance of butteriness, saltiness, and toasty nuttiness—like a good bucket of movie popcorn. In fact, it's just as addictive.

Italians serve Pecorino Toscano alongside a meal, not as a garnish or grated touch. The balance of flavor comes from pressing and salting this cheese when it's young, then massaging it with olive oil or, in some cases, tomato paste. The result is a firm, slightly granular wheel that is sold fresh (*fresco*) or aged (*staggianato*). Try snacking on it. The Italians have for centuries. In fact, Pecorino is thought to be the first hard cheese ever invented.

Good matches: Serve this for a traditional Tuscan lunch, alongside fresh fruit, salami, olives, bread, red wine, and a fava bean salad tossed with olive oil, lemon juice, and fresh rosemary. After dinner, it's great with walnuts, honey, and pears or apples.

Wine/beer: For aged Pecorino Toscano, choose a Tuscan red; otherwise go for a crisp white, like Sauvignon Blanc. A light lager works well, too.

PEPATO

ITALY, SHEEP'S MILK
PERSONALITY: A Pecorino with hot wheels.

Pepato yearns for motorcycle rides. Pack it in your saddlebags and take it on a picnic. Studded with peppercorns, this firm, salty character can endure a sultry afternoon, as long as you shield it from the sun. High winds, sea air—these things bring out its Sicilian accent and conjure the rugged coast where it's produced, deep in the heart of Pecorino country.

If you want to impress a date, just mention that Pepato originated in the first century, where it was reputedly made by Romulus, twin brother of Remus and founder of Rome. Pepato, meaning "pepper," is most similar to Locatelli (page 194), so if you want to add variety to pasta night, this is an excellent choice. It's also a good snacker, especially when you need a quick boost of protein.

Good matches: Pepato is a terrific grating cheese for pasta, especially if you like a cheese with zest. On an Italian snack plate, it's a good accent, especially alongside pickled vegetables and other Italian cheeses.

Wine/beer: Pair Pepato with a robust Italian red, like Chianti. Light beers and lagers add crispness. For a late brunch, this is a perfect cheese to serve with Bloody Marys.

PROVOLONE

ITALY, COW'S MILK
PERSONALITY: A sturdy old steady, always up for a tailgate.

Forget the tasteless slices of provolone you've grown numb to at deli counters. Real provolone pops with flavor, like a boxing glove to the tongue. The real stuff also hangs from the ceiling as it ages; it doesn't come in blocks. In southern Italy, this is the ultimate working man's cheese, and you won't find an icebox without a chewy morsel to pair with a hunk of cured meat. Even in South Philly, everyone's got their "Brovolone."

Like mozzarella, provolone comes from pulling cheese curds into feathery strands, then shaping them into tubes or spheres. If you look carefully at the texture, you'll notice fine onion-like layers. A little brine patted around the outside helps to draw out the moisture as the cheese cures, salami-style, hanging from a rope. Today, provolone is made throughout Italy and across the United States. Di Bruno Bros. carries Auricchio Provolone from Cremona and Grande Provolone from Wisconsin. If you like yours dagger-sharp, ask for Provolone *Stravecchio*, aged three years.

Good matches: Take this with you to the bleachers, along with a stick of pepperoni. Or, make a proper antipasti with olives, cured meats, pickled artichoke hearts, roasted red peppers, and baked garlic.

Wine/beer: Why not do like the original Di Bruno brothers did: sit out on your stoop with your provolone and a can of Schlitz? If you want to get all fancy (tongue in cheek), grab a Chianti in a basket.

RAGUSANO

ITALY, RAW COW'S MILK
PERSONALITY: A cowboy of the Italian cheese world—big, sinewy, and salty.

Buttered sweet corn. That's the taste of a well-aged hunk of Ragusano, a cheese that was once traded throughout the Mediterranean and now appears on a series of cheese-related postage stamps that celebrate Italian food culture. This hard, sweet-salty character can mingle with Pecorinos, but it's definitely made of cow's milk—something that's unusual in cheeses from this area. Most Italian island cheeses are made from ewes' milk, which imparts a savory flavor. In Sicily, Ragusano's bovine sweetness is considered a delicacy, especially when it's aged for more than six months. That's when it becomes succulent.

Ragusano begins as a stretched cheese, much like mozzarella. It's made from the raw milk of cows that graze on the herb-rich pastures of the Iblean Plateau, near the city of Ragusa. Once the curds are formed, they are left to ripen, then kneaded into giant loaves the size of cinder blocks, usually between twenty and thirty pounds. Fresh Ragusano is eaten as a table cheese, while the tangy, aged version is saved for special occasions.

Good matches: Few things are better than a simple supper of shaved Ragusano over sautéed broccoli rabe. Add some orecchiette pasta, plenty of chopped garlic, a hefty splash of olive oil, maybe even a little ground pork sausage, and you'll have a splendid supper.

Wine/beer: An aged Ragusano needs a full-bodied red. Try a Merlot. A citrusy beer works, too, but as far as hard cheeses go, this one tastes best with big wine.

REMEKER

THE NETHERLANDS, RAW COW'S MILK

PERSONALITY: Like Aristotle, a stargazer's delight with classic undertones.

This hard Dutch cheese is chock full of starry crystals staggered like Milky Ways across its cut surface. Although the makers use a recipe for Gouda, this cheese is so much more: in addition to toasted almonds and brown butter, you'll taste a deep and lingering fruitiness that's traditionally found only in aged Parm and Asiago. Note how quickly each bite melts on your tongue, like a lump of maple sugar.

Irene and Jan Dirk van der Voort make Remeker by hand on their farm in the Netherlands. They pasture a hundred Jersey cows and focus on sustainable, non-chemical-based agriculture. Note that Remeker is sold at two ages: seven months and sixteen. The latter, often referred to as Olde Remeker or *Oude* Remeker, is exceptional. Try to find a crunchier morsel for a more esoteric cheese.

Good matches: This is a great dessert, served with candied nuts and sliced green apple.

Wine/beer: Try a glass of lightly smoky Pinot Noir or Madeira. The cheesemakers serve Remeker with coffee, which is delicious. So is coffee stout.

A FIRST ENCOUNTER WITH REMEKER

Staring down into Jan Dirk's hand as he offered me a sample of his cattle's feed, I had to decide whether to take a leap of faith. "It's safe," he assured me as my fingers sifted through the coarse powder. I leapt.

Jan Dirk van der Voort feeds his herd a ground up mélange of nuts and spices, heavy on the hazelnuts and cloves. As he proved to me, it is safe for human consumption. But here's what is even more unique: Jan Dirk does not sear the horns of his calves the way most farmers do. After commissioning a study that compared the milk of horned and hornless cattle, he made a groundbreaking discovery: without the protection of their horns, cattle live in a constant state of anxiety. This alters the chemical structure of their milk.

Jan Dirk believes this chemical change may be linked to lactose intolerance in humans. To test his theory, he asks every lactose-intolerant guest, me included, to drink his milk. Not only was it the most delicious milk I had ever tasted, I had no trouble digesting it. This guy is my hero.

-CHEESEMONGER HUNTER FIKE

RONCAL

SPAIN, SHEEP'S MILK
PERSONALITY: Like Hemingway, scruffy
and sweet with an aroma of straw.

Northern Spain is known for its wine, its hard cheese, and its idiosyncratic inhabitants who love to feast and brawl. This rich sheep's milk cheese embodies that spirit, carrying the ruggedness of the landscape on which it's produced—a valley in the Navarre, the same province where Papa Hemingway set his novel *The Sun Also Rises.*

Roncal bears the distinction of being Spain's first name-controlled cheese, which means that the government regulates its production to ensure quality and preserve tradition. Villagers of the Roncal Valley have produced these firm, natural-rinded wheels since the Middle Ages, drawing on the milk of native, pasture-raised sheep. If you're a fan of Manchego (page 51), leave the door open for Roncal. Olivey notes crossed with herbaceous sweetness make this a perfect snack for book club night or a rainy day of reading and noshing on the couch.

Good matches: On a cheese plate, pair Roncal with Spanish olives, smoked meat, Marcona almonds, and pickled white asparagus. You can also grate it on salads or pasta.

Wine/beer: Go Spanish all the way with a red or white from the Navarre. A Tempranillo is especially nice. Otherwise, try a Pilsner.

SCAMORZA

ITALY AND UNITED STATES, COW'S MILK
PERSONALITY: With a name that means
"beheaded," this one's a retired mobster in
disguise.

You want a taste of tradition? Scamorza (pronounced Ska-MORT-sa) is the Scarface of the cheese world. It comes with a noose around it, let's put it that way. At Di Bruno Bros., these are made in-house from mozzarella that is salted and hung to dry for about a week. The exterior turns waxy, the inside tightens up, and you end up with an Old School Tough.

Italian grandpas tend to order Scamorza (sometimes they refer to it as *Manteche* or *Manteca*), a cheese that's popular in Lombardy, where it's often twisted into animal shapes around the holidays. Around here, Scamorza just looks like a big ear, or a broken face. Mild and chewy, this is basically mozzarella jerky. Keep it in the fridge for a snack, or put a hunk in your lunch for a reminder of days past.

Good matches: The concentrated milky flavor of Scamorza makes this an especially good cheese for grating onto pizza or lasagna. For an appetizer, slice it thinly and toast it on bread schmeared with pesto or sundried tomatoes. Purists eat Scamorza toasted on crusty Italian bread with a drizzle of good Tuscan olive oil and a crank of black pepper.

Wine/beer: Serve this with a big red wine at dusk, preferably with a symphony of crickets around a bocce court. An easy drinking beer works, too.

TESTUN AL BAROLO

ITALY, MIXED MILK
PERSONALITY: An Italian widow, shrouded in netting.

Few cheeses look as rustic as this one, packed in spent grape skins. Look for a big purple wheel with a gravelly textured surface. When you get up close, you'll see that the rind is made of Nebbiolo grape must, left over from making Barolo wine. Yes, you can and should eat that. In Piedmont, eating the rind is part of the experience. The grape seeds form a crackly crust, and the skins have a lovely raisiny quality that permeates the paste to form a deeply satisfying—some would say mesmerizing—boozy sweetness.

Testun is a firm cheese made from a combination of cow, goat, or sheep milk—sometimes all three. The texture is moist but crumbly. The taste: lush, complex, faintly tangy. The earthy sweetness calls to mind burial rituals, tobacco, and wine stomps.

Good matches: This is an impressive party cheese, in part because of its curious appearance. Set out a big hunk before or after dinner, and keep the accompaniments simple. You really don't even need bread.

Wine/beer: Serve this with a Barolo wine or a beer like Dogfish Head's Raison D'Etre.

ON FLAVORED CHEESE

In general, our mongers are not proponents of cheese with stuff in it. Sure, there are a few that we carry because demand is so high, like Cotswold and Lemon Stilton, but there are certain atrocities that we just refuse to bring into our offering. Mango and ginger Stilton? Who decided that it would be a good idea to take the king of British cheese and flavor it with a fruit from the tropics and a spice from the Orient? No, thank you.

Certain flavored cheeses, though, make sense, and have become staples of our product offering. Testun al Barolo is a classic example. This hearty mixed-milk cheese hails from the Piedmont, and is washed with Barolo wine. Then, the Nebbiolo grape skins, remnants of the wine-making process, are pressed into the rind for additional flavor and a striking aesthetic. Because both cheese and wine are made in the same area, the grape skins serve to amplify the otherwise subtle hints of terroir in the milk. Logical and delicious!

—CHEESEMONGER HUNTER FIKE

TRUGOLE

ITALY, COW'S MILK

PERSONALITY: Your basic Italian lumberjack, hard-working and bold.

"Midnight snack" is the first phrase that comes to mind when someone mentions Trugole. It's a sharp, affable cheese with a lingering taste of caramelized onions. The texture is not unlike aged provolone, but the taste is more characteristic of Parm or Asiago, two cheeses with fruity sweetness. It's exactly what you want in a table cheese, or at night when you're rummaging around for something to convert a turkey sandwich into a small miracle. In a word, this cheese is versatile.

Trugole (pronounced True-GOH-lay) comes from the foothills of the Alps in Italy's Piedmont region. Wheels are aged for sixty days and rubbed daily with a brine solution to add moisture and enhance flavor. The name refers to a particular pasture where Alpine cattle graze, a mountain meadow surrounded by firs. Dream your Wagnerian dreams.

Good matches: Trugole is great for a tailgate hamper (page 205) or a ploughman's lunch. Set it out with cured meats and pickles, along with bagel chips or garlicky flatbread. It's also a good cheese to tuck into casseroles and quiches. Try it in Tomato and Pancetta Strata (page 203).

Wine/beer: Pour a glass of Chianti or Pinot Noir, or serve a nut brown ale or lager.

TOMATO AND PANCETTA STRATA

Here's a remedy for those stale baguette rounds you have left over after a party: make strata. It's a savory bread pudding, and if you assemble it before bed and pop it in the fridge, the bread will soak up all the eggy goodness and become very fluffy when you bake it the next morning. This recipe calls for specific cheeses and ingredients to make a very presentable dish for company, but you can always substitute whatever cheese lumps and veggies you have on hand. Note the variations listed at the bottom of this recipe.

SERVES 6 TO 8

Unsalted butter, as needed
½ pound pancetta, thinly sliced
5 cups cubed stale baguette or crusty bread
½ pound Trugole, grated or cubed
¼ pound Parmigiano Reggiano, grated
½ cup chopped scallions (white and green parts)
½ cup basil leaves, sliced into ribbons
1 medium red pepper, chopped
10 large eggs
4 cups whole milk
1 tablespoon Dijon mustard
1 teaspoon salt
2 large Roma tomatoes, sliced

Variations

- Cheddar, ham, apple, sautéed onion
- Brie, sautéed mushrooms, fresh chives
- Ricotta (spoonfuls), pesto, roasted red pepper, sun-dried tomato
- Goat cheese, bacon, and roasted veggies (mushrooms, onions, and zucchini)

Butter a 9 x 13 x 2-inch baking dish.

Heat a skillet over medium-high heat and fry the pancetta until the edges are crispy, about 5 minutes. Drain on paper towels.

Spread the baguette cubes evenly across the greased baking dish, and crumble the pancetta over the top, followed by a sprinkling of the cheeses, scallions, basil, and chopped peppers.

In a large bowl, whisk together the eggs, milk, mustard, and salt. Pour the egg mixture over the bread mixture in the baking dish. Give the whole thing a stir with a large spoon, just so that the ingredients are mixed.

Add the tomato slices in rows across the top, and press them down into the casserole with the back of your spoon.

Cover with foil and chill for at least 4 hours or overnight.

Preheat the oven to 350°F.

Uncover the baking dish and bake the strata for 50 to 60 minutes or until the top becomes golden brown and the center appears set. Reserve the foil in case the strata browns too quickly. Serve hot.

TUMA PERSA

ITALY, RAW COW'S MILK
PERSONALITY: A perfect cheese for the lovelorn—strong and boozy.

Several years ago, an esteemed Sicilian cheese-maker named Salvatore Passalaqua opened a closet in an old house and found a cheese recipe that hadn't seen daylight in a hundred years. He set out to create a batch and ended up producing something wondrous, a kicky pro-volone-like cheese that finished with a grapey sweetness. He dubbed it *Tuma Persa*, or "lost treasure." The secret is a wine wash and a good rubdown with black pepper.

Passalaqua doesn't produce much of this cheese because he makes everything by hand. His output is something dinky, like fifty wheels per week, which means that tracking down a hunk requires diligence. But oh my stars, it's worth pestering your local cheesemonger. Tuma Persa is like tasting wine and cheese together for the first time. Put on a scratchy record and nurse your heartache.

Good matches: Bread and grapes are all you need. Serve at nostalgic moments or on ceme-tery picnics. If you can't find Tuma Persa, try Ubriaco.

Wine/beer: Sip a glass of Primitivo or, even better, Nero d'Avola made with the black grapes of Sicily. Because this is a wine-washed cheese, skip the beer unless you offer something raisiny.

UBRIACO

ITALY, RAW COW'S MILK
PERSONALITY: Your tipsy uncle around the holidays—sweet, buzzed.

Rumor has it that Ubriaco was invented when cheesemakers hid wheels in barrels of wine to avoid paying tax collectors. Back in the day, producers were required to hand over a tariff on every cheese sold. The system resulted in a wine-steeped style of cheese that is boozy, fruity, and much loved on cheese plates. The name "Ubriaco" literally means "drunk." Cheesemakers in Lombardy use various mari-nades, depending on what's local or in season: Chianti, Prosecco, Merlot.

For a summer party, try Ubriaco Prosecco. You can actually taste the effervescence in the rind. This is a cheese that buzzes on your tongue, turning crisp and spicy. For a jammier taste, pick up a wedge of Ubriaco Chianti or Merlot. All Ubriacos are firm with a Cheddar-like paste. Once you discover them, you'll want to slip slices into your lunch sack for a secret nip. If you develop a habit, be sure to try Testun al Barolo (page 200), which is packed in grape must.

Good matches: Slice up fresh or dried fruit, and set out an array of Italian cheeses. Candied nuts pair perfectly. So do pretzels.

Wine/beer: Serve Ubriaco alongside what-ever wine it's been drinking. Skip the beer on this one.

CHEESE BOARD: Emilio's Ultimate Tailgate Hamper

The official tastebuds of Di Bruno Bros. belong to Emilio Mignucci, a third-generation Di Bruno and trained chef. When he's not traveling the world in search of the next great cheese, he's stoopin' it South Philly-style with his old friends and neighbors in the Italian Market. On game day, he loves to put together these homey favorites to showcase Old World flavor. This board combines grandfatherly favorites, like fudgy Taleggio and boxing-glove shaped Caciocavallo, alongside new discoveries, from oniony Trugole to luxuriant Cremificato Verde Capra—a cheese that Emilio likes to call "New World Gorgonzola."

"I dream of enjoying these cheeses with thinly sliced Prosciutto Rotondo Dolce from Parma," Emilio says. "It's very rustic with a light gaminess from being cured the Old School way—on the bone for the first sixteen months, then finished off the bone for another six months. Exquisite."

Taleggio (page 158) or Quadrello di Bufala (page 152)
Trugole (page 202)
Caciocavallo (page 181)
Fiore Sardo (page 181)
Cremificato Verde Capra (page 234)

Suggested accompaniments: Crusty bread, assorted olives, roasted red peppers, long-stem artichokes in oil, grilled vegetables, pepper shooters (cherry peppers over-stuffed with sharp provolone, wrapped in prosciutto), Cacciatorini al Diavolo spicy salami, fig jam, and Acacia honey.

CHEESE 101: Charcuterie Demystified

Charcuterie refers to any smoked, cooked, or cured meat, including salami, bacon, and even *pâté*. It's a French term, which harkens back to an earlier era when preserving food often required salting and smoking. In the last decade, charcuterie has found a new band of devotees, making it impossible to walk through Brooklyn, or even South Philly, without stumbling into a rogue butcher carrying a ham under his arm. It also means that meat counters have started to look like aquariums with more mysterious eel-shaped, gill-thin offerings than ever.

The following guide provides a quick reference to some favorites, along with pairing suggestions for cheese. It's maddening to buy a quiet morsel and a random stick of salami, only to realize when you serve them on a cheese board that the meat is so chock full of peppercorns it steals the spotlight. Curtain, please! Here are some harmonious sensations:

Prosciutto di Parma

This ribbon-thin cured ham is salty and silky. Of the many kinds available, Di Bruno Bros. is partial to Greci & Folzani, the real deal from Parma. Pair it with Wise Guys (page 179), like Grana Padano (page 184), or with fresh mozzarella (page 34). A sweet Cheddar, like Fiscalini (page 169), works, too.

Duck Prosciutto

A slice of River & Glen's duck prosciutto looks like a lace hem. It's delicate enough to serve with triple crèmes, like Délice de Bourgogne (page 95), and even gentle blues, like Chiriboga (page 233). On the side: serve Amarena cherries for a wild tryst.

Dulce De Leche and Serrano Ham Appetizers

For a quick *amuse bouche* alongside Spanish cheeses, try topping crostini or Petit Toasts with a thin layer of Dulce de Leche and a ribbon of Jamón Sérrano. Cheesemonger Ian Peacock loves using this sweet-salty pairing to echo the burnt sugar notes that appear in Spanish cheeses like Abbaye de Belloc (page 40) and Idiazábal (page 49).

Finnochiona

This Tuscan-style salami is seasoned with fennel, making it a nice breath freshener for Stinkers (page 141). Have it sliced thin and serve it with cheeses that are soft and robust: try Taleggio (page 158) or La Serena (page 103).

Bresaola

Distinguished by its deep purple color, Bresaola is lightly seasoned air-cured beef. In northern Italy, it's served paper-thin on a bed of arugula with a drizzle of olive oil, lemon juice, and grated Parmigiano for an appetizer. Try it with Alpine cheeses, like Fontina (page 125) or Gruyère (page 127), which take well to cured meats.

Soppressata

A pungent Italian salami full of peppercorns and marinated in wine, this one needs big, fatty cheeses. Try those made with sheep's milk or buffalo milk, in particular. Moliterno (page 187) and Quadrello di Bufala (page 152) are good partners. Soppressata comes in two flavors: sweet or spicy.

Saucisson Sec

Similar to Soppressata but more finely ground, this rustic French salami is cured with red wine and peppercorns. Try it with Raclette (page 129), a mountain cheese from the Alps, or other firm French Mountain Men (page 117).

Speck

Lightly smoky and aged with juniper berries, this dry-cured ham is similar to prosciutto but less salty. Its complex taste is a good fit for many cheeses, including Quiet Types (page 39), but especially Mountain Men (page 117) and Stinkers (page 141). On a hot day, pair it with peaches and mozzarella (page 34) or mascarpone (page 32). It's also great wrapped around fresh figs.

Jamón Sérrano (Serrano Ham)

Spain's iconic dry-cured ham tends to be dry and nutty, a good fit for Spanish cheeses, like Manchego (page 51), that contain almond notes. Quince paste is traditionally paired alongside. Try Quiet Types (page 39) for other good matches. For an exceptional treat, try Jamón Ibérico, made from wild boar.

Good Pairings for a Charcuterie Board

On a cheese board with charcuterie, add pickles, mustard, horseradish, onion jam, olives, apple slices, radishes, and good bread. Tapenade (recipe, page 183) can be a great addition; lavender mustard (recipe, page 122) is wonderful for cleansing the palate and cutting through decadent cured meats.

CHAPTER IX

SUGAR MAMAS

(sweet, desserty)

When you want to lean on something rich and sweet at the end of a meal, these are the cheeses that call to mind butterscotch candy. Watch out, they're habit-forming and oh-so-friendly with after-dinner drinks. Though most of these mamas are Goudas, you'll also find a few sweet-smiling blues in the mix.

Basajo I Bleu d'Auvergne I Coolea I Evalon I Ewephoria I Gorgonzola Dolce I Blue Velvet Pudding I L'Amuse Gouda I Midnight Moon I Nylander I Old Gold I Prima Donna I Rogue River Blue I Rogue River Sushi I Wilde Weide Gouda I Cheese Board: Three Picnics I Cheese 101: How to Pair Cheese and Fruit

BASAJO

ITALY, RAW SHEEP'S MILK
PERSONALITY: The Mae West of blue cheese —big 'n' saucy.

Have you ever walked by hyacinths and detected a sweet, bubblegummy smell? Well, there's a luxurious blue cheese that beckons with the same seductive scent. Basajo, an uncommon little number from the Veneto, gets its lush floral sweetness from a long bath in Sicilian white wine and a rubdown with booze-infused golden raisins. Call this a dessert cheese with benefits.

As blue cheeses go, Basajo (pronounced Bah-SIGH-oh) is on the velvety end of the spectrum. It's got the consistency of rum-soaked cake, and its blue crags aren't pronounced. The salty rage that lurks in other blue wheels is tamed here, making this an easy lover for newcomers. Be sure to eat the plump raisins along the rind—each one is like the worm at the bottom of the Tequila bottle. Wheeee!

Good matches: Set this out after sunset and enjoy ample hunks amid fireflies and sweet wine. Because it's so distinct, Basajo doesn't need any accompaniments, except baguette.

Wine/beer: Serve flutes of Sauternes or, ideally, the wine in which this cheese is embalmed: Passito de Pantelleria. Barley wine or a garnet-colored Belgian Quadrupel would be fantastic.

BLEU D'AUVERGNE

FRANCE, COW'S MILK
PERSONALITY: Roquefort without attitude—supple and uncomplicated.

Most people think of Roquefort when it comes to French blues, but lo, Roquefort has a little sister and her name is Bleu d'Auvergne (BLUH-doh-vair-nyah). She's got kick, but it's short-lived—kind of like Lisa on *The Simpsons*. Don't look for too much nuance or feisty backtalk. When you want a creamy, slightly crumbly blue that looks rich and rustic, Bleu d'Auvergne is a good call. Be prepared for guests to fall all over it, particularly those who claim they "can't stand Roquefort." There's a grassy quality to the milk, which appeals to any fan of French cheese.

Bleu d'Auvergne is made in the fertile region of Auvergne in south-Central France, where families have produced it since the 1800s. It's pricked twice to encourage plenty of mold growth, and the "bluing," as its called, is notable for its lichen-green color that forms in bloom-like clusters. It's very different from Gorgonzola, which develops evenly spaced pinstripes. For a tasting of French blues, try this cheese against authentic Roquefort (page 92) and Fourme d'Ambert (page 236). They're surprisingly different in flavor but all very sumptuous.

Good matches: Serve this for dessert with biscotti and pears, or toss it into hot linguini with sautéed mushrooms and toasted walnuts or smoky bacon. Cheesemonger Dan Black believes in serving Bleu d'Auvergne on top of Delmonico steaks for Valentine's Day.

Wine/beer: Look for a dessert wine that's not too sweet when you serve Bleu d'Auvergne on its own: try Vouvray or sherry. A porter is excellent, but the magical love pairing has to be Pretty Things Brown Ale, a cheesemonger favorite.

COOLEA

IRELAND, COW'S MILK
PERSONALITY: Buttery, nutty, candy-like—
a Valedictorian Gouda.

If Gouda were crossed with sweet corn, it would taste like Coolea (Coo-LAY). This sweet-salty cheese is made from a traditional Dutch recipe, but it uses lush Irish milk. Cut into it, and you'll notice how cleanly it slices without flaking or crumbling. No yellow dye is added; Coolea's golden hue reflects the quality of milk used by cheesemakers Dicky and Sinead Williams of County Cork. The couple pastures their cows, which accounts for high levels of beta carotene in the milk, hence the sunny color.

Recently, this cheese nabbed a lot of attention at the British Cheese Awards where it won Best Irish Cheese. If you're a fan of sweet, nutty Goudas like L'Amuse (page 216), you'll appreciate the richness of this cheese. If you've been raised on Gouda in red wax, you're in for an unbelievable treat.

Best matches: For game night, set out a wedge of Coolea alongside a bowl of caramel-corn and candied nuts. For something more refined, serve this for dessert alongside toasted almonds, thinly sliced apples or pears, and oat crackers.

Wine/beer: Grab a roasty, malty beer, like Yards Extra Special Ale, or pour everyone a dram of sherry in Grandma's teardrop crystal glasses.

EVALON

UNITED STATES, RAW GOAT'S MILK
PERSONALITY: The Gouda prodigy of
America, freakishly delicious.

No one in the dairy world will ever forget how 25-year-old Katie Hedrich won the U.S. Cheese Championship in 2011. Her yet-unknown raw-milk goat cheese, Evalon, scored 99.06 points out of a possible 100, making her one of the most talked-about cheesemakers among the lacto cognoscenti. Hedrich, the daughter of Wisconsin goat farmers, had recently graduated from college with a marketing degree, but a family trip to Holland got her hooked on Gouda. She came home, enrolled in a program for cheesemakers, and started making some bad (as in good) cheese.

Evalon tastes like spun honey. It's sweet; it's smooth; it does not have the acidic lilt of a goat cheese. Put a slice on your tongue and it melts, releasing nutty notes typified by aged Goudas, but then—hello, dancer!—an unexpected fruitiness unfurls on the finish, calling to mind a sprightly Asiago. For cheese geeks, Evalon is a must-try. Although there are some great Goudas on the market, few are made with this much precision and imagination. Every wheel is remarkably consistent and delicious.

Good matches: On a cheese board, pair this with some caramelized pecans or apple slices. Otherwise, this showpiece needs little in the way of accompaniment.

Wine/beer: Try a dry Riesling or a nut-brown ale.

EWEPHORIA

EWEPHORIA

HOLLAND, SHEEP'S MILK
PERSONALITY: A sweet tooth's lifelong dream, a cheese that tastes like butter-scotch.

Most people who enter into a relationship with sheep's milk cheese expect a salty hunk: think of your Pecorinos from Sardinia, your Manchegos from La Mancha. These hard, earthy cheeses can be addictive, but they often require a sugary sidekick, like honey or quince paste, to offset their briny temperaments. And sometimes they're a bit gamey.

Ewephoria is all brown sugar. It was created in part by a Seattle importer who wanted a sheep's milk cheese to please the American palate. A Dutch dairyman in Friesland offered to make an aged Gouda using sheep's milk. After ten months of ageing, these wheels are so sweet they taste like pineapple upside-down cake. A freshly cut wedge of Ewephoria smells like rum and tastes—I kid you not— faintly of pineapple.

Good matches: Play off the butterscotchy notes here with a dish of toasted almonds, hazelnuts, popcorn, or pretzels. For an elegant dessert, serve nut brittle and sliced green apple. Dried figs, dates, and apricots also pair well.

Wine/beer: A glass of sherry or a pint of stout or porter works beautifully alongside this cheese. Try a coffee stout.

GORGONZOLA DOLCE

ITALY, COW'S MILK
PERSONALITY: A blue cheese in kitten heels.

Goopy. That's the first word that comes to mind when someone mentions Gorgonzola Dolce, Lombardy's most beloved cheese. Bring a slice to room temp, and it turns to ice cream cake, melting into moussey oblivion. The taste should be just as desserty, sweet and unctuous. Emilio Mignucci of Di Bruno Bros. says it reminds him of chocolate-covered cherries. After a big Italian dinner, this double-crème serves as a perfect interlude between the last savory bite and the first round of sugary espressos.

In blue-cheese circles, Gorg Dolce is viewed as a tabby cat. It's mild, in part because it's only aged a few months. Originally, this cheese was made in the little town of Gorgonzola, outside of Milan, a spot where shepherds led their cows to rest after they descended from high pastures, but today it's produced by about fifteen different manufacturers, and the town of Gorgonzola has become—woe is me— a suburb! Quality varies among Gorg producers, so always ask for a taste. Seek out the Mauri label. We think it's especially goopy.

Good matches: On a dessert plate, serve Gorgonzola with honey and ripe pears, or drizzled with Amarena cherries in syrup. For an appetizer, schmear it on crostini with a layer of smoky speck. Or do the unthinkable: make Blue Velvet Pudding (page 214).

Wine/beer: Asti Spumante, Moscato, or a Barbaresco are all ideal wines, depending on how much sweetness you like. Veer toward lighter styles of dark beer, like porters, or for something pitch perfect: a bottle of Balladin Nora, an Italian ale spiced with orange peel.

BLUE VELVET PUDDING

Blue cheese and chocolate have a strange affinity for one another, kind of like David Lynch and dark highways. In this pudding, which is crossed between soft custard and a thick *pots de crème*, something amazing happens. Gorgonzola noir? If you want a very forward bluesy note, add another tablespoon of blue cheese. In my opinion three tablespoons is perfect—subtle but distinct. Some people may not even be able to tell you what's in this dessert if you don't give away the secret. Be sure to use Gorgonzola Dolce (page 213), not Piccante. You can also use Cremificato Verde Capra (page 234).

SERVES 6 TO 8

FOR THE PUDDING:

12 ounces semi-sweet chocolate chips

2 cups half-and-half

6 egg yolks

3 tablespoons Gorgonzola Dolce, softened

FOR THE GARNISH:

½ cup pistachios, shelled

¼ cup Turbinado sugar

½ cup halved green grapes

½ cup halved red grapes

For the pudding: in a double boiler, gently stir the chocolate and half-and-half together over medium heat. Do not boil. Once the chocolate melts and the mixture is smooth, set the pan aside to cool briefly.

In a blender, combine the egg yolks and Gorgonzola Dolce on low speed until smooth. Leave the blender running and carefully remove the lid. Pour the chocolate from the pan in slowly. The key is to combine the two mixtures without making scrambled eggs, so do not stop the blender while it's whirring. Blend until smooth.

Return the mixture to the double boiler and gently heat it, stirring constantly with a wooden spoon, about 8 to 10 minutes. It will thicken gradually to the consistency of gravy. Remove the pan from the heat and strain the pudding through a mesh sieve into a glass or metal bowl to remove any lumps. They're not your fault.

If you prefer to make individual servings, ladle the mixture into ramekins or teacups before chilling. Otherwise, put the bowl straight into the fridge to chill for at least two hours.

For the garnish: Toast the pistachios in a small skillet over medium heat for 5 to 7 minutes. Add the sugar and allow to melt, then toss to coat the nuts. Continue to cook, stirring frequently for 4 to 5 minutes, then place on a lightly greased cookie sheet to cool. Add the grapes and nuts to the pudding just before serving.

L'AMUSE GOUDA

HOLLAND, COW'S MILK
PERSONALITY: An old sweetheart, bejeweled and bedazzling—full of crystals.

This amber beauty has only been available in the United States for a few years, and already it's become a much-requested dance partner. Look for its golden glow in the cheese case; the butterscotch paste and tiger-orange wrapper are distinct, and so are the snowy flecks of tyrosine that crunch between your teeth. These amino acid crystals, visible along the cut surface, evolve as the cheese ages over a two-year period.

L'Amuse Gouda is the specialty of a famous "Gouda midwife" named Betty Koster, who owns the L'Amuse Cheese Shop just outside of Amsterdam. Koster selects the wheels from a nearby cooperative, then uses her expertise to mature the wheels at a slightly warmer temperature than most caves, thereby creating a product all her own. You'll taste burnt sugar, toasted nuts, even a little bacon. Simply glorious. No other Gouda tastes quite like this old queen.

Good matches: On a holiday cheese plate, pair this with nut brittle or a dish of shelled pistachios, toasted almonds, and dried cranberries. After dinner, serve L'Amuse with almond biscotti and dessert wine.

Wine/beer: Serve with Madeira, Amontillado sherry, or any wine with a raisiny quality. For beer, pick something toasty and malty.

MIDNIGHT MOON

HOLLAND, GOAT'S MILK
PERSONALITY: Think Pink Floyd on Gouda, sweet and psychedelic.

Midnight Moon doesn't need a lot of introduction. If you like salt caramel, you're done. If you're a Cheddar head, you're done. While this cheese is technically of the Gouda ilk, Midnight Moon exhibits more brown butter sweetness than most year-old wheels in this category. It's dense and chewy, with little amino acid crystals that crunch pleasurably under your teeth.

Midnight Moon is made in Holland, then imported by cheese doyenne Mary Keehn of Cypress Grove (the mother of Humboldt Fog, page 74). People who claim to be goat-cheese averse rarely recognize that this baby comes from our bearded caprine friend. Be careful: it's freakishly addictive. In 2002, it was awarded Best New Product at the Fancy Food Show.

Good matches: This is a great one for the cheese plate, especially alongside dried apricots, candied almonds or pecans, and green grapes. For dessert, try serving it alongside nut brittle.

Wine/beer: For a spectacular pairing, try Midnight Moon with Dogfish Head's Midas Touch, a cross between mead and barleywine that is spiced with honey and saffron. It would also work with a stout or porter. Otherwise, try a jammy red or a dessert wine.

NYLANDER

HOLLAND, RAW COW'S MILK
PERSONALITY: A Narnia-like Gouda that's
the stuff of legends.

Let's talk about Jersey cows for a moment. Their
high-fat milk makes beautiful butter and cheese.
When that milk is left unpasteurized and when
those Jerseys have been grass fed on organic pasture, the flavor and texture together are pretty
much ideal. That's the basis for Nylander
(rhymes with "highlander"), a Gouda with so
much TLC in its production that Di Bruno
cheesemongers still wax poetic about particular
wheels in the same way that sommeliers crow
about vintages. Mention Nylander around
cheesemonger Hunter Fike, and he'll swoon.
"Like cream and eggs, like sweet custard," he'll
tell you, "but that was the first wheel. Let me
tell you about the second wheel. . . ."

Tasting a cheese like Nylander against a
commodity Gouda wrapped in wax is a good
way to sense how a particular cheese style can
vary. One is the result of careful artistry and
land stewardship, the other comes about
through mass production. Both can be satisfying
in different situations, but there's no doubt that
they will differ in terms of complexity. Nylander, which is made by Otto Jan Bokma in north
Holland, is nuanced—nutty-sweet and rustic
with changing notes like switchbacks in a
stream. It's the kind of cheese you might see in
a Dutch Master painting, rustic and ochre, lovingly rendered into a luminous moon.

Good matches: Eat this rare cheese straight
up. A dish of unshelled nuts and some yellow
apples are all you need.

Wine/beer: Because wheels of Nylander tend
to vary, always taste a sample before you consider a pairing. A pint of stout or a glass of
Madeira will probably serve you best.

OLD GOLD

UNITED STATES, RAW COW'S MILK
PERSONALITY: The locavore's dreamboat, a
big cheese from a tiny herd.

This beautiful aged Gouda from Lori Sollen-
berger in central Pennsylvania is sharp and
bright with just a twinge of caramel. It's the
kind of cheese you crave before bed or even for
breakfast, alongside toast and coffee. The flavor
notes swing low and savory, then bend into
grassy sweetness. The striking golden color
appears naturally, a sign that Lori pastures her
Jerseys—since cows can't digest beta carotene, it
appears in the milk and, naturally, the cheese. A
year of ageing concentrates the hue.

One thing that's special about Hidden
Hills's Old Gold is that it comes from a small
herd (at last count, Lori had eight cows). Most
traditional Goudas come from dairy cooperatives in Holland where milk is mixed from
many farms. The cheese can be excellent, but
it's a very different kind of experience from
tasting a product made from a single set of
cows. Because Lori knows her herd well, she
tweaks her recipe to fit their production cycle.
In this case, she uses only summer milk, when
the grasses are the sweetest, and she adjusts her
recipe to fit the changing complexity of her
milk. If you try this cheese from one year to the
next, or even from one wheel to the next, you
can learn a great deal about nuance and terroir.

Good matches: Savor this cheese. Try to
notice the flavors, how they swell and shift. If
you add an accompaniment, keep it simple with
some sliced apples or almonds.

Wine/beer: Tröeg's Javahead Stout from Har-
risburg, PA is the quintessential pairing here.
Notes of oatmeal, cocoa, and coffee pick up on
the subtlety of this cheese. Try a glass or
Madeira or sherry.

PRIMA DONNA

HOLLAND, COW'S MILK
PERSONALITY: The Miss America of Gouda-style cheeses—big flavor, wide appeal.

If the characters on *Friends* had hosted more cheese parties, you can be sure that Prima Donna would have become a household name. At Di Bruno Bros., this is one of the most requested wheels, and the reason is obvious. It's a cheese that can dance, put on a one-piece and look gorgeous, and smile in an evening gown. No, really, it sparkles—those are little crystals of an amino acid called tyrosine—and you're right, Prima Donna does taste like butterscotch candy! It's also light on fat (38%), so it's technically not even a Gouda, which requires 48% butterfat.

Prima Donna combines the flavor profiles of Gruyère and Parmigiano to play up the nutty, sugary notes that Americans tend to love. In Holland, it's aged at least a year before it's released, making for a cheese that's almost as good as salt caramel. Is it as complex as some of the fine aged Goudas in this chapter? Perhaps not, but for an indulgence that's light on fat and fairly easy on the wallet, this is a good cheese to keep in your stash.

Good matches: Before the game, after the game: Prima Donna with honey-roasted nuts.

Wine/beer: Pick a big red, like a Merlot or Cabernet Sauvignon. This is an exceptional cheese to pair with beer; try a saison or, for dessert, a coffee porter.

ROGUE RIVER BLUE

UNITED STATES, RAW COW'S MILK
PERSONALITY: A rumpled boyfriend with pear brandy on his breath and leaves stuck to his sweater.

If you're the kind of person who spends a lot of time daydreaming about blue cheese or even a little time thinking about it, you need to know about Rogue River Creamery. The company hand-makes a dozen different blues, and this one is their grand champion. It's THE cheese to buy if you need to impress a date or that person's parents. It's snow white and very pretty, first of all, and it's wrapped in brandy-soaked grape leaves that have been harvested from the Rogue River Valley, just behind the creamery. This, my love, is one sweet-smelling and sweet-tasting cheese.

In 2011, Rogue River Blue won the equivalent of the cheese Oscars in the United States, so finding it can require a bit of a chase. I sense you like a chase, though, if you're reading to this second paragraph. Now go tell a cheesemonger that your life depends on this cheese, and he or she will probably be able to scare up a secret hunk in the back. If you are offered another blue by Rogue River, specifically a wedge of Cave Man Blue or Rogue River Smokey (page 239), close your eyes and say yes.

Good Matches: A cheese this good doesn't need much to go with it. Treat it like a great Roquefort—which inspired Thomas Vella, the original cheesemaker who started Rogue River Creamery—and slice up a ripe pear. A dish of toasted walnuts is a nice foil.

Wine/beer: Give this puppy a nice big red: a juicy Cab or Syrah, or even a port. Weyerbacher's Blithering Idiot is an exquisite coupling, if you are not opposed to the sweet kick of a barleywine. Otherwise, grab a stout.

ROGUE RIVER SUSHI

This appetizer, designed by cheesemonger Rocco Rainone, is a fun way to kick off a BBQ, and you can easily make it ahead or double the recipe. The combination of smoked blue cheese, salty cured ham, and sweet *membrillo* (also known as quince paste) is eye-opening, and the membrillo really does look like raw tuna at the center of a sushi roll. If you can't find Rogue River Smokey Blue (page 239), try Strathdon Blue (page 240).

SERVES 4

4 ounces Surryano ham or prosciutto, thinly sliced

5 ounces Rogue River Smokey Blue, at room temperature

4 ounces membrillo, cut into two ¼-inch strips

Tear off a 12-inch length of plastic wrap and spread it on your counter or cutting board. On it, arrange the ham length-wise so that the slices overlap each other. Trim the ends with kitchen scissors so that you have a rectangle that resembles a sheet of nori.

Using a butter knife, spread the blue cheese across the ham, leaving about ¼ inch on all sides. If the cheese doesn't spread easily, you may need to dampen your fingertips with water and gently press it into a thin layer.

Arrange the membrillo strips in a single line along the width of the roll, about an inch from the edge closest to you. Starting with the edge closest to you, form a tight roll, using the plastic wrap to hold all the ingredients in place.

Keep the roll in plastic wrap and refrigerate for at least 30 minutes, or until the log feels firm. Then remove the plastic, place the roll seam-side down on a cutting board, and slice into 8 pieces. Serve cut-sides up on a platter, like sushi.

WILDE WEIDE GOUDA

HOLLAND, RAW COW'S MILK

PERSONALITY: The Walt Whitman of Goudas, full of wild sweetness and wild grasses.

Jan van Shie and his wife Roos produce this bright, floral Gouda on an island that is one square kilometer. While most Gouda has become a commodity product, Wilde Weide represents small-batch cheesemaking at its finest. Jan and Roos are the sixth generation to farm their land, and the care they put into producing organic raw milk cheese from their herd of Montbéliarde and red Friesian cows is evident in every wheel. They produce fewer than twenty-five per day.

When you taste Wilde Weide, look for balance. Sweetness meets savory somewhere in the middle. Daphne Zepos, who discovered this Gouda and began importing it, points out the "whiskey quality" that develops in this cheese after fifteen months. The flavor profile is more scotchy than butterscotch—think of wood, burnt caramel, citrus peel, wildflowers. It all adds up to the true meaning of Wilde Weide: *wild meadow.* This is a cheese for poetry readings.

Good matches: Serve Wilde Weide with fresh or dried fruit and caramelized pecans.

Wine/beer: The mix of flavors in this cheese is best paired with beer or whiskey. Try Abita's Pecan Harvest Ale or la Chouffe, a Belgian Strong Pale Ale.

CHEESE BOARD: Three Picnics

All of these selections are easy to pack, and they store well as long as you keep your picnic basket out of the sun and let the softies sit on ice packs. Stow a blanket, grab a bottle of wine, and toss in some berries, apples, honey, and baguette. Voilà: you have just made yourself irresistible.

The Call of the Forest: Leaves, 'Shrooms, and Straw

Pick up a leaf-wrapped Banon (page 88), a 'shroomy Camembert (page 46), and a sweet hunk of Evalon (page 211) or Wilde Weide Gouda (page 220), which translates to mean "Wild Meadow." A hunk of sweet Valdéon (page 240) wrapped in brandy-soaked grape leaves is the perfect finish.

Under the Stars: Romantic Cheeses

Start with a 2-person crock of Saint Marcellin (page 108) or a lush cake of Harbison (page 96), then meander on to boozy Ubriaco (page 204), followed by a golden snap of Ewephoria (page 213). To finish: how about a breath-freshening bite of Pecorino Ginepro (page 191) or a sensual morsel of Gorgonzola Dolce (page 213)?

Lunch on the Beach: Salt and Sea

If you're packing shrimp, take along Pantaleo (page 56). If you want a coastal beauty that will shimmy onto bread: Humboldt Fog (page 74). Beecher's Flagship Reserve (page 164) is the must-have sweet-salty Cheddar, and no beach picnic would be complete without a lump of Strathdon Blue (page 240) or Point Reyes Original Blue (page 239).

CHEESE 101: How to Pair Cheese and Fruit

Most berries and stone fruits bed down with cheeses just beautifully, but occasionally you'll discover an off pairing. For the world's best guide to working with flavors, check out *The Flavor Thesaurus,* by Nikki Segnit. Or, just follow some of these tried-and-true combos.

Berries

The acidity in raspberries and strawberries helps cut through luxurious cheeses, especially Vixens (page 87), and tempers the tang in fresh goaty numbers. Brambly blackberries are especially nice with rustic leaf-wrapped cheeses, like Banon (page 88) and ash-rolled dandies, like Monte Enebro (page 78). Blueberries are strangely wonderful with sweet blues. Try Chiriboga (page 233).

Cherries

Cherries are the great equalizer. Dried or preserved, they pair well with myriad cheeses, from Vixeny triple crèmes to bold Robiola (page 107) to fetching blues. In Spain and France, they're also favored for firm sheep's milk cheeses, like Petit Basque (page 58). Amarena cherries, imported from Italy in dark syrup, make a wonderful topping for Stilton (page 234) and Délice de Bourgogne (page 95).

Grapes

Look for tiny Champagne grapes to enliven this age-old pairing. Mild cheeses are especially fond of grapes, like Wensleydale (page 60) and Mrs. Kirkham's Tasty Lancashire (page 54). Otherwise, dark, plump grapes are a good palate cleanser, particularly for blues or hunky Mountain Men, like Fontina (page 125).

Peaches

Try peak-of-summer peaches with sumptuous cheeses, like mascarpone (page 32) or sweet blues, like Gorgonzola Dolce (page 213). Mozzarella (page 34) interlaced with fresh basil and sliced peaches reframes the classic Caprese.

Cook down bruised peaches into a compote (recipe, page 98) to serve with Red Hawk (page 154), Taleggio (page 158), and Harbison (page 96). Top grilled peaches with plush slabs of Quadrello di Bufala (recipe, page 153).

Apples and Pears

Sliced pears are great dunkers for gooey rounds, like Harbison (page 96) and Vacherin Mont d'Or (page 136). They're also a classic accompaniment for Camembert (page 46) and Roquefort (page 92). Try Asian pears with goat cheese; the floral quality is exquisite against delicate Capricho de Cabra (page 30) or zesty Shellbark Sharp II (page 80). Pair apples, apple pie, or apple-pepper jelly with clothbound Cheddars always and forever.

Figs

Like cherries, figs can dance to anything: they're a classic pairing for Stilton (page 234) and other blues, but they also do well with sheep's milk cheeses, like Manchego (page 51). Goat's milk cheeses adore them, fresh or dried. If you keep a jar of fig jam or Balsamic Poached Figs (page 182) on hand, you will always have a fitting condiment for a cheese board.

Oranges

Feta (page 70) and fresh goat cheese can be crumbled onto a salad of fresh oranges, purple onion, and dark olives. Serve marmalade with washed rind cheeses, like Winnimere (page 112). Candied orange peel is fantastic with Taleggio (page 158).

On Jams, Chutneys, Pastes, and Stewed Fruit

Many cultures have developed classic pairings around preserved or cooked fruits; caramelized sugars offset salty notes in cheese and play well off nutty tones. In Spain, quince paste (or *membrillo*) is almost always served with firm sheep's milk cheese from the Basque region. In fact, eating Manchego (page 51) or Idiazábal (page 49) any other way would seem strange. In England, chutney is often part of a winter cheese board, especially if it features musty clothbound Cheddars and blues. Chutneys often contain mustard seeds and onions, which impart a savory note alongside their sweet stew of apples, pears, or mango. A horseradishy wheel of Montgomery's Cheddar (page 172) is perfectly tempered by this. The Italians favor mostarda, a sweet, fruity delicacy spiked with mustard oil. It pairs well with fatty Italian cheeses and tastes bright and clearing.

CHAPTER X

PIERCED PUNKS

(intense, blue)

Blues will always be in a class of their own—they scare some people, but everyone knows they're the cool kids. If you think you're not thick-skinned enough to hang out with the toughs, think again. Some are very chill, especially when served with stouts and porters.

Bayley Hazen | Birchrun Blue | Bleu des Basques | Blu di Bufala | Dessert Grilled Cheese | Cabrales-Stuffed Dates | Cabrales | Chiriboga Blue | Colston Bassett Stilton | Cremificato Verde Capra | Cremificato with Chocolate and Artichokes | Fourme d'Ambert | Gorgonzola Piccante | Harbourne Blue | La Peral | Point Reyes Original Blue | Rogue River Smokey Blue | Strathdon Blue | Valdéon | Cheese Board: A Fireside Party | Cheese 101: How to Pair Cheese and Digestifs

BAYLEY HAZEN

UNITED STATES, RAW COW'S MILK
PERSONALITY: A true Vermonter, rugged and yet refined.

Few American blues can claim the complexity and all-around vivacious spirit of this Vermont blue from Jasper Hill Farm. If America has a Stilton, this is it, and yet you won't find the smoke-and-leather elements that turn British Stilton into a gentleman's cheese. Bayley Hazen epitomizes Vermont; it's twangy, herbaceous, nutty, grassy, and smooth, with a hint of licorice. The Kehler Brothers, who developed this cheese, have won every award possible, and their approach to farming and cheesemaking inspires everyone in the business.

The key to this cheese is, as always, milk quality and technique. The Kehlers practice sustainable farming, and they draw on knowledge they learned from apprenticing with the best in the business. French cheesemakers taught them the process, and affineurs (master agers) at Neal's Yard Dairy in London schooled them on maturation. Once you get a taste of this dazzling blue, you'll want to seek out Jasper Hill's other cheeses. Try Constant Bliss (page 94), Moses Sleeper (page 106), and Winnimere (page 112).

Good matches: Parker Pie in West Glover, Vermont has made a classic out of Bayley Hazen pizza, topped with apple slices and smoky bacon. Replicate it, or just enjoy the hell out of a good wedge and some baguette. If you want to play off the fennel-y notes in this cheese, try crumbling some over a fennel-apple salad dressed with walnut oil and a splash of fruity vinegar.

Wine/beer: Pick Zinfandel or Canadian ice wine. This is an excellent blue to pair with stout. Grab a Lancaster Milk Stout or, for a sterling Vermont-on-Vermont match: Dark Angel Imperial.

BIRCHRUN BLUE

UNITED STATES, RAW COW'S MILK
PERSONALITY: **An honest blue cheese in overalls, a Pennsylvania favorite.**

In Philadelphia, there's one blue cheese that you're bound to see on restaurant menus, and that's Sue Miller's wonderful Birchrun Blue. It's creamy, earthy, and grassy, with a twinge of mushroom, a characteristic common in cheeses from Chester County. Nearby Kennett Square is famous for being America's 'shroom HQ, so perhaps there's something in the soil. The terroir definitely cries out, "Champignons!"

Miller has an interesting story. She and her husband Ken are life-long dairy farmers, and when milk prices hit bottom a few years ago the family risked losing their land. One night, Sue went to bed with a brainstorm: she would learn to make cheese in order to add value to her milk supply. In the morning, she registered for a class, and within a few months she was making her first batch of blue. Di Bruno Bros. became her first customer, and Sue is now one of the area's most successful raw-milk cheesemakers. Look for her at Philadelphia-area farmers' markets, including the Market at Headhouse Square. Sue's Red Cat and Fat Cat (page 146) are also local faves.

Good matches: This cheese can swing sweet or savory. Figs and walnuts harmonize on a cheese plate, but you can also crumble Birchrun Blue into a leek-and-mushroom quiche or use it as a topper for a mushroom burger. In Philly, local confectioner Betty's Tasty Buttons uses this cheese to make Birchrun Blue fudge!

Wine/beer: Since this cheese is modeled after Stilton, try serving a glass of port or barleywine. In summer: a late-harvest Riesling. Porters and stouts make for dreamy combos, but one of the most interesting pairings is local to the Miller's farm: Victory Golden Monkey, a big Belgian ale brewed in Downingtown, Pennsylvania.

BLEU DES BASQUES

FRANCE, RAW SHEEP'S MILK
PERSONALITY: A royal weirdo, a blue blood with crazy taste (think *Grey Gardens*).

This earthy blue princess from the Pyrénées is firm, flinty, and full of intrigue. Like Roquefort, it's made entirely of ewe's milk, and yet Bleu des Basques is a completely different beast. Unlike Roquefort, which is extremely moist and neatly wrapped in foil, Bleu des Basques is dry and rustic, with a rind that looks like an ambient-mold pincushion. This is a sniffy cheese, lots going on here: shellfish, mutton, and grass, along with flavors of nuts and pine. What a fascinator.

Bleu des Basques belongs at a garden party in a blue-green frock with cat-eye glasses and a big knitting bag. She'll melt at a glance, but she loves deep conversation. Consider serving this on a marble platter to keep it cool; this one weeps in the heat. Like all ewe's milk cheeses, care should be taken not to let Bleu des Basques sit out for too long. The fat beads, oh how the fat beads.

Good matches: Break out the dried figs and walnuts, then put on some waltzes. For a contrast, serve this with a hunk of Ossau-Iraty (page 56) produced by the same French company, Onetik.

Wine/beer: This one needs a tawny port or barleywine. Try Weyerbacher's Blithering Idiot, a sweet thing full of dark fruit and spice.

BLU DI BUFALA

ITALY, BUFFALO'S MILK
PERSONALITY: A big, tatted-up cowboy with wild, animal-filled dreams.

Gorgonzola fans, clear the table. This unusual newbie from Lombardy doesn't have the centuries-old history of Italy's most famous blue, but its renegade spirit likes to ride neck and neck with the best. Made from the milk of water buffalo, this square-shaped cheese brings nutty, salty, tart, faintly gamey notes to the mat. For those who like more savoriness in their blues, this one wrangles deep, dark flavor. The texture? Well, think of calfskin. Buffalo milk is famously lush.

Blu di Bufala is produced by one of Italy's great buffalo farms, Quattro Portoni, near Bergamo. The two brothers who released this cheese to the world in 2005 also make Quadrello di Bufala (page 152) and Casatica di Bufala (page 93). These are great cheeses for decadent nights or for taking on a vision quest when you need a substitute for pemmican.

Good matches: This is a fatty, spicy cheese so it can stand up to other intense flavors. Try smoky meats, like speck, or fruit pastes. We can't recommend our Dessert Grilled Cheese enough (page 230).

Wine/beer: Pair this with a Moscato d'Asti or a leather-tinged shiraz. Tröeg's Mad Elf, a Belgian Strong Dark Ale, has complimentary notes: cloves, tart cherry, caramel. You could also try a smoked beer.

RECIPE

DESSERT GRILLED CHEESE

This is a rather glamorous sandwich, one that calls for some creative thinking, since the ingredient list is rather wild. It comes from cheesemonger Jamie Png, a twee Australian with a taste for buffalo milk, blue cheese, and chocolate. Jamie likes to use chocolate-cherry bread from Philadelphia's Metropolitan Bakery, which is divine (and can be purchased online), but you can easily substitute raisin-walnut bread. If you can't find buffalo butter, just use the regular kind. Jamie likes to serve this savory-sweet sandy with strong black tea.

SERVES 1

4 ounces Blu di Bufala, at room temperature
2 thick slices chocolate-cherry bread
½ firm Bosc or D'anjou pear, thinly sliced
2 to 3 tablespoons buckwheat honey
1 tablespoon butter, preferably Delitia
    Buffalo Milk

Preheat the oven to 350°F.

Spread Blu di Bufala on one side of each slice of bread, making sure to cover them from edge to edge. Lay the pear evenly across one cheesy slice. Drizzle with honey, then cover with the other slice of cheesy bread.

Wrap the sandwich in foil, and bake it in the oven for 8 minutes to meld the flavors and soften the pear. The cheese should melt but not liquefy, so keep an eye on it if your oven runs hot.

Melt the buffalo butter in a skillet over medium-high heat. Place the unwrapped sandwich in the pan and fry it on both sides until very crisp.

CABRALES-STUFFED DATES

Cabrales takes a lot of flack for being too spicy, but plug it into plump dates and wrap them in *guanciale*, or cured pork jowl, and this wild Spanish blue becomes one more vivid flavor. If you can't find guanciale, you can substitute bacon or prosciutto, but cured pork cheeks have a gaminess that pairs especially well with this cheese. Serve these at your next rodeo, your next rave. They're good warm or at room temperature.

SERVES 6 TO 8

12 Medjool dates
4 ounces Cabrales, at room temperature
12 slices guanciale

Preheat the oven to 400°F, and line a cookie sheet with foil.

Slice open the dates like hot dog buns and remove the pits, then stuff each cavity with about a tablespoon of Cabrales. Wrap a slice of guanciale around each date, rolling it tightly. You can use a toothpick to hold everything together, but you shouldn't need one as long as you place the wrapped dates seam-side down on the cookie sheet.

Bake for 5 to 7 minutes, until the cheese has begun to melt. Serve with a powerhouse stout.

CABRALES

SPAIN, COW, GOAT, AND SHEEP'S MILK
PERSONALITY: A big, bad blue—fierce
enough to make grown men cry.

Cabrales is a blue known for its horseradish-y heat. Behind the counter, it's also known as "the nine-volt battery." Don't be surprised if a bite of this cheese makes your eyes tear and your tongue go numb. Not all wheels are quite so fierce, so ask for a taste, but generally Cabrales is revered for its voltage. Russian customers like to use it as a chaser for vodka.

Beyond its fire, Cabrales is complex. After the initial kick, you'll notice a range of flavors that can veer from sweet to sour to bitter. The damp limestone caves, where the wheels are aged, contribute a wonderful minerality. Cabrales is considered one of the great cheeses of Spain. Its production is tightly controlled to ensure quality. Only cheesemakers in the tiny town of Cabrales produce this cobalt-blue namesake.

Good matches: Tame the flames with melon or sliced green apple. On a cheese plate, add peppery cured meats and other robust flavors, like Balsamic Poached Figs (see page 182), fresh endive leaves, honey, toasted walnuts, and pears. Cabrales-Stuffed Dates (see opposite page) make great party fare.

Wine/beer: Reach for a sweet pick-me-up, like rich stout, Port, or Sauternes. Hard cider is often served as an accompaniment in northern Spain. Don't be afraid to break out ice cold gin or vodka on a hot night.

CHIRIBOGA BLUE

GERMANY, RAW COW'S MILK
PERSONALITY: A saintly, soft blue that
embodies purity in taste and texture.

Arturo Chiriboga produces this topical salve of mellow blue butter in the town of Bad Oberdorf. It's a blue so chaste and delicate that you almost want to genuflect before eating it. When it first appeared at Di Bruno Bros. back in the spring of 2012, it spawned a flurry of tweets from excited cheesemongers. Few European blues are this quietly beautiful, without any gaminess or rough sparkle. Set a shard on your tongue, and it melts like butter. No, like vanilla ice cream.

Chiriboga Blue comes from a turn-of-the-century recipe for Bavarian Blue, a cheese known for its enticing texture and demure vibe. Cheesemaker Arturo Chiriboga adapted it to fit the milk of a dairy cooperative near his home in the Bavarian Alps. An Ecuadorian by birth, he relocated to Germany for love, which perhaps explains why his cheese has been dubbed by some "the perfect Valentine's Blue."

Good matches: Serve this with slices of crisp apples and a light-colored honey, or schmear it on baguette rounds and eat it naked. This is an excellent dessert cheese. Try it with thin wafers of dark chocolate.

Wine/beer: Serve a grass-kissed Grüner Veltliner or a flute of Champagne. For something desserty, pick out a porter or oyster stout.

COLSTON BASSETT STILTON

ENGLAND, COW'S MILK

PERSONALITY: The British royalty of blue cheeses, distinguished and earthy.

When you taste this particular Stilton, it's impossible not to think of a library—you get a whiff of leather, a hint of pipe smoke. This is the cheese Sherlock Holmes might have served on a wintry evening, a blue that reveals its mystery one flavor at a time. If you've succumbed to lesser Stiltons, with mango bits (horrific!) or grainy textures (don't tell us!), you'll appreciate this nuanced wedge from the tiny village of Colston Bassett. Only a handful of dairies in England are licensed to make true British Stilton, and Colston Bassett is the smallest producer of the bunch.

A true Stilton has a nubby natural rind and a biscuity crumb. The texture should be a twinge moist, and yet the wedge should break apart like a scone. Because this is such a nuanced cheese, you may taste slightly different notes from batch to batch. It's not uncommon to observe the following: licorice, flint, yeast, black pepper, wood, chocolate. Try comparing it to the highly prized raw-milk version of Stilton, called Stichelton (page 174).

Good matches: There's nothing better than a spot of Port and a wedge of good Stilton by the fire. Set out a dish of walnuts for cracking, along with a pot of chutney or honey, and some dark chocolate.

Wine/beer: Port or sherry is the classic pairing for Stilton; look for a bottle of Pedro Ximénez (otherwise known as PX). For something properly British, seek out J. W. Lees barleywine. A thick, malty Russian Imperial Stout can be brilliant; the same goes for Scotch—look for one that's big and peaty with caramel notes.

CREMIFICATO VERDE CAPRA

ITALY, GOAT'S MILK

PERSONALITY: A sexy diva of a goat cheese with blue satin stripes.

This may be our planet's most gorgeous blue cheese. It is glacier white with midnight-blue veins that are dagger straight. Then there's texture to consider. Have you ever fantasized about blue cheese pâté? Cremificato might as well be; it's sensual, a real seductress. Even the blue cheese-averse tend to be swayed.

On the nose, Cremificato calls to mind lemons and mushrooms. This is no ordinary blue; in fact, it's one of the few blues made from goat's milk, hence the slight acidity. It hails from a single maker in Lombardy, Ambrogio Arnoldi, who is well known for his beefy Taleggio (page 158). Cremificato is his newest creation, and it's surprisingly gentle—perfect for tweens and anyone yearning for a late-night blue cheese tryst.

Good matches: Ripe pears, dark grapes, walnuts or spiced pecans, and biscotti all make wonderful accompaniments. Because this blue is very light, owing to the goat's milk, Cremificato is a good choice before dinner. Consider serving your adventurous friends an appetizer of Cremificato with Dark Chocolate and Artichokes (page 235).

Wine/Beer: To start a party, try a sparkly Vouvray (a bottle of 2005 Vouvray Pétillant Brut from Domaine Huet is perfect, according to cheesemonger Hunter Fike). For a surprise, pick out a milk stout.

CREMIFICATO with CHOCOLATE and ARTICHOKES

This "salad" is one of those revelations that makes a roomful of people at a party stop, look at each other, and laugh with delight. The recipe, developed by cheesemonger Ian Peacock, is arrestingly vegetal and earthy with a wild range of textures. If you can't find long-stemmed artichokes, use a drained jar of artichoke hearts marinated in oil. Serve this as an appetizer or teaser, along with baguette rounds.

SERVES 4 TO 6

6 oil-marinated long-stemmed artichokes,
    thinly sliced into ribbons
¼ pound Cremificato Verde Capra, crum-
    bled
2 ounces dark chocolate, shaved or grated

Combine the artichokes, crumbled cheese, and grated chocolate in a bowl or a glass jar with a tight-fitting lid. Stir or shake until the mixture is well combined. The cheese should coat the other ingredients, creating a milky dressing of sorts. Serve at room temperature.

"Mind's Mouth" Pairings

The cheesemongers have a name for recipes like the one listed above; they call them snacks from the "mind's mouth." The term refers to a cheesemonger's ability to imagine unexpected pairings on the job. As cheesemonger Rocco Rainone explained, "We spend all day tasting cheese and studying the ingredients we carry on the shelves, so we're always inventing new combinations and trying to amaze each other with them." For other Mind's Mouth pairings, check out the recipes for Rogue **River Sushi** (page 219) and **Scharfe Maxx S'mores** (page 156).

FOURME D'AMBERT

FRANCE, COW'S MILK

PERSONALITY: The gamer's delight—an ancient blue once loved by Druids.

Mild, mushroomy, and medieval are the words that come to mind when someone mentions Fourme d'Ambert. Of France's many blue cheeses, this one tends to be the mellowest and least salty, and yet it's not without nuance. The smell is earthy, and the taste makes you lust for burgers or grilled portabellas, or both. Why not? The texture is creamy, spreadable. Try serving it at your next Solstice party.

Two thousand years ago, Fourme d'Ambert was made around the village of Ambert in central France. Today, it's mostly produced in factories, but the quality—particularly of raw-milk versions, if you can find them—is quite good, since government regulators oversee production. Look for half-moon slices that are alabaster in color with plenty of navy stippling. The rind is naturally nubby—you may find it to your liking, but don't hesitate to cut it off if it's not your thing.

Good matches: This is an excellent cheese for cooking. Toss it into stuffing, pack it into mushroom caps, or slather it on a bacon-mushroom burger. On a cheese plate, it pairs well with pears or green apples, along with walnuts and light-colored honey.

Wine/beer: Try a Loire Valley Chinon, Vin Jaune, or Beaujolais. This is a good cheese to serve with a lightly smoked beer.

A Blue for Every Mood

Blue cheeses are the misunderstood loners of the dairy case. The emphasis here is on "misunderstood" because people tend to think all blues are pretty much the same. That's like saying that all jazz or all punk music sounds alike. Hundreds, if not thousands, of blues are produced around the world, and they vary wildly in taste and texture. Here's a brief list of greatest hits for the blue-cheese beginner:

Sweet: Gorgonzola Dolce (page 213), La Peral (page 238)
Savory: Point Reyes Original Blue (page 239), Fourme
   d'Ambert (page 236)
Spicy: Gorgonzola Piccante (page 237) Carles Roquefort
   (page 92)

GORGONZOLA PICCANTE

ITALY, COW'S MILK
PERSONALITY: A blue cheese in stilettos.

When you walk through a piazza and see women in high heels passing briskly across the cobblestones, you can be sure they are thinking of Gorgonzola Piccante. Like the cheese, they tend to be firm in form and full of zest. Gorgonzola Piccante has always had its place at the Italian table: its versatility makes it a lovely snowcap for salads and steaks, and its rich history extending back to the tenth century makes it a touchstone for Italian families who have served it for generations.

Gentle palates tend to reach for Gorgonzola Dolce (page 213), which is mild and ultra moist, almost runny. The more aged Piccante version leaves a thick impression on the palate and finishes with a spicy flourish. The mold in both of these cheeses tends toward blue-green, rather than indigo or navy, which is common in other wheels that are inoculated with *Penicillium*. That's right, blue cheeses are pierced with needles, or spikes, creating fissures so that blue mold can form. Originally, this mold occurred naturally in caves, but today it's usually added at the beginning of the cheese-making process. The greenish blue veins in Gorgonzola are referred to as *erborinato*, meaning "parsley."

Good matches: Buckwheat honey is marvelous as a Gorg foil. So is fig jam. It's also great slathered onto a panini or burger, crumbled on top of a spinach salad, or stirred into a cream sauce. If you need a gutsy, inexpensive blue, this will give you plenty of bang for your buck.

Wine/beer: This needs a rowdy red, like a Barolo. Otherwise, veer sweet to offset the peppery finish; try barleywine, apple ice wine, or an apple schnapps, like Apfelkorn. Beer lovers, rev your chocolate stouts.

HARBOURNE BLUE

ENGLAND, GOAT'S MILK
PERSONALITY: A songstress, lyrical and wholly original—the Billie Holiday of blue.

A morsel of Harbourne is like a spring walk. The first bite is often floral—think lilacs, violets—then it turns woodsy and sweet, only to finish on a flinty note. You might also detect hints of citrus and licorice. The texture is dry, flaky, and reminiscent of feta, or as longtime Di Bruno cheesemonger Ezekial Ferguson once said: "It's like Astronaut Ice Cream."

Esteemed cheesemaker Robin Congdon of Devon, along with cheesemaker Ben Harris, produces this delight. Although this blue is highly sought after by cheesemongers, its existence is still something of a secret from the public. In part, this is because most seekers of British Blue ask for Stilton (page 234) or Stichelton (page 174), with good reason. They're gorgeous. Deviants recognize that a goat's milk blue from England is nothing short of anomalous. When they taste it, they are often stunned. As one British friend exclaimed when he ate this cheese for the first time, "Oh, sandy beaches! I'm in East Sussex!"

Good matches: Harbourne is an excellent cheese to eat with chocolate. Pick a dark bar of high quality, like Éclat, made in Philadelphia. Because this cheese is rather precious (read: spendy), you don't want to gussy it up with knick-knacks. Serve it alone in the afternoon, or make it the dessert of someone's dreams.

Wine/beer: Find an aromatic wheat beer, or something light and simple. Di Bruno cheesemongers favor Stouts Pilsner. A summery wine with mineral notes pairs well, too. A cheese this complex needs an understated pairing.

LA PERAL

SPAIN, COW AND SHEEP'S MILK
PERSONALITY: A sweet señorita with kid gloves.

Northern Spain is known for three blue cheeses, and La Peral is the gentlest one. You don't even have to like blue cheese to fall for La Peral. She's rich and flirtatious, a blue blood but without a whole lot of blue markings. Her sisters, Valdéon (page 240) and Cabrales (page 233) have more fire, which can be fun for those who enjoy spice, but if you want a blue to cuddle with? This is the luxuriant choice.

La Peral is made in the region of Asturias on Spain's northern coast. Picture rocky beaches, fishing villages, and lush pastures. There, a single family produces this beauty, using a recipe passed down through three generations. This cheese only appeared recently in the States, and it's much beloved by cheese geeks for its fudgy, slightly granular texture. Whenever I eat La Peral, I taste white chocolate on the front end and mushrooms on the finish, so you can swing sweet or savory in terms of pairings.

Best matches: On a cheese plate, serve this with fresh figs or tiny Champagne grapes. For an appetizer, spread La Peral on toasted baguette rounds and top with sautéed mushrooms or caramelized onions; serve with a dish of plump Spanish olives.

Wine/beer: Follow the season: in high summer, pour a Spanish sparkler or a Tempranillo; in winter, choose an Oloroso sherry. Otherwise, pick a dark beer with hints of chicory or chocolate.

How Blue Cheese Gets Its Color

I named the cheeses in this chapter "Pierced Punks" because they really are pierced. Cheesemakers puncture the wheels with needles in order to create air vents, not to inject mold, as many people suspect. The mold is actually introduced early in the cheesemaking process when a cocktail of *Penicillium roqueforti* is stirred into curds. Blue mold in cheese is harmless, but if the veins scare you look for a sample with very little "bluing," like Cremificato Verde Capra.

POINT REYES ORIGINAL BLUE

UNITED STATES, RAW COW'S MILK
PERSONALITY: A salty bloke, well-loved for his punchy attitude and burger-friendly vibe.

Year-round grass feeding makes Point Reyes Creamery a special place. The Holsteins that wander along Tomales Bay graze on pastures that are laced with sea spray, a detail that you can actually taste in this stunning cheese. As far as blues go, this one leans toward the salty end of the spectrum, much like Roquefort. But don't let that scare you. A salty blue is perfect for topping burgers and steaks, which is why you'll find this cheese on pub menus across the country.

At Point Reyes Creamery, farm duties are shared by members of the Giacomini family. When they founded Point Reyes Creamery in 2000, they brought Italian cheesemaking roots with them. That means they handle all of their own milking and produce a beautiful, briny wonder that is as stunning to look at (the blue veining is usually quite pronounced) as it is to eat.

Good matches: The big spice here loves a drizzle of light-colored honey. Serve with black grapes, oatmeal crackers, or wafer-thin gingersnaps, along with dried pears or fig jam. For an intriguing dessert combination, serve this cheese with Amarena cherries and a spot of dark chocolate.

Wine/beer: Try oatmeal or milk stout, or a glass of sherry or Sauternes.

ROGUE RIVER SMOKEY BLUE

UNITED STATES, RAW COW'S MILK
PERSONALITY: A burly, outdoorsy blue with bacon-like appeal.

Very few smoked cheeses make the cut at Di Bruno Bros., where the mongers frown on smoke flavorings, often used in commercial cheesemaking. Rogue River Smokey is special, however. This wonderful blue from the Pacific Northwest is cold-smoked over hazelnut shells to produce a creamy, caramel-tinged opus that is sharp and sweet. Under the delicate layer of smoky flavor, you can still taste milk—the sign of a good smoked cheese.

Rogue River Smokey is made at Oregon's Rogue Creamery, which was established in the 1930s. Although the business has changed hands, Rogue remains one of the all-time great cheese operations in the United States. The company produces about a dozen handmade blues, many of them award-winning. Something about the Rogue spirit makes this an especially good cheese for camping trips; it fulfills those morning bacon cravings, especially alongside pancakes.

Good matches: For a snack or fireside conversation piece, break out the hard liquor and candied pecans or walnuts. Fig cake, dried cherries, maple syrup, nut brittle, and even fudge all pair nicely.

Wine/beer: Play off the smoky-salty notes with a fruity lambic, a sweet-leaning whiskey, or oatmeal stout. Believe it or not, smoked beer works well with smoked cheeses. The folks at Rogue River Creamery recommend a glass of Cabernet Franc or Zinfandel.

STRATHDON BLUE

SCOTLAND, COW'S MILK
PERSONALITY: A beachcomber with gentle
eyes and a craggy smile.

Cheesemaker Ruaraidh ("Rory") Stone lives in
a converted brewery at the tippy top of Scotland. There, his herd of Ayrshire cattle munches
along the seacoast, and the salty mist that settles
on the grass finds its way into the cheese. Yes,
this is a blue for the beach. Not only does it
taste of saline and cream, there is something
rocky here—flint? slate?—that makes you feel as
if you have wandered into a sea cave. If you're a
fan of Point Reyes Original Blue (page 239), a
coastal creamy from California, try this one for
the sake of comparison. Both cheeses are lush
and briny, but Strathdon definitely has more
wilderness in its flavor profile.

Strathdon Blue showed up on the scene a
few years ago, and it's still morphing and
improving. It started as a crumbly bard, but in
recent years it's become a rich crooner. Careful
handling at London's Neal's Yard Dairy, where
this cheese is aged, brings out the best in it, in
terms of balance. Although this cheese might
look intimidating (avoid eye contact with the
furry blue pockets), Strathdon is surprisingly
mellow. It looks and tastes like a velvet asteroid.

Good matches: Pack a beach hamper full of
fresh fruit, bread, figs, and dark chocolate. On a
cheese plate, serve Strathdon with pears or
chutney, oat cakes, and caramelized pecans. If
you want a buddy cheese, add a hunk of Isle of
Mull Cheddar (page 170) for a gorgeous Scottish duet.

Wine/beer: A salt-tinged stout, like Exit 1
Bayshore Oyster Stout from Flying Fish Brewery,
is an extraordinary pairing. You can always lean
on Port, Scotch, or late harvest Riesling. Look
for plums, pears, or flint in the flavor profile.

VALDÉON

SPAIN, COW AND GOAT'S MILK
PERSONALITY: Elegant and assertive, a
spunky Spanish grandmother wrapped in
a heavy shawl.

Valdéon is one of the all-time great blue
cheeses from Spain, and it's always easy to recognize because it's wrapped in sycamore leaves.
The leaves keep the cheese moist and contribute to the flavor, which is peppery and
earthy with a sweet finish. Because Valdéon is
ripened in limestone caves, you may also detect
a faint minerality, a lovely quality, especially if
you choose to drape a wedge over steak.

In the blue cheese realm, Valdéon is considered one of the saltier selections, which
makes it a good fit for sweet pairings. It's often
compared to its sister cheese, Cabrales (page
233), a fire breather, but despite the fact that
these are both cave-aged blues from northern
Spain, they taste very different. Valdéon tends to
be a good gateway blue, ever popular, while
Cabrales attracts thrill-seekers.

Good Matches: This is a lovely capper for a
Spanish cheese plate, alongside Monte Enebro
(page 78) and Idiazábal (page 49). Serve it with
honey, dried figs, and Marcona almonds.

Wine/beer: Try a Riesling or an Oloroso
sherry, or swing toward barleywine.

CHEESE BOARD: A Fireside Party

If you can't find time to prepare a holiday feast, throw up your hands and head to the cheese counter. It's the best time of year to find unusual selections and seasonal treats to pamper your guests, and you can create an unforgettable cheese crèche. Skip chocolates on the pillow, and pick up an assortment of the following cheeses and special sundries for a fireside tasting. Or, celebrate with a pairing or two each night.

Brie de Meaux (page 89)
With pears or baked into puff pastry (see recipe, page 90)
Truffle Tremor (page 110)
With roasted chestnuts or hazelnuts
Vacherin Mont d'Or (page 136) or Winnimere (page 112)
With marmalade or candied orange peel
Midnight Moon (page 216)
With candied pecans
Sparkenhoe Red Leicester (page 173)
With dried cranberries and pistachios
Foja de Noce (page 184)
With honey and walnuts
Colston Bassett Stilton (page 234)
With dark chocolate

Suggested accompaniments: Dried or fresh fruit, Finnochiona (fennel salami) or speck (smoked ham), pâté, pickles, ginger thins, biscotti, plenty of baguette. If you're serving wine, offer Champagne, Pinot Noir, and Madeira or Tawny Port to cover all the bases. If you're serving beer, select something effervescent, like Duvel, to pair with the first three cheeses; a nut brown ale to accompany Midnight Moon and Sparkenhoe; and Imperial Stout to pair with the Pecorino and Stilton. A mellow Scotch would not be out of place, especially with the last four cheeses.

CHEESE 101: How to Pair Cheese and Digestifs

Few things are lovelier than ending a meal with a spot of cheese. The French have done it for years without any trauma to their collective girth, which suggests that indulging in a morsel or two of cheese after supper, instead of a brownie sundae, just might be better for all of us. In fact, eating cheese at the end of a meal is supposed to be good for your teeth. Thank you, food scientist Harold McGee, for that important dental insight.

For after-dinner inspiration, try ordering a cheese course for dessert next time you go out. The Fountain Restaurant in Philadelphia is famous for its cheese cart, which is wheeled to each table like an elaborate pram; the Gramercy Tavern in Manhattan offers an impeccable assortment which sits, veiled, on a slate in its tavern dining room, so that's it's impossible not to steal furtive glances. Cheese after a meal should be so exquisite; it should arouse desire.

Here are a dozen pairings for you to play with after dinner, and while I would like to say they are foolproof, I hope you'll seek the confirmation of a cheese-monger. Cheeses vary by season and change moods as they age. Like the best of us, they can bristle or lose energy without the right touch, so try to sample them and learn about their needs before you serve an ill-conceived match to a room full of bigwigs or even littlewigs.

Tawny Port

Port is the ultimate fall and winter spirit. While some may complain that it's too sugary, assure them that a good tawny is light and not too sweet. Its plumminess caresses the leather notes in Colston Bassett Stilton (page 234) and balances the salt in Point Reyes Original Blue (page 239).

Sauternes

This white dessert wine from Bordeaux tranquilizes ultra salty blues like Roquefort (page 92), its soul mate. Any French or Danish blue succumbs. You might also try Bleu d'Auvergne (page 210). This combination is a great way to finish a spring or summer meal, especially with pears.

Moscato d'Asti

Sparkly and sweet conjoin here, a magical touch for Gorgonzola Dolce (page 213). Make like the Italians and serve thinly-sliced biscotti for dunking, dipping, slathering, etc. You can also pair Vin Santo, a blended sweet wine from Tuscany, with Gorgonzola.

Sherry

Spanish cultures produce a variety of sherries, which pair nicely with their dry, flinty blue cheeses, like Valdéon (page 240), and buttery Spanish sheep's milk cheeses, like Manchego (page 51) and Idiazábal (page 49). Try serving these cheeses with an Oloroso sherry, which is moderately sweet.

Late Harvest Riesling

For something light and versatile, serve a clean-tasting Alsatian Riesling, or explore New York's burgeoning Riesling empire. This is a good choice for a cheese board that includes a variety of cheeses made from different milks. Choose from Monte Enebro (page 78), Morbier (page 151), Emmentaler (page 121), Piave (page 190), and Harbourne Blue (page 237).

Calvados

This amber spirit distilled from cider can be a welcome shift from sweet dessert wines. Because it's from Normandy, it loves Camembert (page 46), but it's also a beautiful accompaniment to Cabot Clothbound Cheddar (page 165) and well-aged Parmigiano Reggiano (page 189). Serve it outdoors around a fire.

Whiskey or Scotch

A soft mellow whiskey can harmonize with a butterscotchy Cheddar, like Cabot Clothbound (page 165), or pick up on the spirits in a leaf-wrapped Banon (page 88). An Irish whiskey likes a fudgy wedge of Ardrahan (page 142). Pair Scotch with Isle of Mull Cheddar (page 170) or a salty, flinty blue like Strathdon (page 240). A 14-year Oban is rumored to be the perfect mate for Humboldt Fog (page 74).

Stouts and Porters

Heavy, earthy stouts were made for cheese, especially blues and Goudas. Try a coffee stout with Ewephoria (page 213) or a hunk of L'Amuse (page 216). Oyster stout with a briny wedge of Strathdon Blue (page 240) is not to be believed. Chocolate stout heaps love on peanutty washed rinds—check out Red Hawk (page 154). If you need less horsepower, choose a porter.

Tea and Coffee

For those who don't care to imbibe, prepare a light-bodied green tea to serve with goat cheese, like Capricho de Cabra (page 30); the grassy notes will compliment each other. Smoky oolongs pair well with firm sheep's milk cheeses, like Berkswell (page 44), and caramel-rich Goudas. Earl Gray, with its bracing note of Bergamot, pairs with many strong cheeses, including blues. In Holland, coffee is a traditional pairing for aged Goudas, like Remeker (page 197).

APPENDIX

USEFUL BOOKS, WEBSITES, AND ORGANIZATIONS

The world is full of wonderful resources about cheese. The ones on this list were invaluable during the writing of this book. Many of them make excellent bedtime or kitchen table reading.

BOOKS

Beckett, Fiona. *Fiona Beckett's Cheese Course.* London: Ryland, Peters & Small, 2009.

Chartier, François. *Tastebuds and Molecules: The Art and Science of Food with Wine.* Toronto: McClelland & Stewart Ltd., 2010.

Dalby, Andrew. *Cheese: A Global History.* London: Reaktion Books, 2009.

Davies, Sasha. *The West Coast Guide to Cheese.* Portland: Timber Press, 2010.

Dorenburg, Andrew, and Karen Page. *What to Drink with What You Eat.* New York: Bulfinch Press, 2006.

Fletcher, Janet. *Cheese and Wine: A Guide to Selecting, Pairing, and Enjoying.* San Francisco: Chronicle Books, 2007.

Grescoe, Taras. *The Devil's Picnic: Travels Through the Underworld of Food and Drink.* New York: Bloomsbury, 2005. (See chapter 3 on Epoisses.)

Harbutt, Juliet. *World Cheese Book.* New York: DK Publishing, 2009.

Herbst, Sharon Tylor, and Ron Herbst. *The Cheese Lover's Companion: The Ultimate A-to-Z Cheese Guide.* New York: William Morrow, 2007.

Jenkins, Steven. *Cheese Primer.* New York: Workman, 1996.

Kaufelt, Rob. *The Murray's Cheese Handbook.* New York: Broadway Books, 2006.

Kindstedt, Paul. *Cheese and Culture.* Burlington: Chelsea Green, 2012.

Linford, Jenny. *Great British Cheeses.* London: DK Publishing, 2008.

Masui, Kazuka, and Tomoko Yamada. *French Cheese.* 3rd ed. New York: DK Publishing, 2005.

McCalman, Max, and David Gibbons. *Mastering Cheese: Lessons for Connoisseurship From a Maître Fromager.* New York: Clarkson Potter, 2009.

McGee, Harold. *On Food and Cooking.* New York: Scribner, 2004.

Michelson, Patricia. *The Cheese Room.* London: Penguin Books, 2001.

Mogannam, Sam, and Dabney Gough. *Eat Good Food.* Berkeley: Ten Speed Press, 2011.

Oliver, Garrett. *The Oxford Companion to Beer.* Oxford: Oxford University Press, 2011.

Roberts, Jeffrey. *The Atlas of American Artisan Cheese.* White River Junction: Chelsea Green Publishing, 2007.

Segnit, Niki. *The Flavor Thesaurus.* New York: Bloomsbury, 2010.

Slow Food Foundation. *Italian Cheese: A Guide to Its Discovery and Appreciation.* Milan: Slow Food Editore, 2005.

Thorpe, Liz. *The Cheese Chronicles.* New York: Harper Collins, 2009.

Weinzweig, Ari. *Zingerman's Guide to Good Eating.* New York: Houghton Mifflin Harcourt, 2003.

Werlin, Laura. *The New American Cheese.* New York: Stewart, Tabori, & Chang, 2000.

MAGAZINES
Culture
www.culturecheesemag.org

Cheese Connoisseur
www.cheeseconnoisseur.com

The Art of Eating
www.artofeating.com

WEBSITES
Cellars at Jasper Hill
www.cellarsatjasperhill.com

Cowgirl Creamery's Library of Cheese
www.cowgirlcreamery.com/library.asp

Culture Magazine's Online Cheese Library
www.culturecheesemag.com/cheese-library

Cutting the Curd (podcasts by Anne Saxelby)
www.heritageradionetwork.com/programs/14-Cutting-the-Curd

Neal's Yard Dairy
www.nealsyarddairy.co.uk

ORGANIZATIONS
American Cheese Society
www.cheesesociety.org

National Association for the Specialty Food Trade (NASFT)
www.specialtyfood.com

Slow Food USA
www.slowfoodusa.org

Slow Food International
www.slowfood.org

CHEESE GLOSSARY

AFFINEUR
A person who specializes in ageing cheeses. This may involve rubbing, washing, turning, and tasting wheels at various points as they mature.

ALPINE
A term for cheeses that originate in the Alps. Usually these are mountain cheeses from Switzerland, France, or Italy, but even Vermont cheeses, for example, may be referred to as "Alpine" in style if they exhibit particular flavors and textures.

ANNATTO
A natural orange coloring derived from annatto seeds. See Cheesemonger Note (page 43).

ARTISAN
The term implies artistry by a craft person, but this is loosely defined in the cheese world where many large companies label their cheeses "artisan." In the context of this book, artisan is used to describe high-quality cheeses that are made by hand in small quantities.

BLOOMY
A reference to white-rinded cheeses that have a thin layer of downy mold on their surfaces, thanks to *Penicillium candidum*. Brie is a good example.

BLUE CHEESE
A type of cheese with blue veins or markings, created by mixing mold spores (usually *Penicillium roqueforti*) into the milk or the curds during the cheese-making process. The blue color only develops when the wheels are pierced, usually with long needles, to create air vents. Contrary to popular belief, blue cheeses are not injected with blue mold.

BRINE
A salt-water solution that is sometimes used to wash cheeses; these are often referred to as "washed-rind" cheeses. The brine solution encourages some bacterial growth, inhibiting others; it also keeps the surface moist. Brine-washed cheeses are often recognizable by their orange rinds (Taleggio, page 158, is a good example). Some cheeses, like feta, are stored in brine.

CHEESEMONGER
A person devoted to the care and study of cheese as part of his or her livelihood, typically at a cheese counter.

CHÈVRE
Soft, fresh goat's milk cheese, from the French word for "goat." Note that it comes in many shapes, from logs to small rounds.

CLOTHBOUND

Usually applied to traditional British Cheddars that are bound in muslin or calico. Cheeses that are clothbound, or "bandaged," often have a slightly musty flavor. The cloth protects the cheese as it ages and prevents a rind from forming.

CREAMLINE

A viscous layer below the rind of certain cheeses, usually a positive sign of ageing. Cheeses that ripen from the outside in develop this as bacteria begin breaking down the paste. Gorwydd Caerphilly (page 170) is a good example.

CROTTIN

A muffin-sized cylinder of goat cheese. The word derives from old French, meaning "animal dropping."

CURD

The solid matter that forms when milk is curdled.

FARMSTEAD

A cheese that is made from the milk of a single farm where the cheesemaker is often involved in raising animals. Use of the word "farmstead" usually indicates that a cheese is made in small batches, by hand.

GRASS-FED MILK

Refers to milk from animals that have been pasture-raised. Typically, grass-fed milk has more flavor than milk from animals that have been fed corn and silage.

MOLD

This can refer to spores that are stirred into the milk or into the curds during the cheesemaking process, or it can refer to ambient molds that live in cheese caves and contribute to the development of certain cheese rinds. Common molds used in cheesemaking include *Penicillium candidum*, *Penicillium glaucum*, and *Penicillium roqueforti*. The latter two are used in making blue cheese.

MONASTIC CHEESE

Any cheese that was developed by monks in a monastery. Usually these are fairly potent. Monastic cheeses often pair well with abbey beers, for obvious reasons.

NAME-PROTECTED

A term used in this book to refer to cheeses that are carefully regulated by their countries of origin, like Stilton, for example. Within the industry there are more formal designations for these cheeses. The European Union uses the term Protected Designation of Origin (PDO) to regulate products sourced or manufactured in certain geographic regions. Various national systems have evolved to refine this designation, including the French AOC (Appellation d'Origine Contrôllée) and the Italian DOC (Denominazione d'Origine Controllata).

PASTE

The part of the cheese that is not the rind.

PASTEURIZED MILK

The United States government defines this as milk that has been heated to a minimum of 143°F for at least thirty minutes or a minimum of 161°F for at least fifteen seconds.

RAW MILK

Fresh milk, straight from the udder, that has not been pasteurized according to government specifications. By law, cheese made from raw milk must be aged sixty days or more before it can be sold.

RENNET

An ingredient used in cheesemaking to coagulate fresh milk. Traditionally, rennet was extracted from the stomach lining of animals. Today, a variety of microbial rennets are available from labs, including vegetarian rennet.

RIND

The exterior layer of some cheeses (not all cheeses have rinds). Many rinds are edible; some are not, especially if the cheese has been dipped in wax. As a rule of thumb: eat the rind if it looks appealing to you.

TOMME

A French term that refers to a rustic round of cheese, usually affiliated with its region of origin. Tomme de Savoie (page 135) is a classic example.

WASHED-RIND

A style of cheese where brine or spirits are applied to the surface as it ripens. "Washing" cheese enhances its flavor and texture. Epoisses (page 143) is the classic example.

INDEX

NOTE: *Italicized* page references indicate photographs. Colored page references indicate recipes.

A

Abbaye de Belloc, 40, 138, 206
Acapella, 66
Almond
Marcona, and Manchego Pesto, *52, 53*
Smoked, and Sicilian Olive
Tapenade, 183
American cheese
Acapella, 66
Ascutney Mountain, 118
Bayley Hazen, 227
Beecher's Flagship Reserve, 164
Bijou, 66
Birchrun Blue, 228
Cabot Clothbound Cheddar, 165
Constant Bliss, 94
Evalon, 211
Fat Cat, 146
Fiscalini Bandaged Cheddar, 169
Grayson, 146
Harbison, 96, *97*
Haystack Queso de Mano, 49
Hooligan, 148
Hudson Red, 148
Humboldt Fog, 74, *75*
Hummingbird, 99
Kunik, 102
Largo, 104
Lazy Lady La Petite Tomme, 76
Mont Saint Francis, 151
Moses Sleeper, 106
Noble Road, 106
Old Gold, 217
Old Kentucky Tomme, 78
Old Man Highlander, 127
Pleasant Ridge Reserve, 128
Point Reyes Original Blue, 239
Reading Raclette, 129
Red Hawk, 154
Rogue River Blue, 218
Rogue River Smokey Blue, 239
Rush Creek Reserve, 132
Scamorza, 199
Sea Smoke, 79
Seven Sisters, 60
Shellbark Sharp II, 80
Tarentaise, 132
Tomme Dolce, 174
triple crèmes, about, 94
Truffle Tremor, 110
Vermont Shepherd, 175

vs. imported cheese, 18
Wabash Cannonball, 83
Weybridge, 111
Winnimere, 112
Anchovy and Mascarpone Toasts,
35
Annatto seed extract, about, 43
Anton's Red Love, 88
Appenzeller, 118, 138
Appleby's Cheshire, 41, *42*
Apples, pairing with cheese, 222
Apricots and Pears, Baked Brie
with, 90, *91*
Ardrahan, 142, 243
Artichokes and Chocolate,
Cremificato with, 235
Ascutney Mountain, 118
Asiago d'Allevo Stravecchio, 180
Australian cheese
Seal Bay, 108
Avonlea, 37, 164

B

Baby Faces
burrata, 27
Capricho de Cabra, 30
cheese board suggestions, 35
mascarpone, 32, *33*
mozzarella, 34
ricotta, 34
Bacon
Maple Grilled Cheese, Zeke's, 168
Tomato and Pancetta Strata, 203
Balsamic Poached Figs, 182
Balsamic vinegar, pairing with
Parm, 189
Banon, 36, 88, 186, 221, 222, 243
Basajo, 210
Basil
Burrata with Heirloom Tomatoes,
28, *29*
Goat Cheese Terrine with Fig Jam
and Pesto, 31
Peaches, and Speck, Mascarpone
with, 35
and Pine Nut Pesto, 185
Bayley Hazen, 227
Beaufort, 37, 119
Beecher's Flagship Reserve, 164
Beer

Cheddar Ale Soup, 166, *167*
IPAs, pairing with cheese, 50
pairing with cheese, 21, 50, 176,
177, 243
stouts and porters, pairing with
cheese, 243
Berkswell, 44, *45*, 243
Berries, pairing with cheese, 222
Bijou, 66, 115
Birchrun Blue, 228
Bleu d'Auvergne, 210, 243
Bleu des Basques, 186, 229
Blu di Bufala, 229, 230, *231*
Blue cheese. *See also* **Pierced Punks;**
specific blue cheeses
blue coloring in, 238
pairing with honey, 85
recommended for beginners, 236
storing, 161
Blue Velvet Pudding, 214, *215*
Bresaola, about, 207
Brie de Meaux, 37, 89, 90, *91,* 241
Bûcheron, 67
Buffalo's milk cheese
Blu di Bufala, 229
Casatica di Bufala, 93
mozzarella, 34
Quadrello di Bufala, 152
Bulgarian cheese
Feta, 70, *71*
Burrata, 27, 28, *29*

C

Cabot Clothbound Cheddar, 37,
61, 165, 168, 177, 243
Cabrales, 186, 232, 233
Caciocavallo, 181, 205
Cacio di Bosca al Tartufo, 180
Calvados, pairing with cheese, 243
Camembert du Normandie, 46,
222, 243
Caña de Cabra, 67, 68
Canadian cheese
Avonlea, 164
Cantal, 48, 63
Capricho de Cabra, 30, 31, 85,
222, 243
Carles Roquefort, 92, 113, 236
Carre du Berry, 63, 69, 84, 186
Casatica di Bufala, 93

Challerhocker, 119, 122, *123,* 160

Champagne, pairing with cheese, 21, 36, 37

Charcuterie
guide to, 206–7
The Incredible Bulk, 130, *131*

Cheddar, 85, 166, *167. See also specific types*

Cheese. *See also* Cheese 101; Cheese boards; Pairings; *specific cheese types*
American vs. imported, 18
buying, at cheese shops, 17, 23
buying tips, 161
dried out, reviving, 161
eight styles of, 23
fat and cholesterol in, 20
flavored, note about, 200
leftover, uses for, 159
mold, scraping off, 159
rinds, about, 23, 89

Cheese 101
how cheese is made, 114–15
how to taste cheese, 139
pairing cheese and beer, 177
pairing cheese and charcuterie, 206–7
pairing cheese and digestifs, 242–43
pairing cheese and fruit, 222
pairing cheese and honey, 84–85
pairing cheese and olives, 63
pairing cheese and wine, 36
storing cheese, 161

Cheese boards
All-Goat Blow-Out, 84
charcuterie and cheese, 207
Craft Beers and Artisan All-Stars, 176
creating, tips for, 21
Desk Bento for One, 61
educational value of, 18
Emilio's Ultimate Tailgate Hamper, 205
Evening in Paris, 113
Fireside Party, 241
Monastic Traditions, 138
Pinochle with Grandpa, 160
Tapas on the Patio, 35
Three Picnics, 221

Cheesemakers
Allison Hooper, 115
James Montgomery, 172
Jan Dirk van der Voort, 197
Judy Schad, 115
Mary Keehn, 115
Soyoung Scanlan, 105

Cherries, pairing with cheese, 58, 222

Chiriboga Blue, 206, 233

Chocolate
and Artichokes, Cremificato with, 235
Blue Velvet Pudding, 214, *215*
Dessert Grilled Cheese, 230, *231*
Scharfe Maxx S'mores, 156, *157*

Chutney, pairing with cheese, 223

Cocktails, pairing with cheese, 186

Coffee, pairing with cheese, 243

Colston Bassett Stilton, 177, 234, 241, 243

Comté, 37, 113, 121

Constant Bliss, 94

Coolea, 211

Cow's milk cheese
Anton's Red Love, 88
Appenzeller, 118
Appleby's Cheshire, 41, *42*
Ardrahan, 142
Ascutney Mountain, 118
Asiago d'Allevo Stravecchio, 180
Avonlea, 164
Banon, 88
Bayley Hazen, 227
Beaufort, 119
Beecher's Flagship Reserve, 164
Birchrun Blue, 228
Bleu d'Auvergne, 210
Brie de Meaux, 89
burrata, 27
Cabot Clothbound Cheddar, 165
Cabrales, 233
Caciocavallo, 181
Camembert du Normandie, 46, *47*
Cantal, 48
Challerhocker, 119, *120*
Chiriboga Blue, 233
Colston Bassett Stilton, 234
Comté, 121
Constant Bliss, 94
Coolea, 211
Délice de Bourgogne, 95
Emmentaler, 121
Epoisses, 143, *144–45*
Fat Cat, 146
Fiscalini Bandaged Cheddar, 169
Fontina Val d'Aosta, 125, *126*
Fourme d'Ambert, 236
Frumage Baladin, 169
Gorgonzola Dolce, 213
Gorgonzola Piccante, 237
Gorwydd Caerphilly, 170
Grana Padano, 184

Grayson, 146
Gruyère, 127
Gubbeen, 147
Harbison, 96, *97*
Hooligan, 148
Hudson Red, 148
Hummingbird, 99
Isle of Mull Cheddar, 170
Juni, 186
Keen's Cheddar, 171
Kunik, 102
Laguiole, 187
L'Amuse Gouda, 216
La Peral, 238
Largo, 104
La Tur, 104
Limburger, 149
Lincolnshire Poacher, 171
Mahón, 50
mascarpone, 32, *33*
Mimolette, 54
Montasio, 188
Montgomery's Cheddar, 172
Morbier, 151
Moses Sleeper, 106
mozzarella, 34
Mrs. Kirkham's Tasty Lancashire, 54
Munster, 152
Noble Road, 106
Nylander, 217
Ogleshield, 173
Old Gold, 217
Old Man Highlander, 127
Parmigiano Reggiano, 189
Piave, 190
Pleasant Ridge Reserve, 128
Point Reyes Original Blue, 239
Prima Donna, 218
Provolone, 196
Raclette, 129
Ragusano, 196
Reading Raclette, 129
Red Hawk, 154
Remeker, 197
ricotta, 34
Robiola Bosina, 107
Rogue River Blue, 218
Rogue River Smokey Blue, 239
Rush Creek Reserve, 132
Saint Marcellin, 108
Saint Nectaire, 154
Scamorza, 199
Scharfe Maxx, 155
Seal Bay, 108
Seven Sisters, 60

Sottocenere, 109
Sparkenhoe Red Leicester, 173
Stichelton, 174
Strathdon Blue, 240
Taleggio, 158
Tarentaise, 132
Testun al Barolo, 200, *201*
Tomme Crayeuse, 133
Tomme de Savoie, 135
Tomme Dolce, 174
Trugole, 202
Tuma Persa, 204
Ubriaco, 204
Vacherin Mont d'Or, 136
Valdéon, 240
Wensleydale, 60
Weybridge, 111
Wilde Weide Gouda, 220
Winnimere, 112
Cremificato Verde Capra, 84, 205,
234, 235
Croatian cheese
Paški Sir, 188
Crottin de Chavignol, 70, 84

D

Dates, Cabrales-Stuffed, 232
Délice de Bourgogne, 37, 61, 95,
113, 206, 222
Dessert Cheeses. *See* **Sugar Mamas**
Digestifs, pairing with cheese,
242–43
Duck prosciutto, about, 206
Dulce de Leche and Serrano Ham
Appetizers, 206
Dutch cheese
Ewephoria, *212,* 213
L'Amuse Gouda, 216
Midnight Moon, 216
Nylander, 217
Prima Donna, 218
Remeker, 197
Wilde Weide Gouda, 220

E

Emmentaler, 121, 122, *123,* 124,
243
Endive, Caramelized, Marmalade,
45
English cheese
Appleby's Cheshire, 41, *42*
Berkswell, 44
Colston Bassett Stilton, 234
Harbourne Blue, 237
Keen's Cheddar, 171
Lincolnshire Poacher, 171
Montgomery's Cheddar, 172
Mrs. Kirkham's Tasty Lancashire, 54
Ogleshield, 173
Sparkenhoe Red Leicester, 173
Stichelton, 174
Ticklemore, 110
Wensleydale, 60
Epoisses, 37, 138, 143, *144–45,* 177
Evalon, 211
Ewephoria, *212,* 213, 221, 243

F

Fat Cat, 146
Feta, 63, 70, *72, 73,* 222
Fig(s)
Baked Brie with Pears and
Apricots, 90, *91*
Balsamic Poached, 182
and Goat Cheese Crostini, 81
Grilled, with Manchego, 51
Jam and Pesto, Goat Cheese Terrine
with, 31
pairing with cheese, 222
Finnochiona, about, 207
Fiore Sardo, 181, 182, 205
Fiscalini Bandaged Cheddar, 169,
206
Flagship Reserve, 221
Foja de Noce, 183, 184, 241
Fondue
Swiss, 126
Vacherin, 136
Fontina Val d'Aosta, 37, *124,* 125,
207, 222
Fourme d'Ambert, 236
Free Spirits
Acapella, 66
Bijou, 66
Bûcheron, 67

Caña de Cabra, 67
Carre du Berry, 69
cheese board suggestions, 84
Crottin de Chavignol, 70
Feta, 70, *71*
Humboldt Fog, 74, *75*
Lazy Lady La Petite Tomme, 76
Leonora, 76
Monte Enebro, 78
Old Kentucky Tomme, 78
Sea Smoke, 79
Selles-Sur-Cher, 80
Shellbark Sharp II, 80
Valençay, 82
Wabash Cannonball, 83
French cheese
Abbaye de Belloc, 40
Banon, 88
Beaufort, 119
Bleu d'Auvergne, 210
Bleu des Basques, 229
Brie de Meaux, 89
Bûcheron, 67
Camembert du Normandie, 46, *47*
Cantal, 48
Carles Roquefort, 92
Carre du Berry, 69
cheese board suggestions, 113
Comté, 121
Crottin de Chavignol, 70
Délice de Bourgogne, 95
Epoisses, 143, *144–45*
Fourme d'Ambert, 236
Laguiole, 187
Mimolette, 54
Morbier, 151
Munster, 152
Ossau-Iraty, 56
Petit Basque, 58
Raclette, 129
Saint Marcellin, 108
Saint Nectaire, 154
Selles-Sur-Cher, 80
Tomme Crayeuse, 133
Tomme de Savoie, 135
Valençay, 82
Frosting, Mascarpone, 32, *33*
Frumage Baladin, 138, 169

G

Garrotxa, 48, 63, 103
German cheese
  Anton's Red Love, 88
  Chiriboga Blue, 233
  Limburger, 149
Gin
  pairing with cheese, 186
  A Pecorino-Perfect Martini, 192, *193*
Goat's milk cheese
  Acapella, 66
  Banon, 88
  Bijou, 66
  Bûcheron, 67
  Cabrales, 233
  Caña de Cabra, 67
  Capricho de Cabra, 30
  Carre du Berry, 69
  cheese board suggestions, 84
  Cremificato Verde Capra, 234
  Crottin de Chavignol, 70
  Evalon, 211
  flavor of, 82
  French vs. American, 79
  Garrotxa, 48
  Goat Cheese Terrine with Fig Jam
    and Pesto, 31
  good matches for, 82
  Harbourne Blue, 237
  Haystack Queso de Mano, 49
  Humboldt Fog, 74, *75*
  Kunik, 102
  La Tur, 104
  Lazy Lady La Petite Tomme, 76
  Leonora, 76
  Midnight Moon, 216
  Monte Enebro, 78
  Mont Saint Francis, 151
  Nevat, 55
  Old Kentucky Tomme, 78
  pairing with honey, 85
  Pantaleo, 56
  ricotta, 34
  Sea Smoke, 79
  Selles-Sur-Cher, 80
  Shellbark Sharp II, 80
  Testun al Barolo, 200, *201*
  Ticklemore, 110
  Truffle Tremor, 110
  Valdéon, 240
  Valençay, 82
  Wabash Cannonball, 83

Gorgonzola Dolce, 213, 214, *215,*
  221, 222, 236, 243
Gorgonzola Piccante, 63, 236, 237
Gorwydd Caerphilly, 160, 170, 176
Gouda. *See under* Dutch cheeses;
  Sugar Mamas; *specific Gouda
  cheeses*
Grana Padano, 184, 185, 206
Grand Old Man, 191
Grapes
  Blue Velvet Pudding, 214, *215*
  pairing with cheese, 222
Grayson, 146
Gruyère, 37, *126,* 127, 207
Gubbeen, 147

H

Ham. *See also* Prosciutto
  Mascarpone with Peaches, Basil,
    and Speck, 35
  Rogue River Sushi, 219
  Serrano, about, 207
  Serrano, and Dulce de Leche
    Appetizers, 206
  speck, pairing with cheese, 207
Harbison, 94, 96, 98, 222
Harbourne Blue, 237, 243
Haystack Queso de Mano, 49
Herbs, Fresh, Lemon Zest, and
  Olive Oil, Ricotta with, 35
Honey
  Dessert Grilled Cheese, 230, *231*
  Fig and Goat Cheese Crostini, 81
  Grilled Figs with Manchego, 51
  pairing with cheese, 84–85
  and Pine Nuts, Baked Caña de
    Cabra with, 68
Hooligan, 148, 160
Hooper, Allison, 115
Hudson Red, 148, 177
Humboldt Fog, 74, 177, 221, 243
Hummingbird, 99, 100, *101*

I

Idiazábal, 49, 206, 223, 243
The Incredible Bulk, 130, *131*
Irish cheese
  Ardrahan, 142
  Coolea, 211
  Gubbeen, 147

Isle of Mull Cheddar, 170, 176
Italian cheese
  Asiago d'Allevo Stravecchio, 180
  Basajo, 210
  Blu di Bufala, 229
  burrata, 27
  Caciocavallo, 181
  Cacio di Bosca al Tartufo, 180
  Casatica di Bufala, 93
  Cremificato Verde Capra, 234
  Fiore Sardo, 181
  Foja de Noce, 184
  Fontina Val d'Aosta, 125, *126*
  Frumage Baladin, 169
  Gorgonzola Dolce, 213
  Gorgonzola Piccante, 237
  Grana Padano, 184
  Juni, 186
  La Tur, 104
  mascarpone, 32, *33*
  Moliterno, 187
  Montasio, 188
  mozzarella, 34
  Nuvola di Pecora, 55
  Pantaleo, 56
  Parmigiano Reggiano, 189
  Pecorino di Fossa, 190
  Pecorino di Pienza, 191
  Pecorino Ginepro, 191
  Pecorino Romano, 194
  Pecorino Toscano, 195
  Pepato, 195
  Piave, 190
  Provolone, 196
  Quadrello di Bufala, 152
  Ragusano, 196
  ricotta, 34
  Robiola Bosina, 107
  Scamorza, 199
  Sottocenere, 109
  Taleggio, 158
  Testun al Barolo, 200, *201*
  Trugole, 202
  Tuma Persa, 204
  Ubriaco, 204

J

Jam, Rhubarb Refrigerator, 77
Juni, 186

K

Keehn, Mary, 115
Keen's Cheddar, 85, 171
Kunik, 102

L

Lactose sensitivity, 20
Laguiole, 187
L'Amuse Gouda, 216, 243
La Peral, 236, 238
Largo, 94, 104, 176
La Serena, 103, 186, 207
La Tur, 104
Lavender Mustard, 122, *123*
Lazy Lady La Petite Tomme, 76
Leonora, 76, 77, 85, 186
Limburger, 149, 150
Lincolnshire Poacher, 171

M

Mac 'n' Cheese, Limburger, 150
Mahón, 50, 103
Manchego, 51, 51, *52*, 63, 103, 207, 222, 223, 243
Marmalade, Caramelized Endive, 45
Martini, A Pecorino-Perfect, 192, *193*
Mascarpone, 32, 32, *33*, 35, 61, 69, 207, 222
Membrillo
 pairing with cheese, 223
 Rogue River Sushi, 219
Midnight Moon, 84, 216, 241
Mimolette, 54
Moliterno, 186, 187, 207
Montasio, 188
Monte Enebro, 78, 84, 222, 243
Montgomery, James, 172
Montgomery's Cheddar, 172, 223
Mont Saint Francis, 151
Morbier, 113, 151, 243
Moscato d'Asti, pairing with cheese, 243
Moses Sleeper, 69, 94, 106
Mostarda, pairing with cheese, 223
Mountain Men
 Appenzeller, 118

Ascutney Mountain, 118
Beaufort, 119
Challerhocker, 119, *120*
cheese board suggestions, 138
Comté, 121
Emmentaler, 121
Fontina Val d'Aosta, 125, *126*
Gruyère, 127
Old Man Highlander, 127
Pleasant Ridge Reserve, 128
Raclette, 129
Reading Raclette, 129
Rush Creek Reserve, 132
Tarentaise, 132
Tomme Crayeuse, 133
Tomme de Savoie, 135
Vacherin Mont d'Or, 136
Mozzarella, 34, 37, 206, 222
Mrs. Kirkham's Tasty Lancashire, 54, 222
Mull Cheddar, 243
Munster, 37, 152, 160
Mustard
 Lavender, 122, *123*
 Truffle, 122

N

Nevat, 55
Noble Road, 94, 106
Nut(s)
 Manchego and Marcona Almond Pesto, *52*, 53
 Pine, and Basil Pesto, 185
 Pine, and Honey, Baked Caña de Cabra with, 68
 Sicilian Olive and Smoked Almond Tapenade, 183
Nuvola di Pecora, 55
Nylander, 217

O

Ogleshield, 173
Old Gold, 217
Old Kentucky Tomme, 78, 115
Old Man Highlander, 127
Olive(s)
 Cerignola, and Strawberries, Pickled Feta with, *72, 73*
 The Incredible Bulk, 130, *131*
 pairing with cheese, 63

A Pecorino-Perfect Martini, 192, *193*
 Sicilian, and Smoked Almond Tapenade, 183
Oranges, pairing with cheese, 222
Ossau-Iraty, 56, 57, 63

P

Pairings
 cheese and beer, 21, 50, 176, 177, 243
 cheese and breakfast foods, 69
 cheese and cocktails, 186
 cheese and digestifs, 242–43
 cheese and honey, 84–85
 cheese and olives, 63
 cheese and preserved or cooked fruits, 223
 cheese and prosciutto, 206
 cheese and red wine, 37
 cheese and Scotch, 44
 cheese and seafood, 57
 cheese and white wine, 37
 cheese and wine, 21, 36, 37, 243
 guidelines for, 21, 36
 note about, 20
 Parm and balsamic, 189
Pancetta and Tomato Strata, 203
Pantaleo, 56, 61, 63, 186, 221
Parmigiano Reggiano, 37, 63, 85, 127, 189, 203, 243
Paški Sir, 188
Peach(es)
 Balsamic Compote, 98
 Basil, and Speck, Mascarpone with, 35
 Grilled, with Quadrello di Bufala, 153
 pairing with cheese, 222
Pears
 and Apricots, Baked Brie with, 90, *91*
 Dessert Grilled Cheese, 230, *231*
 pairing with cheese, 222
Pecorino, 85, 192, *193*
Pecorino di Fossa, 190
Pecorino di Pienza, 186, 191
Pecorino Ginepro, 186, 191, 221
Pecorino Romano, 194
Pecorino Toscano, 84, 195
Pepato, 195
Pesto
 Basil and Pine Nut, 185
 and Fig Jam, Goat Cheese Terrine with, 31

Manchego and Marcona Almond, *52, 53*

Petit Basque, 58, 222

Piave, 37, 190, 243

Pierced Punks

Bayley Hazen, 227

Birchrun Blue, 228

Bleu des Basques, 229

Blu di Bufala, 229

Cabrales, 233

cheese board suggestions, 241

Chiriboga Blue, 233

Colston Bassett Stilton, 234

Cremificato Verde Capra, 234

Fourme d'Ambert, 236

Gorgonzola Piccante, 237

Harbourne Blue, 237

La Peral, 238

Point Reyes Original Blue, 239

Rogue River Smokey Blue, 239

Strathdon Blue, 240

Valdéon, 240

Pine Nut(s)

and Basil Pesto, 185

and Honey, Baked Caña de Cabra with, 68

Pleasant Ridge Reserve, 128

Point Reyes Original Blue, 85, 176, 221, 236, 239, 243

Porters, pairing with cheese, 243

Prima Donna, 218

Prosciutto

de Parma, about, 206

duck, about, 206

Rogue River Sushi, 219

Provolone, 196

Pudding, Blue Velvet, 214, *215*

Q

Quadrello di Bufala, 152, 153, 205, 207, 222

Quiet Types

Abbaye de Belloc, 40

Appleby's Cheshire, 41, *42*

Berkswell, 44

Camembert du Normandie, 46, *47*

Cantal, 48

cheese board suggestions, 61

Garrotxa, 48

Haystack Queso de Mano, 49

Idiazábal, 49

Mahón, 50

Manchego, 51

Mimolette, 54

Mrs. Kirkham's Tasty Lancashire, 54

Nevat, 55

Nuvola di Pecora, 55

Ossau-Iraty, 56

Pantaleo, 56

Petit Basque, 58

Seven Sisters, 60

Wensleydale, 60

R

Raclette, 129

Ragusano, 37, 196

Raw milk cheese

Abbaye de Belloc, 40

about, 18

Appenzeller, 118

Appleby's Cheshire, 41, *42*

Ascutney Mountain, 118

Asiago d'Allevo Stravecchio, 180

Avonlea, 164

Basajo, 210

Bayley Hazen, 227

Beaufort, 119

Berkswell, 44

Birchrun Blue, 228

Bleu des Basques, 229

Challerhocker, 119, *120*

Chiriboga Blue, 233

Comté, 121

Emmentaler, 121

Evalon, 211

Fat Cat, 146

Fiscalini Bandaged Cheddar, 169

flavor of, 20

Fontina Val d'Aosta, 125, *126*

Frumage Baladin, 169

Gorwydd Caerphilly, 170

Grana Padano, 184

Grayson, 146

Haystack Queso de Mano, 49

Hooligan, 148

Hudson Red, 148

Idiazábal, 49

Isle of Mull Cheddar, 170

Juni, 186

Keen's Cheddar, 171

Laguiole, 187

La Serena, 103

Lincolnshire Poacher, 171

Montasio, 188

Montgomery's Cheddar, 172

Mont Saint Francis, 151

Mrs. Kirkham's Tasty Lancashire, 54

Nylander, 217

Ogleshield, 173

Old Gold, 217

Old Kentucky Tomme, 78

Old Man Highlander, 127

Parmigiano Reggiano, 189

Pecorino Ginepro, 191

Pecorino Romano, 194

Pleasant Ridge Reserve, 128

Point Reyes Original Blue, 239

Ragusano, 196

Reading Raclette, 129

Remeker, 197

Rogue River Blue, 218

Rogue River Smokey Blue, 239

Rush Creek Reserve, 132

Scharfe Maxx, 155

Seven Sisters, 60

Sparkenhoe Red Leicester, 173

Stichelton, 174

Tarentaise, 132

Tomme de Savoie, 135

Tomme Dolce, 174

Tuma Persa, 204

Ubriaco, 204

Vermont Shepherd, 175

Wilde Weide Gouda, 220

Winnimere, 112

Reading Raclette, 129, 130, *131,* 207

Recipes

Baked Brie with Pears and Apricots, 90, *91*

Baked Caña de Cabra with Pine Nuts and Honey, 68

Balsamic Poached Figs, 182

Basil and Pine Nut Pesto, 185

Behind-the-Counter Winnimere Dip, 112

Blue Velvet Pudding, 214, *215*

Burrata with Heirloom Tomatoes, 28, *29*

Cabrales-Stuffed Dates, 232

Caramelized Endive Marmalade, 45

Cheddar Ale Soup, 166, *167*

Cremificato with Chocolate and Artichokes, 235

Dessert Grilled Cheese, 230, *231*

Dulce de Leche and Serrano Ham Appetizers, 206

Fig and Goat Cheese Crostini, 81

Goat Cheese Terrine with Fig Jam and Pesto, 31

Grilled Bread with Fresh Tomatoes, Garlic, and Ricotta Salata, 35

Grilled Figs with Manchego, 51
Grilled Peaches with Quadrello di Bufala, 153
The Incredible Bulk, 130, *131*
Lavender Mustard, 122, *123*
Limburger Mac 'n' Cheese, 150
Manchego and Marcona Almond Pesto, *52,* 53
Mascarpone and Anchovy Toasts, 35
Mascarpone Frosting, 32, *33*
Mascarpone with Peaches, Basil, and Speck, 35
Peach Balsamic Compote, 98
A Pecorino-Perfect Martini, 192, *193*
Pickled Feta with Cerignola Olives and Strawberries, *72, 73*
Rhubarb Refrigerator Jam, 77
Ricotta with Fresh Herbs, Lemon Zest, and Olive Oil, 35
Rogue River Sushi, 219
Scharfe Maxx S'mores, 156, *157*
Semolina Crackers with Sea Salt, 100, *101*
Sicilian Olive and Smoked Almond Tapenade, 183
Swiss Fondue, 126
Taleggio and Salami Ravioli, 158
Tomato and Pancetta Strata, 203
Truffle Mustard, 122
Vacherin Fondue, 136
Zeke's Bacon Maple Grilled Cheese, 168
Red Hawk, 98, 154, 177, 222, 243
Remeker, 197, 243
Rhubarb Refrigerator Jam, 77
Ricotta, 34, 35, 37, 61, 69
Ricotta Salata, 34, 35
Riesling, pairing with cheese, 243
Rinds, cheese, 23, 89
Robiola Bosina, 107, 222
Rockstars
  Avonlea, 164
  Beecher's Flagship Reserve, 164
  Cabot Clothbound Cheddar, 165
  cheese board suggestions, 176
  Fiscalini Bandaged Cheddar, 169
  Frumage Baladin, 169
  Gorwydd Caerphilly, 170
  Isle of Mull Cheddar, 170
  Keen's Cheddar, 171
  Lincolnshire Poacher, 171
  Montgomery's Cheddar, 172
  Ogleshield, 173
  Sparkenhoe Red Leicester, 173
  Stichelton, 174

  Tomme Dolce, 174
  Vermont Shepherd, 175
Rogue River Blue, 176, 218, 219
Rogue River Smokey Blue, 239
Rogue River Sushi, 219
Roncal, 199
Roquefort, 37, 85, 222, 243
Rush Creek Reserve, 132, 137

S

Saint Marcellin, 108, 221
Saint Nectaire, 154
Salads
  Pickled Feta with Cerignola Olives and Strawberries, *72, 73*
  topping with Petit Basque, 58
Salami
  pairing with cheese, 207
  and Taleggio Ravioli, 158
Sandwiches
  Dessert Grilled Cheese, 230, *231*
  The Incredible Bulk, 130, *131*
  Zeke's Bacon Maple Grilled Cheese, 168
Saucisson sec, about, 207
Sauternes, pairing with cheese, 243
Scamorza, 199
Scanlan, Soyoung, 105
Schad, Judy, 115
Scharfe Maxx, 155, 156, *157,* 160
Scotch, pairing with cheese, 44, 243
Scottish cheese
  Isle of Mull Cheddar, 170
  Strathdon Blue, 240
Seafood, pairing with cheese, 57
Seal Bay, 108
Sea Smoke, 79
Selles-Sur-Cher, 69, 80
Semolina Crackers with Sea Salt, 100, *101*
Seven Sisters, 60, 61
Sheep's milk cheese
  Abbaye de Belloc, 40
  Basajo, 210
  Berkswell, 44
  Bleu des Basques, 229
  Cabrales, 233
  Cacio di Bosca al Tartufo, 180
  Carles Roquefort, 92
  Ewephoria, *212,* 213
  Feta, 70, *71*
  Fiore Sardo, 181
  Foja de Noce, 184

  Hummingbird, 99
  Idiazábal, 49
  La Peral, 238
  La Serena, 103
  La Tur, 104
  Manchego, 51
  Moliterno, 187
  Nevat, 55
  Nuvola di Pecora, 55
  Ossau-Iraty, 56
  Paški Sir, 188
  Pecorino di Fossa, 190
  Pecorino di Pienza, 191
  Pecorino Ginepro, 191
  Pecorino Romano, 194
  Pecorino Toscano, 195
  Pepato, 195
  Petit Basque, 58
  ricotta, 34
  Robiola Bosina, 107
  Roncal, 199
  Testun al Barolo, 200, *201*
  Vermont Shepherd, 175
Shellbark Sharp II, 80, 81, 85, 222
Sherry, pairing with cheese, 243
Sicilian Olive and Smoked Almond Tapenade, 183
Smoked cheese
  Idiazábal, 49, 206, 223, 243
  Rogue River Smokey Blue, 239
S'mores, Scharfe Maxx, 156, *157*
Soppressata, about, 207
Sottocenere, 109
Soup, Cheddar Ale, 166, *167*
Spanish cheese
  Cabrales, 233
  Caña de Cabra, 67
  Capricho de Cabra, 30
  cheesemonger notes, 103
  Garrotxa, 48
  Idiazábal, 49
  La Peral, 238
  La Serena, 103
  Leonora, 76
  Mahón, 50
  Manchego, 51
  Monte Enebro, 78
  Nevat, 55
  Roncal, 199
  Valdéon, 240
Sparkenhoe Red Leicester, 173, 241
Speck
  about, 207
  Peaches, and Basil, Mascarpone with, 35

256 DI BRUNO BROS. HOUSE OF CHEESE

Stichelton, 61, 160, 174
Stilton, 37, 186, 222
Stinkers
Ardrahan, 142
cheese board suggestions, 160
Epoisses, 143, *144–45*
Fat Cat, 146
Grayson, 146
Gubbeen, 147
Hooligan, 148
Hudson Red, 148
Limburger, 149
Mont Saint Francis, 151
Morbier, 151
Munster, 152
Quadrello di Bufala, 152
Red Hawk, 154
Saint Nectaire, 154
Scharfe Maxx, 155
Taleggio, 158
Stout, pairing with cheese, 243
Strata, Tomato and Pancetta, 203
Strathdon Blue, 177, 221, 240, 243
Strawberries and Cerignola Olives,
    Pickled Feta with, *72, 73*
Sugar Mamas
Basajo, 210
Bleu d'Auvergne, 210
cheese board suggestions, 221
Coolea, 211
Evalon, 211
Ewephoria, *212,* 213
Gorgonzola Dolce, 213
L'Amuse Gouda, 216
Midnight Moon, 216
Nylander, 217
Old Gold, 217
Prima Donna, 218
Rogue River Blue, 218
Wilde Weide Gouda, 220
Swiss cheese
Appenzeller, 118
Challerhocker, 119, *120*
Emmentaler, 121
Gruyère, 127
Raclette, 129
Scharfe Maxx, 155
Vacherin Mont d'Or, 136

T

Taleggio, 37, 127, 158, 158, 205,
    207, 222
Tarentaise, 132

Tawny Port, pairing with cheese, 243
Tea, pairing with cheese, 243
Terrine, Goat Cheese, with Fig
    Jam and Pesto, 31
Testun al Barolo, 200, *201*
Ticklemore, 37, 110
Tomato(es)
Fresh, Garlic, and Ricotta Salata,
    Grilled Bread with, 35
Heirloom, Burrata with, 28, *29*
and Pancetta Strata, 203
Tomme Crayeuse, 133
Tomme de Savoie, 135
Tomme Dolce, 174
Truffle cheeses
Cacio di Bosca al Tartufo, 180
Sottocenere, 109
Truffle Tremor, 110, 115, 241
Truffle Mustard, 122
Truffle Tremor, 110, 115, 241
Trugole, 202, 203, 205
Tuma Persa, 63, 204

U

Ubriaco, 204, 221

V

Vacherin Mont d'Or, 136, 136,
    137, 222, 241
Valdéon, 221, 240, 243
Valençay, 37, 82, 113
Vermont Shepherd, 85, 175
Vixens
Anton's Red Love, 88
Banon, 88
Brie de Meaux, 89
Carles Roquefort, 92
Casatica di Bufala, 93
cheese board suggestions, 113
Constant Bliss, 94
Délice de Bourgogne, 95
Harbison, 96, *97*
Hummingbird, 99
Kunik, 102
Largo, 104
La Serena, 103
La Tur, 104
Moses Sleeper, 106
Noble Road, 106
Robiola Bosina, 107

Saint Marcellin, 108
Seal Bay, 108
Sottocenere, 109
Ticklemore, 110
Truffle Tremor, 110
Weybridge, 111
Winnimere, 112
Voort, Jan Dirk van der, 197

W

Wabash Cannonball, 83
Welsh cheese
Gorwydd Caerphilly, 170
Wensleydale, 60, 85, 222
Weybridge, 111
Whiskey, pairing with cheese, 186,
    243
Wilde Weide Gouda, 220, 221
Wine, pairing with cheese, 21, 36,
    37, 243
Winnimere, 112, 112, 137, 222, 241
Wise Guys
Asiago d'Allevo Stravecchio, 180
Caciocavallo, 181
Cacio di Bosca al Tartufo, 180
cheese board suggestions, 205
Fiore Sardo, 181
Foja de Noce, 184
Grana Padano, 184
Juni, 186
Laguiole, 187
Moliterno, 187
Montasio, 188
Parmigiano Reggiano, 189
Paški Sir, 188
Pecorino di Fossa, 190
Pecorino di Pienza, 191
Pecorino Ginepro, 191
Pecorino Romano, 194
Pecorino Toscano, 195
Pepato, 195
Piave, 190
Provolone, 196
Ragusano, 196
Remeker, 197
Roncal, 199
Scamorza, 199
Testun al Barolo, 200, *201*
Trugole, 202
Tuma Persa, 204
Ubriaco, 204